Principles of
Maritime Power

Principles of
Maritime Power

Bruce A. Elleman
With Foreword by S. C. M. Paine

ROWMAN & LITTLEFIELD
Lanham • Boulder • New York • London

Published by Rowman & Littlefield
An imprint of The Rowman & Littlefield Publishing Group, Inc.
4501 Forbes Boulevard, Suite 200, Lanham, Maryland 20706
www.rowman.com

86-90 Paul Street, London EC2A 4NE

British Library Cataloguing in Publication Information Available

Library of Congress Cataloging-in-Publication Data

Names: Elleman, Bruce A., 1959- author. | Paine, S. C. M., 1957- writer of foreword.
Title: Principles of maritime power / Bruce A. Elleman ; foreword by S. C. M. Paine.
Description: Lanham : Rowman & Littlefield Publishers, [2022] | Includes
    bibliographical references and index.
Identifiers: LCCN 2021046358 (print) | LCCN 2021046359 (ebook) |
    ISBN 9781538161043 (cloth) | ISBN 9781538161067 (ebook)
Subjects: LCSH: Sea-power. | Naval art and science.
Classification: LCC VA10 .E45 2022 (print) | LCC VA10 (ebook) |
    DDC 359/.03—dc23/eng/20211001
LC record available at https://lccn.loc.gov/2021046358
LC ebook record available at https://lccn.loc.gov/2021046359

To RADM Jeffrey A. Harley USN (ret.), PhD

President, U.S. Naval War College, 2016-2019

Officer, Scholar, Gentleman

Contents

List of Acronyms   ix

Foreword: Maritime Solutions to Continental Conundrums   xi
S. C. M. Paine

Acknowledgments   xix

Introduction   1

1   Mutiny   5

2   Blockades   17

3   Coalitions   31

4   Piracy   41

5   Expeditionary Warfare   55

6   Commerce Raiding   71

7   Non-military Naval Operations   93

8   Sea Control   107

9   Sea Denial   117

10   Conclusions: Sea Powers vs Land Powers   127

Compiled List of Naval Case Studies   137

Contents

List of Strategic Terms   143

Selected Bibliography   171

Index   205

List of Acronyms

AIS	Automatic Identification System
COG	Center of Gravity
DOD	Department of Defense
EEZ	Exclusive Economic Zone
FON	Freedom of Navigation
GWOT	Global War on Terror
IMO	International Maritime Organization
ISPS	International Ship and Port Facility Security
LLOC	Land lines of communications
MALSINDO	Malaysia, Singapore, Indonesia
MDA	Maritime Domain Awareness
MOOTWA	Military Operations Other Than War
PLAN	People's Liberation Army Navy
PRC	Piracy Reporting Center
ReCAAP	Regional Cooperation Agreement on Combating Piracy and Armed Robbery against Ships in Asia
ROE	Rules of Engagement
SLOC	Sea lines of communications
SOLAS	International Convention for the Safety of Life at Sea
UNCLOS	United Nations Convention on the Law of the Sea 1982
VLCC	Very Large Crude Carrier

Foreword

Maritime Solutions to Continental Conundrums

CONTINENTAL POWERS COVET CONQUESTS; MARITIME POWERS COMPOUND WEALTH[1]

Since the Industrial Revolution, the currency of international power has shifted from land to commerce. The incoming global maritime order focuses on compounding wealth by minimizing transaction costs, while the outgoing order of competing continental empires focused on pounding each other.[2] The old system destroyed wealth; the new one creates it, as the statistics show. In 2020, an article from the Center for International Maritime Security suggested a 66-70-80-90-99 rule, highlighting that 66 percent of global wealth comes from or near the sea; 70 percent of the globe is oceanic; 80 percent of its population is coastal; 90 percent of goods arrive by sea; and 99 percent of international digital traffic goes by submarine cable.[3]

As the 19th century gave way to the 20th, the United States began its transition from a continental to a maritime security paradigm and, after World War II, became champion of a maritime world order as the result of a three-phase transformation. The U.S. Navy has played a key role in the transition.

A Continental United States

The U.S. conquest of much of North America defined the continental phase. The United States unsuccessfully invaded Canada twice (1775, 1812); negotiated treaties with the British and Spanish empires (straightening the northern border in 1818 and gaining Florida in 1819); cut large checks for the central and western United States (the 1803 Louisiana Purchase from Napoleon Bonaparte and the 1867 purchase of Alaska and points south from Tsar

Alexander II); and fought Mexico for Texas and the Southwest (the Mexican-American War, 1846–48).

The Monroe Doctrine, this period's most famous foreign policy proclamation, was a classic continental, sphere-of-influence, "stay out of my exclusive zone" warning to European powers. Meanwhile, the U.S. Army completed America's longest war: the conquest of the west, which its original inhabitants fought to retain their lands. It ended in an 1890 massacre at Wounded Knee, the same year Alfred Thayer Mahan published his seminal book, *The Influence of Sea Power upon History: 1660–1783*, grounded in an understanding that commerce had become the currency of power. Mahan ushered in the second phase of the U.S. maritime metamorphosis when he made the case for investment in a blue-water navy that became the mantra of navalists worldwide.

Becoming a Maritime Power

Much earlier, Britain by necessity had developed a maritime security paradigm suited to its island geography and neighboring large continental foes. Britain's preeminent maritime theorist, Sir Julian S. Corbett, quotes Britain's great philosopher, scientist, lawyer, and statesman, Sir Francis Bacon: "[H]e that commands the sea is at great liberty, and may take as much and as little of the war as he will. Whereas those that be strongest by land are many times in great straits."[4]

Vice Admiral Satō Tetsutarō, president of Imperial Japan's Naval War College, published the 1908 *History of Imperial Defense*, making him among Japan's most influential naval officers. Satō highlighted the first fundamental discriminator between maritime and continental powers: "Among the Powers in the World, there are only three countries that can defend themselves primarily with navies. They are the UK and the US and Japan."[5] In other words, maritime powers can defend themselves primarily by sea, whereas continental powers cannot. Each must prioritize spending on naval versus ground forces accordingly.

Nicholas Spykman, a naturalized U.S. citizen from Amsterdam, The Netherlands, finished his most famous work, *The Geography of the Peace*, in 1943 while Nazis occupied his homeland. He emphasized oceans as access both for oneself and for one's enemies, and ships as the main conduit: "The United States will have to depend on her sea power communications across the Atlantic and Pacific to give her access to the Old World. The effectiveness of this access will determine the nature of her foreign policy."[6] In other words, U.S. security was a function of sea power.

Land powers, however, seek security by accumulating spheres of influence and exclusion zones, often in concentric rings around their borders.

Typically, they try to prevent the rise—or seek the dismemberment—of bordering powers. They tend to prefer weak neighbors and have often assumed responsibility for their neighbors' foreign policies. The Chinese, Mongol, Russian, Napoleonic, Soviet, and Nazi empires followed this pattern.

In contrast, sea powers (such as Britain and the Dutch Republic) have tried to expand the reach of international law and, eventually, of international institutions to share the oceanic commons to trade in safety. Indeed, the Dutch Republic's Hugo Grotius became the founding father of international law. According to his 1609 *Freedom of the Seas*: "Every nation is free to travel to every other nation and to trade with it."[7] In *Law of War and Peace* (1625), he cited the Roman jurist Celsus: "To all men belong the use of the sea," as well as a Byzantine recodification of Roman law: "By natural law, the following are common to everyone: the air, flowing water, the sea, and in consequence the seashore."[8] Thus, the view of oceans as commons goes far back in Western thinking.

Commerce Over Conquest

Unlike land powers—which face immediate threats on their borders that force a focus on national security—sea powers, given the comparative security afforded by a moat, can focus on national prosperity and oceanic trade as a means to that security. This gives rise to differing preoccupations: Whereas land powers often view both land and sea as sovereign territory and pursue a negative-sum, wealth-destroying quest for its control, sea powers generally view the world in terms of potential markets and maritime commons for positive-sum trade and cumulative economic growth.

Where land powers see territory to be taken, maritime powers see markets to make money. And while land powers divide the world into competing exclusive zones, sea powers desire commons—a shared space—encompassing not only the seas, but in modern times also air, space, and cyber. The land-power imperative for insulation from the world versus the sea-power appetite for global access is a second distinguishing characteristic. From these two discriminators—the in/ability to defend by sea and the desire for open/closed seas—arise two mutually exclusive visions of global order and a source of much conflict.

The transportation revolution arising from the Industrial Revolution upended global economics, with wealth accruing from commerce far outpacing that derived from land. In 1869, the Suez Canal's completion overturned the economics of the once-lucrative Silk Road, marginalizing formerly coveted real estate from Syria to Afghanistan. Henceforth, sea transport became ever cheaper than land transport, rendering internal lines of communication

far less profitable than external ones. The advent of megaships and contain-
erization greatly accelerated the trend.

This is the third characteristic distinguishing sea and land powers—the
reliance on internal versus external lines of communication, particularly in
wartime. Most significant, external lines connecting the far reaches of the
globe can facilitate far-flung alliances.

Maritime Rules

Rising 20th-century nationalism undermined the economics of both continental
and maritime empires by making colonies ungovernable by outsiders unwilling
to commit genocide to stay or money sinks for those who remained. World War
II and decolonization formed the backdrop to the third phase of the U.S. transformation. The administration of President Harry S. Truman played a key role
in the global transition from empires to a maritime, rules-based world order.

Abroad, President Truman supported the creation of the International
Monetary Fund (1944), the International Bank for Reconstruction and
Development (1944), the United Nations (1945), the General Agreement
on Tariffs and Trade (1947; predecessor of the World Trade Organization),
the Organization of American States (1948), the North Atlantic Treaty
Organization (1949), the European Coal and Steel Community (1951), and
the European Economic Community (1957; predecessor of the European
Union). At home, Truman created the Council of Economic Advisers in 1946
and—in 1947—the Central Intelligence Agency, the Department of Defense,
the Joint Chiefs of Staff, the Air Force, and the National Security Council.
The Eisenhower administration doubled down on this foreign and domestic
institutional legacy to hold the peace, a task that post–World War I leaders
had so conspicuously failed to accomplish.

This legacy makes Truman and Eisenhower's the greatest U.S. generation,
not their children who claimed the title. These Presidents, both veterans of the
war to end war, came home to raise families during the Great Depression, only
to send their children's generation to serve in a second world war. Institution-
building was the Presidents' generational response to crisis management when
its members rose to leadership roles. They fully understood the costs of not
having an institutional international order—two devastating world wars sand-
wiching a global economic depression—so they built strong institutions to create forums to hash out problems verbally rather than fight them out militarily.
Those institutions have held the peace in the industrialized world ever since,
though many unindustrialized countries became battlefields instead.

Yet, most countries do not fit cleanly into land or maritime categories. But
those lacking a maritime geographic position can gain its benefits by virtue
of their friends and the international institutions they support. Alliances can

bestow on the whole a collective maritime position and power denied to the parts, by mobilizing not only soldiers and sailors, but also diplomats, lawyers, financiers, and industrialists to wage war in many domains. Land powers focused on negative-sum land grabs from their neighbors make poor partners. Some nevertheless team up at times, but territorial disputes and fears of encroachment by landward neighbors lurk in the background—China and Russia's predicament. Sea powers do not have this problem since trade, not territory, is their main goal.

A maritime global order gives navies an enormous peacetime role.

The Roles of Navies

Although rarely decisive in wartime, navies have an outsized peacetime role as guardians not only of maritime borders, but also of peacetime commerce, making the navy the service most intimately connected with the civilian economy. Like other services, navies deter attacks on the homeland—most potently through difficult-to-track, nuclear-armed, nuclear-powered submarines—but unlike the others, navies also deter attacks on the commons. Navies minimize piracy, keeping insurance premiums down so that vulnerable merchantmen can deliver goods unmolested and at predictable costs. Without secure maritime commons, international trade would grind to a halt, bottlenecks would choke economies, living standards would crumble, and the win-win, wealth-compounding, global maritime order would unravel.

Contrary to Mahan's hype about decisive naval battle, armies have more often been decisive, in the sense of the single silver-bullet, war-winning, objective-delivering instrument. Because unassisted ground forces can deliver strategic victory, if the war's purpose is annihilation of the opposing army, continental powers often equate operational with strategic success. When land was the currency of power, this type of resolution was more possible. Today, no single instrument of power (except perhaps a vaporizing nuclear strike) is likely to be decisive in the instant-communication, rally-the-third-parties present. Even in the past, protracted wars required production, resources, supportive populations, allies, and a long list of complementary capabilities.

Naval forces can target their opposite numbers in wartime, as occurred in the symmetric Pacific fleet-on-fleet battles during World War II. They also can support land forces in peripheral theaters in coastal locations, as in North Africa in World War II. But against a competent land power, navies are unlikely to reach the main theater, probably located inland and defended against coastal attack. They can blockade opposing fleets in port (which eliminates enemy oceanic trade, too), and sea powers' navies play a huge logistical role in commerce protection through convoys. Land powers may counter with commerce raiding by submarines, but, hemmed in by limited access to the seas, they cannot blockade sea powers' coastlines.

The rare occasions when navies have been decisive required fabulously incompetent adversaries. Sparta's destruction of the Athenian fleet at Aegospotami (405 BCE) ended the Athenian empire—but it took a feckless commander to leave his fleet unattended and pulled up ashore to lose it. Tsar Nicholas II ceded Japan its war objective (control over Korea and southern Manchuria) following his fleet's destruction at Tsushima (1905)— even though his supply lines were exclusively overland, Russians greatly outnumbered Japanese in theater, and one more battle would have defeated an exhausted Japan. Even the brilliant British victory at Trafalgar (1805) that guaranteed against invasion was not *decisive*: The Napoleonic Wars continued for another decade.

Instead, navies routinely combine with other instruments of national power, particularly diplomacy, to coordinate allies with complementary capabilities; international law to regularize relations; and the economic capabilities of finance, production, and distribution. To defeat Napoleonic France, Britain developed a grand strategy—grand in its integration of multiple instruments of national power. It began with a three-part cumulative strategy.[9]

First, protect trade and the home economy to prevent invasion and to fund its and its allies' militaries. Second, simultaneously shut down French trade and access to overseas theaters through blockade to squeeze its economy and throw it back on the resources of its increasingly war-impoverished neighbors. Third, open peripheral theaters with better sea than land access to attrite enemy forces disproportionately, relieve pressure on land-power allies fighting on the main front, and divide enemy attention to predispose overextension.

The Continuum of Peace and War

Cumulative effects fed into an overlapping, sequential strategy to deliver British victory: Immediately find, fund, and arm the most directly threatened land-power ally to pin the French-led army in the main theater. Join the fight on the main front only with multiple allies and after large enemy losses in both the main and peripheral theaters. Thus, dodge the continental enemy's primary strength—its army—and leverage British strengths: naval dominance, the ability to create wealth, and, therefore, the ability to endure a protracted war. The key: Enable the allies to win. As much as a continental power might wish to follow this strategy, without command of the sea, which surrounding narrow seas and adjacent adversaries make highly unlikely, it cannot. But this strategy requires both maritime access and sanctuary at home, a tall order in today's era of precision nuclear strike.

After World War II, few were interested in a nuclearized third major war. Containment became the maritime answer to continental problems—leverage external lines of communication to connect a maritime global alliance and wealth-production system. Put time on one's side by keeping continental problems homebound and let growth compound in the *un*contained maritime world, producing an ever starker divergence in productivity and living standards. Eventually, the problems resolved through a change of heart at the top (Mikhail Gorbachev), revolutions from below (Eastern Europe), or ever-deepening decline (Kim Jong-un). During the long wait, land powers suffered from their follies, while citizens of the maritime system prospered.

Navies play an essential role in containment, along a maritime peace-to-war continuum that ranges from antipiracy operations against small players, to sanctions against any-sized players, to blockades against big ones. The continuum focuses on economic denial strategies to dampen enemy growth. An economy doubles in 23 years at a 3 percent growth rate; in 35 years at 2 percent; and in 70 years at 1 percent—revealing the serious compounding effects of shaving down an enemy's growth rate. Just compare the North and South Korean economies to get a feel for the multigenerational consequences.

This maritime peace-to-war continuum includes a range of sanctions, beginning with *I sanction, my friends sanction*, and *everyone sanctions* a targeted country by refusing to buy, sell, or both for one, multiple, or all items. The continuum proceeds to impounding a targeted country's merchantmen in *my ports, my friends' ports*, or *all ports*. It can escalate further to shutting down SWIFT codes (key identifying information for international banks) to exclude the targeted country from the international banking system. Still more escalatory is commerce raiding, ranging from *I hunt, my friends hunt*, to *everyone hunts* the targeted country's ships. The continuum ends with blockade: *leave port and all your ships*—merchant or military—*will be sunk*. The continuum embodies escalatory denial: a time out from the global trading regime for the targeted country. Navies are essential to enforce sanctions—a key peacetime role. They deny desired goods and raise the costs of defying sanctions and finding substitutes, which together suppress growth.

Today, China contests the global order with genocide at home and territorial expansion abroad. China (let alone Russia) cannot exercise a maritime security paradigm without numerous allies. Neither China nor Russia has a moat; rather, no other countries have nearly as many neighbors, let alone so many hostile or dysfunctional ones. China—indeed, any country—can minimize transaction costs only through peaceful cooperation within the maritime, rules-based order. The alternatives are expensive and wealth reducing.

Counterintuitively, China's defiance of global norms offers a rare opportunity to strengthen Asia's regional security architecture through the growing participation of its neighbors. The more dire the threat, the stronger the impetus to build, spread, and strengthen countervailing institutions. As much as the United States and others may wish China would become a constructive member of the international system, that choice rests with China, which for the foreseeable future will more likely double down than change heart, as the Chinese Communist Party clings to power. For outsiders, China is a problem more amenable to management than resolution.

The U.S. Navy can play an essential role in coordinating maritime cooperation among China's many threatened neighbors, so that the accumulating precedents strengthen, rather than weaken, the security architecture of Asia and thereby deepen the global maritime order. Navies are the first responders for institution building—naval exercises can expand, including ever more participants, and institutionalize into permanent coordination and, ultimately, alliance systems. Navies are part of the long game: coordinated prosperity with partners and defense against the defiant to protect us all from a continental relapse.

NOTES

1. This article originally appeared in the U.S. Naval Institute *Proceedings* magazine, August 2021. Copyright U.S. Naval Institute. Reprinted with permission. S. C. M. Paine, "Maritime Solutions to Continental Conundrums," *Proceedings* 147, no. 8 (August 2021): 1, 422.

The ideas are those of the author alone.

2. By global order, I mean the international legal rules, applying to both state and nonstate actors, and the institutions that develop, amend, and administer these rules.

3. Lars Wedin, "Sweden and the Blue Society: New Challenges for a Small Navy," Center for International Maritime Security (CIMSEC), 17 September 2020.

4. Francis Bacon, "Of the True Greatness of Kingdoms and Estates," in *Essays Civil and Moral*, cited in Julian S. Corbett, *Some Principles of Maritime Strategy* (New York: Longmans, Green and Co., 1911), 55.

5. Cited in Tadokoro Masayuki, "Why Did Japan Fail to Become the 'Britain' of Asia?" in John W. Steinberg, Bruce W. Menning, David Schimmelpenninck Van Der Oye, David Wolff, and Shinji Yokote, eds., *The Russo-Japanese War in Global Perspective: World War Zero*, vol. 2 (Leiden, Netherlands: Brill, 2007), 301–302.

6. Nicholas J. Spykman, *The Geography of the Peace*, Helen R. Nicholl, ed. (New York: Harcourt, Brace, and Co., 1944), 57.

7. Hugo Grotius, *Freedom of the Seas*, Ralph van Demen Magoffin trans., James Brown Scott, ed. (New York: Oxford University Press, 1916), 7.

8. Hugo Grotius, *The Law of War and Peace (De Jure Belli Ac Pacis)*, Louise Ropes Loomis, trans. (Roslyn, NY: Classics Club, 1949), 91–92.

9. The cumulative/sequential strategy distinction comes from RADM J. C. Wylie, USN, *Military Strategy: A General Theory of Power Control* (1967, reprint; Annapolis, MD: Naval Institute Press, 1989), 117–21.

Acknowledgments

This book would not have been possible without the contributions (absolutely free except for a few gratis book copies) of, in order of first appearance and number of chapter contributions, Robert Zebroski, Zachary R. Morgan, Paul G. Halpern (5), Michael Epkenhans, Philippe Masson, David Stevens (3), William F. Sater, Christopher M. Bell, Regina T. Akers, Chris Madsen, Bruce A. Elleman (8), Richard H. Gimblett, Wolf Heintschel Von Heinegg, Silvia Marzagalli (2), Wade A. Dudley, Andrew D. Lambert (4), David G. Surdam, S. C. M. Paine (5), Mark L. Hayes, Ken-ichi Arakawa (2), Geoffrey Till, Malcolm M. Muir Jr., Jeffrey G. Barlow, Spencer C. Tucker (2), Richard A. Mobley, Charles W. Koburger Jr. (2), James Goldrick (2), Chris Rahman, Roger W. Barnett, Jane G. Dalton, Steve Ross, Douglas Hurd, Lawrence Sondhaus, T. G. Otte, Gerhard L. Weinberg, Edward J. Marolda, Bradford A. Lee (2), Charles Ingrao, Andrew L. Stigler, Robert J. Schneller Jr., David B. Crist, Andrew Forbes, Penny Campbell, Robert J. Antony, David Rosenberg, Catherine Zara Raymond, Samuel Pyeatt Menefee, Sam Bateman, Robert F. Turner, Arild Nodland, Gary E. Weir, Eric Talbot Jensen, Michael Duffy, Robin Prior, Donald Chisholm, Jeffrey Grey, Eric Grove, Peter Jones, John Reeve, Thomas S. Truxes, Christopher P. Magra, Kevin D. McCranie, David H. Olivier, Kenneth J. Hagan, Michael T. McMaster, Willard C. Frank, Jr., Werner Rahn, Joel Holwitt, George K. Walker, Martin N. Murphy, John Pentangelo, Henry J. Hendrix, Jan K. Herman, Tom Williams, Darlene R. Ketten, Mary Landry, Andrew S. Erickson, and Austin M. Strange.

And a special thanks to senior scholars John A. Hattendorf (5) and Michael F. Pavkovic for their thoughtful Forewords.

At Rowman & Littlefield, I want to thank Janice Braunstein, Cindi Pietrzyk, Haley White, and Michael Kerns. My gratitude also goes to the folks at Deanta for typesetting this book, and especially to Arun Rajakumar.

Funding to support this maritime case study book series over a period of two decades came from Mr. Andrew Marshall and Dr. Andrew May, Office of Net Assessment—Office of the Secretary of Defense. The U.S. Naval War College also supported this work when I was a member of the Strategic Research Department, Maritime History Department, Dean of Academics, reporting directly to NWC president Jeffrey A. Harley, and finally in the College of Leadership and Ethics. The views expressed herein are those of the author and do not reflect the opinions of the U.S. Naval War College, the U.S. Navy, or the U.S. government.

A big "thank you" to all the senior scholars who helped correct and improve the list of strategic terms. All mistakes, however, are mine alone.

Finally, and most importantly, an incredible debt is due to Sarah C. M. Paine, my classmate, spouse, colleague, wonderful mother of Anna and Steven, plus helpmate and grammar teacher over the past forty years.

Introduction

While the seas largely remain the same as hundreds of years ago, the laws governing the seas keep on changing. Grotius was one of the first legal scholars to argue for the "freedom of the seas." Due to technological restraints, cannons could not shoot further than 3 miles out to sea, so anything beyond that range was considered "high seas," and thus open for all countries' use. The 3-mile limit largely remained in effect worldwide until 1945, when President Harry S. Truman issued a unilateral proclamation that natural resources in the waters, the subsoil, and the seabed of the continental shelf adjacent to the United States were subject to its jurisdiction and control. Truman's decision was motivated by the discovery of offshore oil deposits and the realization that it was unlikely that private companies would invest if undersea mineral rights were disputed or rich fishing grounds could not be secured.

Historically, the United States was one of the strongest proponents for the freedom of the seas. But having established a new standard for enclosing the seas, several countries rapidly followed Washington's lead. In 1946, Argentina claimed control of its continental shelf, which extends beyond 200 miles, and of the seas above it. In 1947, Chile and Peru extended their jurisdictions to 200 miles, as did Ecuador in 1950. In 1948, Iceland declared conservation zones beyond its 3-mile limit out to the extent of its continental shelf and then in 1949 unilaterally invoked a "headland to headland" rule, which in 1958 became a self-declared 12-mile territorial sea; in 1976, Iceland then adopted a 200-mile limit on maritime resources.

This process of increasing state jurisdiction over the seas continued around the oceans of the world. In an attempt to negotiate a single international standard for the continental shelf, in 1958 the United Nations convened in Geneva the First Conference on the Law of the Seas. Amid growing concerns over the possible privatization or militarization of the seabed, the UN

1

General Assembly in 1968 established the Committee on the Peaceful Uses of the Seabed and the Ocean Floor beyond the Limits of National Jurisdiction. In 1970, the General Assembly unanimously adopted the committee's Declaration of Principles, which states that the seabed and ocean floor, and the subsoil thereof, beyond the limits of national jurisdiction as well as the resources of the area are the "common heritage of mankind," and should be reserved for peaceful purposes, not to be subjected to national appropriation, explored, or exploited except in accordance with an international regime to be established.[1]

The UN, recognizing that the many problems of ocean space were inter-related and needed to be considered in its totality, also decided to convene a new conference to prepare a single, comprehensive treaty. This new treaty was to encompass all aspects of the establishment of a regime and machinery for the high seas and seabed, the continental shelf, and territorial sea. Adding pressure to the diplomatic efforts, a series of "Cod Wars" between Britain and Iceland ensued after Iceland adopted a 50-mile territorial sea limit in 1972. British warships rammed Icelandic coast guard vessels and shot over their bows, while the Icelanders cut the nets of British fishing trawlers and eventually broke off diplomatic relations with the United Kingdom.

In 1974, the UN convened the Third Conference on the Law of the Sea. By 1982, it had produced a treaty for international ratification. Among its many provisions, the treaty grants coastal states the authority to declare sovereign rights and resource control over an exclusive economic zone (EEZ) up to 200 nautical miles off their coastlines. In the case of countries bordering semi-enclosed seas, like the South China Sea, in such a way that their EEZ claims overlap, the United Nations Convention on the Law of the Sea 1982 (UNCLOS) calls for establishing joint resource management areas and provides guidelines for doing so, even where conflicting territorial claims are unresolved. The treaty entered into force in November 1994. To date, 155 countries have signed this agreement, but the U.S. Senate has declined to ratify it, although the U.S. Navy largely adheres to its provisions.

In accordance with the principles of the 1982 convention, many coastal countries have asserted greater management control over their newly acquired EEZs. In April 2008, the UN agreed to the proposed outer limits of Australia's continental shelf, increasing the size of that shelf from 8,200,000 square kilometers to over 10,700,000. In 2016, however, its Court of Arbitration told China that its claim to the entire South China Sea was invalid; so far, China has refused to abide by this ruling. By the first half of the twenty-first century, therefore, the early tradition of the freedom of the seas had been thoroughly circumscribed by an ocean enclosure movement sanctioned by the United Nations. This in turn has substantially affected how states deal with a whole range of maritime issues, including war.

The purpose of this book is to evaluate one hundred case studies devoted to maritime history in order to discern traditional views of sea use as well as new principles governing the seas. This investigation will first examine seven core elements that all sea powers must contend with: (1) Discipline, or rather the lack of discipline, called Mutiny; (2) Blockades; (3) Coalitions; (4) Piracy, or the illegal taking of ships and goods; (5) Expeditionary warfare, in particular in peripheral campaigns; (6) Commerce Raiding, or the legal taking of ships and goods; and (7) Non-military naval operations, including the promotion of diplomacy, humanitarian aid missions, and assistance after manmade and natural disasters. This book will then turn to an evaluation of two enduring capabilities of sea powers: sea control and sea denial. It will then conclude by examining the competition between sea powers and land powers.

NOTE

1. The controversial phrase "Common Heritage of Mankind" was first used in a speech by Maltese ambassador Arvid Pardo in 1967, earning Arvid Pardo the title "father of the law of the sea." http://wealthofthecommons.org/essay/common-heri-tage-mankind-bold-doctrine-kept-within-strict-boundaries

Chapter 1

Mutiny

When people think "mutiny" they typically think of the 1789 Royal Navy incident where Lieutenant William Bligh was ousted from command of the HMS *Bounty*, often with an image of the 1930s actor Charles Laughton, or the later remakes with Marlon Brando or Mel Gibson as Mr. Christian, firmly entrenched in their minds. While these representations of mutiny are considered by many to be mere entertainment, rather than a scholarly topic worthy of study, the history of mutinies is really a study of naval discipline or, more precisely, cases where onboard discipline was clearly lacking.[1]

Discipline on ships is the norm, so it is only possible to study it when discipline fails, which can then result in mutiny. Rather than being a "positive space" event, mutinies are in fact examples of "negative space" incidents, since something that should be present—discipline among the crew—is clearly lacking. Organization of naval mutinies requires greater effort by the mutinying crew, not less. Unlike cases of insubordination or even outright revolt in land armies, which tend to be isolated chaotic events in set locations that can be easily suppressed by loyal troops, naval mutinies can include the taking of one or more ships, often while at sea. Since these are mobile platforms, the weapons they hold can then be moved and directed against their own governments, making them a potential existential threat.

Once taken, not only can the ship in question be valuable in its own right, perhaps as a bargaining chip if the mutineers threaten to damage or destroy it, but the ship's guns and ammunition supply make it potentially dangerous to both friends and foe alike. Perhaps, most importantly, since naval ships are highly mobile, and the first thing most mutineers decide to do is flee from possible pursuit, simply locating a ship at sea in order to retake it from the mutineers can be problematic. For all of these reasons, beginning a study of maritime principles with a chapter on naval mutiny is highly appropriate.

HISTORIC BACKGROUND TO MUTINY

Mutinies can happen virtually anywhere, in any navy. Great Britain and the United States, great powers with mature democracies, were no more immune to mutiny than lesser powers or authoritarian regimes, including Germany, China, and Russia. The nature and scope of mutinies can vary widely, however, from a single ship, several ships, a fleet, or an entire navy. They can even occur on land, for example, at a naval base like Port Chicago, CA.[2] The mutineers' objectives can vary widely, from demands to overthrow a national government, improvement of conditions in a navy, or even just to provide better food aboard ship. The main factor linking all of these events is they all involved a deliberate act of collective insubordination by members of the naval profession against lawful military authority.

Definitions of mutiny differ, with distinctions drawn between "real" mutinies where violence or threat of violence was used to seize a ship versus any lesser types of revolt, strike, or protests against what might be seen by the crew as unjust leadership. Since the term intrinsically encompasses the whole range of meanings, naval authorities tend to shy away from using it. In a like manner, sailors protesting orders were eager to eschew this term because the traditional penalty for mutiny was death by hanging. As a result of hesitation to use the word mutiny, there were many euphemisms like "incident," "strike," or "disobedience" that can appear in the historical literature, all of them in one way or another describing the failure of naval leaders to maintain discipline among their crew. To complicate things further, naval mutinies are not always directed against individual officers, they often do not employ violence, and they do not necessarily involve the seizure of a ship—indeed, they sometimes do not even take place on a ship at all.

Sailors' grievances are often linked to broader social or political problems that impact society as a whole, while most naval mutinies are usually due to relatively minor causes surrounding the conditions of service. These generally appear in one of two ways. The first of these are ship-specific problems, including dangerous working conditions, unpopular orders and officers, and then what might normally appear to be relatively minor problems, such as poor food, bad pay, or intolerable working conditions. Relatively mundane material grievances can be sufficient to trigger a mutiny. This type of mutiny is usually isolated to a single ship and so can often be easily resolved.

A second kind of mutiny includes two or more ships, entire fleets, or even whole navies. In these cases, the underlying cause of the unrest is probably due to widespread politically linked problems that impact all ships equally, such as poor treatment, bad discipline, or the perception—whether real or unreal is another matter entirely—of inept leadership over the navy and perhaps over the entire state. Because most of these issues impact the navy alone, it is not unusual for mutineers to discover that their grievances do not generate significant support outside of the navy or even beyond a particular fleet or even squadron.

However, on occasion mutinies do stem from more deep-rooted and systemic problems, including tensions due to class, racial, or national differences. Since a ship's crew represents a cross-section of the nation it tends to reflect the social and political values of the nation as a whole. Conflict within a navy may therefore be either partially or predominantly a spillover from a state's social, economic, or political ills.

Because sailors' complaints can reach beyond local conditions, a principal aim of many mutinies is not always to effect a local change in command, but rather to modify conditions of service in the navy generally. In these cases, it is worth emphasizing that mutineers are not always in direct conflict with their immediate superiors, but rather with a more distant authority, either the naval high command or the government itself. But while unfavorable conditions of service can create an atmosphere conducive to insubordination, and will often provide the "trigger" that sets off a mutiny, the goal of the mutineers seldom goes beyond the amelioration of their service-related grievances.

There are exceptions, however, including the 1905 *Potemkin* mutiny in Russia, the 1918 Austro-Hungarian mutiny at Cattaro, and the sensational revolt of the entire German navy during that same year. Sailors who participated in these mutinies had far-reaching political goals, including overthrowing their governments. Mutinies that begin with political objectives are relatively rare, however, and the more normal causes include poor conditions of service. In the *Potemkin* case, for example, the most radical among the mutineers came forward only after the mutiny had already begun over a more mundane issue—poor food.[3] In the case of the 1919 French naval mutinies, the genuine revolutionaries deliberately emphasized service-related grievances in order to gain the support of the rank and file for an uprising against naval authority—an uprising they hoped would grow into a full-blown revolution. There are three major types of mutiny to consider.

THREE TYPES OF MUTINY

While the objectives that mutineers pursue are highly diverse, a basic distinction can be drawn between mutinies that are essentially isolated acts of protest over service, called "promotion of interest" movements versus "secession" or "seizure of power" movement that represents outright rebellion.[4] There is also a third type of political mutiny that falls somewhere in between, in that the mutineers do not protest strictly naval affairs but they fall far short of advocating revolution. Classifying mutinies into (1) promotion of interests, (2) seizure or secession, or (3) political is made difficult by the fact that as a mutiny progresses the goals of the mutineers can change over time. Of these three, "political mutinies" are the most complex, since mutineers can attempt to influence or coerce their government to adopt a particular policy, such as surrender in a war, without intending to challenge directly the authority or legitimacy of their government. Particularly in democratic states, sailors can use mutiny as a means of participating in the political process, similar to civilian workers going on strike to protest a government decision.

Based on an examination of historical cases of mutiny, it can be difficult to generalize about when grievances will become serious enough to provoke a deliberate act of mass insubordination. The number of mutineers or type of participation seems to have little to do with how serious a mutiny can become. For example, the mutineers on the single ship *Potemkin* sought to spark a national revolution in all of Russia, while the much larger and apparently more serious Invergordon mutiny of the Royal Navy in 1931 only put forward relatively moderate and clearly defined objectives to reverse a recently announced service-wide cut in pay.

Conditions that are sufficient to ignite a mutiny in one ship or navy often will not be enough in another. The pay disputes leading to the Canadian mutinies in 1949, for example, would have seemed remarkably trivial to the Russian sailors of 1905, who expected harsh treatment and poor working conditions as a matter of course. Even ships within the same navy will have different reactions to what are essentially the same conditions. The 1943 mutiny in HMCS *Iroquois*, for example, was due to the relative inexperience of the ship's crew: according to one of the officers involved, offensive behavior by the ship's captain would have probably been ignored by a more seasoned crew.[5]

A range of factors determine each crew's "threshold" for mutiny. Perceptions of what constitutes unacceptable treatment play a critical role in determining when the crew will feel that their grievances are serious enough to warrant mutiny. Standards and norms of behavior differ not only between navies but also across time. Two hundred years ago conditions of service were awful: British sailors in 1800 were routinely pressed into a service where flogging was commonplace, work conditions were harsh, food was bad, and pay was poor and irregular. But mutinies were hardly more frequent then than now because sailors in Nelson's navy viewed these appalling conditions as normal. Some practices and conditions acceptable in the American or British navies even fifty years ago would be considered intolerable in the same forces today. Like their more modern counterparts, they usually mutinied only when they believed they were being treated unfairly or with unusual severity according to the standards of their times.

In any ship, a variety of factors will determine when crews reach their breaking point. Calculations of personal risk are probably the most critical consideration. If the likelihood of punishment or suppression is perceived as slight, a crew's "threshold" tends to move downward—that is, the crew will be more likely to mutiny over minor provocations. There is an opposite tendency, however, in wartime, when additional burdens and hardships will usually be borne willingly out of a sense of patriotic duty. One exception to this rule is the Port Chicago mutiny, which occurred on land in 1944, right at the height of World War II. In this case, the fear of exploding ordnance clearly outweighed feelings of national loyalty, in particular when perceived racial bias—African American stevedores commanded by white officers— was added to the mix.

It is normally quite unusual for a ship to mutiny in wartime, especially if the war is a national war being fought against another state. When mutinies do occur during periods of interstate war, mutineers usually stress their loyalty to the government and willingness to return to duty if threatened by enemy action. A good exception to this rule is a civil war, when both sides claim to be the legitimate national government. It was during the Chinese Civil War, for example, when the Chinese flagship *Chongqing* mutinied in early 1949 and switched sides from the Nationalists to the Communists. Since the Communists soon achieved victory over mainland China, the mutineers were treated as heroes, not criminals, in the People's Republic of China.

The interplay of personalities in any particular ship also represents a critical and unpredictable variable. The presence or absence of a popular commander or a charismatic "troublemaker" has often made the difference between the maintenance of discipline and the outbreak of mutiny. Personalities can also impact how successful a mutiny will be in obtaining the objectives of the mutineers. Not surprisingly, if the mutineers are highly organized and resist becoming divided among themselves over minor issues, then their chances for overall success go up.

MUTINY'S RATE OF SUCCESS OR FAILURE

Mutiny tends to be a very successful means of achieving the primary objectives of the majority of participants, so much so that it is strange that they do not occur more frequently. There are, however, natural constraints working against the outbreak of mutiny. Understandably, the most important of these is the threat of punishment. The penalties for mutiny are potentially extreme. Even today, mutineers may face the death penalty, or some other severe punishment meted out by a court martial, not only for taking a leading part in a mutiny, but even for failing to take sufficient steps to report, prevent, or suppress a mutiny. While all participants are legally subject to the harshest penalties, it is almost invariably the "ringleaders" who bear the full brunt of the law. Potential mutineers will be well aware, therefore, that even if a mutiny achieves its immediate aims, its leaders may still have to fear punishment. This naturally acts as a strong disincentive to take a leading role.

Mutineers have also had to overcome the problem of isolation at sea. In the early twentieth century, the most effective form of communication technology—radio—was usually controlled by ships' officers, who could often squelch any information or even rumors of a mutiny in another ship. Where this did not happen, such as India in 1946, mutiny could spread rapidly to distant ships and stations. Technological advances in recent decades have made it much easier for mutineers to maintain contact with each other ships and incite others to join them. The information revolution may therefore have unwelcome side effects for some navies when it comes to maintaining discipline.

Similarly, communications obstacles have made it difficult for aspiring mutineers in the past to plot a fleet- or navy-wide rebellion. Large-scale mutinies in the twentieth century were usually the cumulative result of a series of separate and spontaneous mutinies on individual ships. Each crew essentially had to make its own decision whether to mutiny, a task made easier in port when sailors could see for themselves that others had already done so. It was therefore more common to see large-scale mutinies occur while ships were collected together in harbor, where they were within visual range of each other, and where the crews from different ships had the opportunity to conspire together on shore. Ships at sea are usually too isolated or preoccupied to experience this "domino effect."

Navies usually provide channels for personnel to resolve grievances without recourse to mutinous behavior. The British and American navies, for example, were the most successful in the twentieth century at encouraging their crew to bring complaints directly to their superiors. To ensure that these channels worked, officers were expected to take a genuine interest in the welfare of the lower deck and stay in touch with the state of its morale. By and large, these efforts were met with a feeling that complaints from the lower deck would be addressed fairly and sympathetically by officers.

When the formal and informal machinery for addressing grievances functioned properly, such as when Non-Commissioned Officers smooth tensions over, trouble was normally avoided. It was when the system did not work, or when it encountered a situation that it was not designed to deal with, that sailors were most likely to pursue drastic solutions to their complaints. During the Port Chicago mutiny, which was unusual for being located on land at a naval base, African American mutineers felt that their legitimate concerns over workplace safety had not received proper consideration by their white superiors. At Invergordon, by contrast, it was clear that the existing welfare machinery was inadequate in the face of government-mandated pay cuts.[6] These large-scale breakdowns in discipline were isolated events, however, because goodwill generally existed between officers and men in these navies.

Where the system was inherently suspect—as was often the case in corrupt or authoritarian states—the potential for discontent rose dramatically. For example, in China it is even now common for officers and sailors to speak different regional dialects, making detailed communications difficult. Clearly, the ability of officers to "make the rounds" in order to listen to lower-deck concerns would be remarkably difficult in these circumstances, even if sailors felt comfortable that they could complain about their superiors without fear of retribution. When cooperation between officers and crew is inadequate or non-existent, then what starts as a small isolated mutiny has a greater tendency to spread. This spread can be horizontal, vertical, or both.

HORIZONTAL AND VERTICAL ESCALATION

One of the most intriguing aspects of mutinies is their ability to spread from one ship to another, known as horizontal escalation. There appear to be two reasons for this tendency to grow. First, as already noted, the conditions that trigger a mutiny in one vessel commonly exist in others. Second, once one ship has taken the unusual step of mutinying, the risk for other ships to do so significantly diminishes. Sailors seem to realize instinctively that the more people and the larger number of ships that take part in a mutiny, the more difficult it becomes to punish all of those who participate. There is safety in numbers.

Notably, the tendency for mutiny to spread horizontally from ship to ship was not always accompanied by a similar process of vertical escalation, in which the mutineers' demands became more complex and far reaching as events progressed. In the HMAS *Australia* mutiny in 1919, the American Port Chicago case in 1944, and the Canadian events in 1949, although very different from each other in terms of background, location, and "triggers," the focus remained on the mutineers' immediate concerns pertaining to poor working conditions and it never shifted to larger demands pertaining to navy-wide or even nationwide issues. Even in the Royal Navy's 1931 mutiny at Invergordon, where sailors attempted from the outset to address navy-wide problems, the mutiny's objectives remained focused on the proximate cause of the unrest—pay cuts.

In sharp contrast to the relatively benign nature of mutinies in democratic states, in the more authoritarian states, such as the *Potemkin* mutiny in Russia in 1905 or China's *Chongqing* mutiny in 1949, single-ship mutinies quickly transitioned to revolutionary movements whose unlimited goals ultimately included the overthrow of the national government. In no other cases was such a rapid vertical transition evident. These cases suggest that mutinies in authoritarian states tend to be inherently more volatile than those in democratic countries.

There are many reasons for this process of vertical escalation to appear. At the most basic level, sailors may simply decide that having already taken the drastic step of disobeying authority over one issue, and thus becoming liable to the most dire penalties, there is nothing more to lose by seeking redress of other grievances. The potential for vertical escalation is clearly greatest when sailors' basic complaints go beyond purely naval problems, such as opposing a suicide mission or fearing additional munition explosions, and in particular when a state is suffering from serious political or economic difficulties and feels like it is facing an existential threat.

Escalation can also be linked to the presence of individual sailors with radical views or revolutionary intentions. Efforts to unionize navies is just one example. Even if these elements are not responsible for launching the mutiny, they will generally attempt to direct subsequent events according to a pre-existing political agenda. Once a ship's officers are removed or marginalized, the absence of well-defined leadership provides ample opportunities for the more politically minded sailors to fill the void.

Mutineers may also feel that, having mutinied, they have effectively "painted themselves into a corner." In authoritarian countries, in particular, mutineers will often have little confidence that a just settlement can be made at ship, naval, or government levels to resolve their grievances. Taking the mutiny to its ultimate extreme, the overthrow of the central government may become the only way to avoid punishment. The *Potemkin* mutiny, for example, sought to spark a national revolution. When that failed, simple survival became the dominant concern. Similarly, the 1949 mutiny of the *Chongqing* ended with the ship defecting to the Communist side, which may not have been the crew's intention all along but was perhaps simply considered the best means of escaping punishment. The change of a national regime is rather a large event. For that reason, these are called limited or unlimited goals.

LIMITED AND UNLIMITED MUTINIES

Mutineers in democratic countries have little incentive to force the process of vertical escalation. This is a major difference between conscripted navies and volunteer navies. On the contrary, volunteer navies will usually emphasize that their demands are strictly limited in scope. As a result, most of these mutinies have been resolved peacefully and resulted in concession being

made by the governments. Navies and governments confronted with mutinous sailors face a difficult choice, however. On the one hand, by giving in
to illegal pressure they risk further undermining discipline and encouraging
other acts of disobedience. On the other hand, the early or excessive use of
force has often been counter-productive, leading to a sympathetic response
among crewmen who had not yet decided whether to join the mutiny in its
initial stages.

Because mutiny is so often seen as an exceptional means to draw attention
to intolerable conditions, making concessions has seldom undermined discipline over the long term. Indeed, the willingness of leaders to give way when
complaints are both serious and legitimate may be one of the reasons why
sailors in some navies are willing to trust their superiors and work within the
system when confronted by routine problems. There is clearly the possibility,
however, that "thresholds" can drop below acceptable levels when mutiny
begins to emerge as a legitimate form of protest rather than exceptional measures to be held in reserve, as appears to have happened in the Canadian Navy
over the latter half of the 1940s.

While force has sometimes been successful in ending or suppressing a
mutiny, there are also notable instances where the threat or use of violence
has served only to inflame passions and increase the likelihood of escalation. If drastic punishment or brutal suppression is a certainty, mutineers
have nothing to lose by directly threatening the government or escaping
from its authority. They might as well ignore all limits. They are on "death
ground" anyway. Reports of mutiny in China, including one in August 1999
that resulted in a dozen dead and wounded officers and crew, reflect such
concerns.[7]

But because most mutineers are seeking to redress specific complaints
rather than fundamentally upset the status quo, it is usually obvious to
mutineers that there is little to gain—and potentially much to lose—either
in employing force against the government or in meeting force with force.
Mutinies are always a two-sided affair. The government in question may be
in a strong position to end a mutiny by initiating its own process of escalation.
The use of force against a mutinous ship or fleet can also hasten a conclusion
simply by demonstrating to mutineers that the government still commands the
allegiance of other ships and of the other armed services.

One of the most important lessons from the study of mutinies, therefore, is
that naval mutinies are less of a threat to democratic states than to authoritarian ones. Perhaps for this reason, authoritarian governments have historically
tended to take the threat of mutinies more seriously. This has manifested itself
in a low tolerance for acts of dissent and the search for organizational barriers to horizontal escalation. For example, the division of the Chinese navy
into three regional fleets may be due—in part at least—to a desire to ensure

that different units cannot easily communicate with each other and organize a rebellion against the central government; so long as only one fleet rebels, while the others remain loyal, any anti-government mutiny can almost certainly be isolated and put down.

While such a fleet organization provides an important institutional barrier against mutiny, the potential downside can be seen whenever there are sharp divisions in communication and command structure between the fleets; in times of war, it would potentially be very difficult to coordinate joint operations among the various fleets. Thus, navies with a high escalation potential for mutiny tend, by their very nature, to be less efficient navies; to organize themselves more efficiently would risk more and greater mutinies. Such institutional and organizational factors might help determine modern naval mutinies.

MODERN NAVAL MUTINIES

As might be expected, the most serious or noteworthy mutinies in the years since 1950 have occurred in authoritarian regimes. As the main actors in these events were usually arrested and—in most cases—executed, the details often remain murky. The first major mutiny of the Cold War period took place on November 8, 1975, when the Soviet *Krivak*-class missile frigate *Storozhevoy* ("Guardian") reportedly attempted to defect from Latvia to the Swedish island of Gotland. This mutiny, which provided the basis for Tom Clancy's *The Hunt for Red October*, was led by the ship's political officer, Valery Sablin. The mutiny was unsuccessful; the ship was stopped; and the mutiny leader was captured, court-martialed, and executed. While the official announcement stated that Sablin was defecting, there are reports that he intended to sail to Leningrad and declare his opposition to the Politburo.

Naval mutinies in communist states represent fundamental threats to the authority of the central government. By contrast, mutinies in Western navies have been infrequent, small-scale, and localized affairs. An incident in 1958 on the British fleet minelayer HMS *Apollo* is typical of the discipline problems faced by democratic states since the end of World War II. According to one of the officers present, this event, portrayed by the media as a "notorious mutiny," was in fact "little more than a temporary breakdown in discipline in one of the junior seamen's mess-decks. A rating had come on board drunk, dodged the Officer of the Watch, whose duty it was to take him into custody for his own safety until he had sobered up, and took refuge in his mess, where his messmates battened down the hatches and refused to give him up. This joint refusal to obey an order was," he concluded, "indeed an act of mutiny."

But, if the incident had not been reported to the *Daily Mirror*, "it could have been dealt with at a local level."[8]

Episodes like this one hardly fit the popular image of a mutiny. Demonstrations in the U.S. Navy have taken a more serious turn. During the final years of the conflict in Vietnam, for example, racially motivated demonstrations and sit-ins took place on four U.S. warships, including the aircraft carriers *Constellation* and *Kitty Hawk*, in 1972.[9] Mutinous activities there ranged from passive "sit-ins" to violent and destructive rioting. But while these incidents show that the U.S. Navy, like American society as a whole, was going through a turbulent period, there was little danger that they would escalate into anything more serious than isolated protest movements. Post-Vietnam reforms have addressed the tensions underlying these incidents and made a repetition virtually unthinkable.

A reported mutiny in the post-Soviet Russian Navy also appears to have been a relatively harmless and isolated incident, making it more similar to those experienced by Western navies. In 1998, sailors on the small missile ship *Uragan* staged a protest to complain about poor living conditions, including damp bedding, insufficient leave, restrictions on personal cameras, and a shortage of films being shown for recreational purposes. According to one source, it was the fault of the deputy captain for educational work, since he had not taken the "opportunity to talk with the seamen not only as a superior but also as a senior comrade and a member of their crew." The captain of the ship "needed a total of a 20-minute conversation with the seamen in order to eliminate all of the complaints and for passions to subside."[10]

CONCLUSIONS

Naval mutinies have been present as long as navies have existed. The downward mutiny trends suggest that major disciplinary incidents are probably a thing of the past for Western, democratic states. Today's all-volunteer forces enjoy greatly improved conditions of service compared to their predecessors of even fifty years ago. They have access to clearly delineated and generally efficient channels for seeking the redress of grievances, in addition to a range of informal means to make their complaints known to higher authorities. When this is combined with institutionalized checks and balances, such as the practice of outside inspections, there appear to be a few problems that existing "systems" will not be able to handle.

Undoubtedly, there will continue to be minor incidents, for several reasons: (1) sailors have a tendency to misbehave from time to time; (2) in this democratic age many sailors will feel that they have an inherent right to protest orders or practices that are objectionable; and (3) the sailors will know that their actions, even if they legally constitute mutiny, will not be perceived or punished as such. The spring 2020 Covid-related events on the USS *Theodore Roosevelt*, resulting in the sacking of the ship's captain and then the sudden retirement of a Secretary of the Navy, are just one possible example. Another is a recently reported mutiny case in Canada when a soldier tried to block the administration of the Covid vaccine.[11]

The prognosis elsewhere is not as good. There are today large portions of the globe governed by unpopular, weak, or corrupt regimes. These states try to deter acts of collective insubordination by the threat of harsh punishment, but such measures might inadvertently ensure that when mutiny does break out there is a higher potential for rapid and dramatic vertical escalation. Foreign actors could even work secretly to exacerbate such tendencies. Therefore, the future instances of naval mutinies are, most likely, far from over.

NOTES

1. The twelve mutiny case studies referred to in this chapter include the 1905 *Potemkin*, 1910 Revolt of the Lash, 1918 Cattaro, 1918 German, 1919 French, 1919 Australia, 1931 Chile, 1931 Invergordon, 1944 Port Chicago, 1946 India, 1949 China, and 1949 Canada, see Bruce A. Elleman and Christopher M., Bell, eds., *Naval Mutinies of the Twentieth Century: An International Perspective* (London: Frank Cass, 2003).

2. Regina T. Akers, "The Port Chicago Mutiny, 1944," in *Ibid.*, 193–211.

3. Robert Zebroski, "The Battleship Potemkin and its Discontents, 1905," in *Ibid.*, 9–31.

4. Cornelis J. Lammers, "Strikes and Mutinies: A Comparative Study of Organizational Conflicts between Rulers and Ruled," *Administrative Science Quarterly*, 14, no. 4 (1969): 559.

5. Michael J. Whitby, "Matelots, Martinets, and Mutineers: The Mutiny in HMCS *Iroquis*, 19 July 1943," *Journal of Military History*, 65, no. 1 (January 2001): 77–103.

6. Christopher M. Bell, "The Invergordon Mutiny, 1931," in Elleman and Bell, *Naval Mutinies*, 170–192.

7. Tien Sui, "Internal Strife Among Naval Officers and Men Leads to Bloodshed Aboard Submarine Chaser," *Hong Kong Cheng Ming*, no. 263 (1 September 1999): 25.

8. *The Times*, 14 February 2002.

9. Paul B. Ryan, "USS *Constellation* Flare-up: Was it Mutiny?" *United States Naval Institute Proceedings*, 102, no. 1 (January 1976): 46–53.

10. Interview with Rear-Admiral Aleksandr Gennadiyevich Dyakonov, *Morskoy Sbornik*, no. 12 (December 1998): 50–53.

11. "Canadian soldier faces mutiny charges for trying to block vaccine distribution," 25 May 2021, *The Guardian*, https://www.theguardian.com/world/2021/may/25/canadian-soldier-mutiny-court-martial-vaccine-coronavirus

Chapter 2

Blockades

There is a popular perception of naval blockades as a line of ships standing duty off an enemy's coastline with blockade runners attempting to break their way through the "wooden wall." While sometimes true, naval blockades frequently take other forms. They are not always directed against a specific port or stretch of coastline, nor do they have to take place at sea at all, so long as their goal of disrupting naval trade is achieved. Naval blockades have also been associated with the "starvation blockade" of World War I, and more recently with the danger surrounding the Cuban Missile Crisis of October 1962. Contrary to these highly publicized blockades, many, if not most, naval blockades have been conducted with little fanfare and relatively little public awareness.

This does not mean that blockades have been ineffective, however, and as a military tactic naval blockades have time after time shown themselves to be one of the most efficient ways to exert pressure on an opponent. When re-examining eighteen of the nineteenth and twentieth century's most important naval blockades, several factors become immediately apparent.[1] While naval blockades have most frequently been conducted by sea powers against land powers—the most well-known examples of this, of course, were the British attempts to blockade Germany in World Wars I and II—a continental country can try to cut an island nation off from international trade, as Napoleon tried to do with Britain's trade with the rest of Europe from 1803 to 1815 or China tried to do with Taiwan in 1995–1996.

Blockades can be very time-consuming affairs, especially if the country being blockaded—and this applies in particular to land powers—can turn away from its sea lines of communications (SLOCs) and instead open new land lines of communications (LLOCs) to help fill the gap. As shown positively by the Crimean War and negatively by the Nationalist blockade of

China during the 1950s, speed is essential, and the longer a land power has to create new communication and trade routes the less effective the blockade will be. Another important factor is the relationship between international law and blockade. By never officially declaring war the belligerents can avoid many restrictions. Calling the conflict a "civil war," for example, rather than an international conflict, allows them to ignore one group of laws, while calling blockades a "quarantine," "embargo," or "sanctions" can also affect how international law regards it.

Blockades can be examined in terms of time, space, force, goals, enemy adaptation, and overall effectiveness. Time includes both the rate of implementation and duration. Space concerns the area under blockade and the SLOCs and LLOCs for both sides. Force refers to the available instruments of national power. Objectives concern both the strategic goal for which the blockade was undertaken and the operational goals of the blockade. Enemy adaptation includes the blockaded country's attempts to adapt to changing circumstances. Finally, effectiveness is measured on both the strategic and operational level. Blockade types include close and distant (in terms of the distance of the blockade perimeter from its focus); near and far (in terms of the distance of the theater from the blockading country); partial and total (in terms of its porosity); and paper, pacific, and belligerent (in terms of the level of coercion). Technological breakthroughs have greatly influenced the cost, execution, and feasibility of all types of blockade, while also widening the distinctions among interdiction, interception, embargo, and full quarantine.

TIME: IMPLEMENTATION AND DURATION

Both the rate of implementation and duration of a blockade can influence its effectiveness. Implementation can be rapid, intermittent, tightening, or loosening, while the duration can be short, medium, or long. For instance, the British and French rapidly blockaded the Baltic during the Crimean War, but for a short period.[2] Meanwhile, the Entente and Allied blockades of Germany during the two world wars gradually tightened over a longer period of time.[3]

Time is especially important in evaluating blockades. Seven rapidly implemented blockades involved sea powers cutting off land powers or other weaker sea powers. These include Crimea, First Sino-Japanese, Spanish-American, Korea, Cuban Missile Crisis, Falklands, and Iraq. In all but two of these conflicts—Korea and Iraq—rapid blockades were also short, forcing a favorable negotiated settlement. Rapid blockades tend to help force the blockaded country into agreeing quickly to a negotiated settlement, suggesting a relationship between speed and effectiveness. In Korea and Iraq, where strategic success was not rapid, Korea was bordering powerful allies including the USSR and China, which enabled North Korea to survive, while long borders and cooperative neighbors also aided Iraq.

In six cases of gradually tightening blockades—Napoleon, World War I, Second Sino-Japanese, World War II, Vietnam, and the Australian reverse blockade—none completely determined the outcome of the wars *except* the Australian reverse blockade, a highly unusual case since it sought to stop illegal immigrants from entering Australian waters.[4] The extensive size of all of these theaters helps to explain why the blockades were not rapid. Yet, if a tightening blockade is being imposed against a land power—Japan's blockade of China in the 1930s and early 1940s is a good example—then the blockaded country should have adequate time to create alternative trade routes, as occurred in Nationalist China.[5] Finally, since tightening blockades tend to take a long time to deliver results, they can really only be adopted successfully by naval powers that enjoy both strong political backing and significant financial resources.

Three intermittent blockades—the War of 1812, the American Civil War, and the PRC missile blockade—while two loosening blockades—ROC-PRC and Rhodesia—were perhaps most strategically effective in what they prevented from happening, in other words, their deterrent effects. For example, the United States did not invade Canada in 1812, the Confederacy did not build a strong navy, China did not invade Taiwan in the 1950s, Rhodesia could not avoid UN censure, and Taiwan did not declare independence in 1996. The main problem with analyzing the effectiveness of deterrent blockades is in not knowing what would have happened had they had never been adopted in the first place. This means examining negative space for critical events that did not occur.

Five blockades were long—Napoleon, Second Sino-Japanese, ROC-PRC, Rhodesia, and the Iraqi wars—averaging ten years or more. With the exception of the rapid development of a coalition opposing Iraq, the first two gradually tightened, while the second two loosened over time. Short and medium-length blockades were usually carried out in combination with either a real, or at least the threat of a land invasion, and the blockaded area generally contained an operational Center of Gravity (COG). In the First Sino-Japanese War, for example, the Chinese navy was trapped in the port of Weihaiwei and was destroyed as a result of the blockade. In the Falklands, the blockaded area encompassed the entire theater of hostilities. In the Cuban Missile Crisis, the ships being blockaded contained missile parts necessary to complete the installation.

In four cases where blockades failed to achieve their primary strategic goal—Napoleon, War of 1812, Second Sino-Japanese, and PRC missile—two of the four were long blockades, while the other two included one short and one medium blockade, so the duration of a blockade probably has less to do with failure than other factors, including the creation of a hostile coalition, the inadvertent strengthening of the enemy's military and naval forces, or the specific nature of the theater.

SPACE: THE NATURE OF THE THEATER

In most cases sea powers impose blockades on land powers. Only extremely rarely do either sea or land powers blockade other sea powers. Blockade distances can vary greatly. The terms "close blockade" and "distant blockade" refer to the distance of the blockade perimeter to the blockaded country, while "near blockade" and "far blockade" refer to the distance of the theater of operations from the country enforcing the blockade. Blockades can be executed unilaterally or in combination with a coalition, and they can be broken by blockade runners or by creating alternate new LLOCs or air routes.

Space includes how close a blockading fleet is to its enemy. The largest number of the blockade cases—seven out of eighteen—involved naval powers conducting close blockades far from their own shores. These include the War of 1812, Crimea, Korea, Vietnam, Rhodesia, Falklands, and Iraq. Arguably all involved sea powers opposing land powers (the United States was not yet a strong sea power in 1812). In these cases the blockaded country was too far away to retaliate effectively against the home territory of the blockading country, for example, Japan during World War II did not blockade the continental United States, so the blockader could afford to patrol closer to the enemy's shores. In other words, all far blockades were also close blockades, although not all close blockades were far. Meanwhile, of the twelve close blockades, five were near, including the Civil War, First Sino-Japanese, Spanish-American, Second Sino-Japanese, and ROC-PRC. In four of these, the theater of operations was near enough to the blockading power that armed retaliation was very likely, and so the enemy's navy became a prime target.

Sea powers do best when blockading islands, peninsulas, or other lesser sea powers that depend primarily on SLOCs, while blockades against land powers tend to be protracted and porous. Land powers can render ineffective a sea power's blockades when their central geographic location provides alternate LLOCs. In particular, if the blockaded country can form land lines with contiguous allies, then the costs of the blockade will increase exponentially and its effectiveness will decline. In such theaters, successful blockades alone did not bring about the strategic success of the blockading sea power; joint and combined operations were also crucial.

Sea powers seeking to blockade a country bordering on Russia should anticipate Russian intervention. Historically, Russia has chosen sides in such conflicts to open up or close down alternate supply routes and sources of supplies. In fully half of all of the case studies—nine cases out of the eighteen—Russian actions have threatened to tip the balance in the blockade effort, including (1) defection from Napoleon's continental blockade of England, (2) defeat in World War I but soon counterbalanced by U.S. participation, (3) opposition to Japan in the Second Sino-Japanese War, (4) cooperating with the Nazis until attacked in 1941, (5) opposition to the Nationalist blockade of China during the 1950s, (6) opposition to the UN blockade of Korea, (7) opposition to the U.S. blockade of North Vietnam, (8) lack of cooperation with the U.S.-led interdiction program in the Persian Gulf, and finally, (9) weapons sales to the PRC during the 1996 missile crisis against Taiwan. In addition, it was Russia being blockaded in the Crimea, while the U.S. blockade in the Cuban Missile Crisis was intended to halt the delivery of Soviet missiles.

More than any other countries, Russia, Britain, and the United Sates figure in multiple naval blockades. This is not too surprising since Russia was the preeminent land power for most of the nineteenth and twentieth centuries, while Britain and the United States have been the two greatest naval powers of the nineteenth and twentieth centuries. Naval blockade is often an indirect strategy chosen by sea powers to exert pressure on land powers, whose armies they do not wish to engage directly.

Based on the evidence presented in the case studies, it would appear that sea powers and island nations require strong navies to overcome a blockade, while land powers can often compensate with alternate LLOCs; conversely, while strong naval powers can successfully conduct quick decisive blockades against land powers—usually leading to a negotiated settlement—land powers can rarely conduct quick operations against sea powers or island nations. Sea powers do particularly well when blockading a diplomatically isolated enemy, and especially when that enemy is an island nation or island colony. Under these circumstances, the blockade serves the dual purpose of attaining a strategic objective and of cutting the enemy off from potential allies. Meanwhile, land powers have a very small chance of successfully blockading anyone, especially an island nation, island colony, or sea power, except perhaps for a deterrent effect.

FORCE: JOINT AND COMBINED OPERATIONS

After time and space, force constitutes a critical dimension of blockade warfare. Enforcement of a naval blockade can include reconnaissance, patrols, and interdiction from the surface, under water, from the air and outer space, and the deployment of armaments like mines, missiles, or bombs. Enforcement often includes joint and/or combined operations between naval,

land, and—in the modern era—air forces, including the invasion of the enemy's sovereign land, sea, or air space. Finally, the duration of the blockade
has an impact on force levels, since protraction can either deplete a set force
or require the deployment of reinforcements.

Surface patrols enforced all but two of the eighteen case studies. The two
exceptions included Napoleon, who mainly used customs officers and police
to halt smuggling from the Continent to England, and the PRC missile blockade of Taiwan, both highly unusual blockades. Underwater mines were extensively used in at least eight of the eighteen blockades—First Sino-Japanese
War, Spanish-American, World War I, Second Sino-Japanese, World War II,
ROC-PRC, Korea, and Vietnam, while submarines factored in four cases—
World War I, World War II, the Cuban Missile Crisis, and the Falklands
War. After the development of aerial bombing, it too was used extensively,
including the Second Sino-Japanese, World War II, the Nationalist blockade
of China, the Korean War, Vietnam, the Falklands, and in Iraq; sea-based
aviation and VSTOL played an especially important role in the Falklands.
Finally, land-based missiles were the primary means of enforcement in only
one of the blockades—the PRC vs Taiwan—but their potential for use in
future blockades is great; blockades of this type have been referred to as
"choke point" blockades.

In at least eight of the blockades, the blockading power was intent on
conquest or reconquest, including Napoleon, the Union, Japan in the Second
Sino-Japanese War, World War II, the Nationalist blockade of China, UN
attempts to reunify Korea, the Falklands War, and the PRC missile blockade.
All but two of these eight, specifically the Nationalists and later the PRC,
included a major invasion of territory.

However, in six other cases there were invasions that were not intended to
be permanent conquests. These included the British attack on the U.S. capital
in the War of 1812, the Anglo-French invasion of the Crimea, the Japanese
invasion of China in the First Sino-Japanese War, U.S. invasion of Cuba in
the Spanish-American War, British deployment on the Continent in World
War I, and UN troops in Iraq. Most, but not all, of the wars of conquest, and
the majority of other blockades that included invasions, lasted over a year.
Many were protracted wars.

Blockades without any land operations were rare. Rather, many naval
blockades entailed joint and combined operations that coordinated sea, land,
and later air operations. The War of 1812, Crimean War, the First Sino-
Japanese War, the Spanish-American War, the Second Sino-Japanese War,
Korea, and the Falklands stand out in this regard. The few exceptions to
this pattern were the Cuban Missile Crisis, Rhodesia, Iraq, the PRC missile
blockade, and the Australian reverse blockade, where operations on land
played little if any role in the blockade (although, in the case of Cuba, the

threat of invasion proved critical to achieving a negotiated outcome to the conflict).

An examination of the force equation, sometimes disparaged as "War by Algebra," suggests that modern blockades are rarely conducted by just surface ships. As submarines and airpower became more available and dependable, they too were used for patrol duty. Joint operations also played an increasingly important role, with joint sea-air operations increasingly substituting for joint land-sea operations in the modern period.

Finally, while wars of conquest usually included invasions—with the two notable exceptions being Chinese (the Nationalist blockade of the PRC and the PRC missile blockade of Taiwan) where a full-blown invasion would have been an enormous undertaking—land invasions were not necessarily intended for permanent conquest. All too often land invasions were merely intended for exerting pressure for a negotiated settlement, as opposed to an unconditional victory, as happened in the War of 1812, the Crimean War, the First Sino-Japanese War, and the Spanish-American War. This is why a careful weighing of strategic and operational goals is critical to success.

STRATEGIC AND OPERATIONAL GOALS

Blockades are a means to an end. At the operational level of warfare, they are simply a way to impede transportation and communications. At the strategic level, however, sometimes alone, but more often in combination with other military strategies, they are also a means to achieve an overarching national goal—often referred to as grand strategy—that provides the rationale for employing coercion. Operational goals include the interruption of trade, the occupation of territory, the destruction of enemy naval or land forces, and the control of population movements. Strategic goals can include deterrence, economic strangulation, military degradation, bottleneck creation, cost escalation, morale erosion, and sanction enforcement. Blockades can be total or something less, hence the terms "total blockade" and "partial blockade." Total blockades completely halt prohibited traffic, while partial blockades, by intent or by default, allow either a percentage or certain categories of trade and population movement to continue. Blockades that are effective at sea, but fail to cut alternate land routes, are still partial, even though they may make critical contributions to victory. Finally, the blockader's goals can be unlimited, meaning the overthrow of the enemy government, or something less, hence the terms "unlimited blockade" and "limited blockade," defined in terms of strategic objective, not in the quantity of resources devoted to the blockade.

In six of the eighteen cases the original objectives were unlimited, and in three more—the Second Sino-Japanese, Korea, and Iraq—the original, limited goals later became unlimited for at least a time. Nine blockades that began as limited conflicts remained so throughout—the War of 1812, Crimea, First Sino-Japanese, Spanish-American, Cuban Missile, Vietnam, Rhodesia, Falklands, and Australia. In many limited wars, blockades were partial, but all total blockades occurred in limited wars and four out of five focused on defeating the enemy's military forces, not on interdicting trade.

Surprisingly, in most limited blockades, the blockading countries instituted a close blockade of their enemy, meaning that their ships and other military assets were very close to the enemy's shores, usually in order to isolate and destroy the enemy's army or navy more than to halt trade. By contrast, a larger number of the distant blockades were part of unlimited wars. In these conflicts blockades were usually intended to disrupt enemy trade as one point of leverage, rather than to eliminate a specific military target or to take a set piece of territory. Unlimited wars by their very nature include a full array of military forces, often in a variety of theaters, so that blockade is just one instrument among many.

Thus, counterintuitively, blockades played a larger role in many limited wars, sometimes even constituting the sole means of coercion. Naval blockades used by themselves are most effective at achieving limited objectives, particularly limited naval objectives, such as blockading an enemy navy in port—in the First Sino-Japanese war—or waiting for the enemy navy to leave port—in the Spanish-American war. Naval blockades alone cannot easily or quickly achieve unlimited goals. In addition, the strategic impact of limited blockades on trade can be difficult to measure, unless there are particular items that the adversary can acquire only through trade and that are essential to continuing the war; for example, preventing Iraq from upgrading its conventional forces and WMD facilitated the overthrow of the Iraqi government in 2003.

The number of cases where land powers tried to use blockades to achieve their overall strategic goals was especially small, and included only Napoleon's continental blockade, the Union in the American Civil War, and the PRC in its missile blockade of Taiwan. All three had unlimited political goals, either the total destruction or absorption of the enemy, but lacked the necessary naval forces to enforce a total blockade. All three were also near blockades, with their enemy close at hand. The results were mixed— Napoleon and the PRC ultimately lost because of third-party intervention, Russia and the United States, respectively, while the Union arguably won in part because the Confederacy, which was also a land power, failed in its efforts to find a strong foreign protector, and, in particular a strong sea power, to come to its aid.

In three cases limited blockades escalated fully or for a time into unlimited blockades—Second Sino-Japanese, Korea, and Iraq. In these cases, the focus of the blockade effort was against the adversary's army, and in particular against their army's logistical lines. In the first two, the geography of China and Korea made it difficult for naval forces, even in conjunction with airpower and an active military presence, to cut the enemy's LLOCs with contiguous land powers. Interestingly, in both of these cases the shift from limited to unlimited proved to be a mistake; only in Iraq, after a thirteen-year blockade, was the unlimited goal achieved and Saddam Hussein removed from power. Arguably, and granted only in hindsight, leaving Saddam in power might have avoided the entire ISIS episode from ever occurring. This shows the importance of considering enemy adaption.

ENEMY ADAPTATION

The enemy is not a potted plant and can adopt their own strategies. Enemies can adapt to changing circumstances and threats, and can show flexibility in their strategic goals, thus making some blockades turn out to be extraordinarily expensive in terms of money, manpower, and prestige so that costs ultimately outweigh benefits. Such outcomes become a nightmare scenario for the blockading country. However, if the blockaded country either lacks effective countermeasures or does not incorporate them in time, or better yet has no allies to help them, then blockades can deliver a quick decisive victory, providing a dream scenario for the blockading country. Most naval blockades fall somewhere between these two extremes.

When examining enemy adaptation, there were three nightmare scenarios—Napoleon, Second Sino-Japanese, and Rhodesia. In the first and second cases, blockade helped forge powerful new enemy coalitions with even more unlimited goals than the blockader, ultimately destroying both Napoleon and Imperial Japan. In the case of the Beira patrol, Great Britain's own UN security resolution ultimately locked it into carrying out the blockade alone. The costs soon exceeded the economic, but not necessarily the prestige, value to Britain, so the blockade dragged on for almost a decade.

Of the five dream scenarios—Crimea, First Sino-Japanese, Spanish-American, Cuban Missile, and Falklands—in four of them the theater of hostilities was focused, with the First Sino-Japanese War being the exception, but this was offset by China's unwillingness to commit its naval forces to destroy Japan's SLOCs. In most of these cases, the blockade ended as a result of negotiations, not unconditional surrender. None of the five entailed fighting on the territory of the blockader and blockaded. In three cases—Spanish-American, Cuban Missile, and Falklands—hostilities took place outside of the core territory of the primary belligerents: Cuba was a colony of Spain and then in the 1960s a client state of the Soviet Union, while the Falklands was not an integral part of Argentina. Such areas have a much lower value than home turf, which probably contributed to the dream-scenario outcome.

In the dream scenarios, the blockaded country largely followed the script anticipated by the blockader. For example, Russia could not create alternate land lines during the Crimean War because it had yet to enlarge its railway system; in the First Sino-Japanese War, the Chinese obliged Japan by anchoring the northern fleet in port where the Japanese navy and army could find, surround, and destroy it; in the Spanish-American War, the Spanish deployed their antiquated fleet in a theater without sufficient coaling stations; in the Cuban Missile Crisis, Soviet remoteness from the theater convinced them to back down in the face of a "quarantine" plus the threat of an invasion of Cuba; finally, in the Falklands, Argentina's air force never damaged the British aircraft carriers, which constituted the COG of the British military effort.

With the exception of the USSR in the Cuban Missile Crisis, therefore, those on the losing side in these dream scenarios were all cooperative adversaries—granted, without necessarily knowing it. Either they lacked key capabilities or they used their capabilities poorly. In three of the five—Crimea, Spanish-American, and Falklands—the losing side had inferior naval forces, while in the Cuban Missile Crisis the USSR had a strong navy, but it was not based near Cuba. Only in the First Sino-Japanese War was there naval parity, but China refused to use her numerically larger and, on paper, more capable fleets to deny Japan sea control.

Ten of the eighteen blockades involved neither dream nor nightmare scenarios. In these cases, both the blockading and blockaded power adapted to each other's strategies. Not all adaptations were effective. For example, the United States in the War of 1812, the South in the U.S. Civil War, the Nationalists opposing Japan's 1930's invasion of China, and the Nazis all embargoed trade with their enemies in response to the blockade. These additional trade restrictions merely served to make the blockades tighter, although not enough to make a crucial difference to the outcome of the war.

Other enemy adaptations worked better. Extensive smuggling by land and sea undermined the effectiveness of many blockades. For example, Britain reflagged its ships and profited from smuggling to the Continent during the Napoleonic Wars. Long coastlines proved difficult to seal in the War of 1812 and the Civil War. In World War I, merchant ships running the blockade were armed. Alternate ports able to handle oil shipments undermined the effectiveness of the Beira patrol. Most importantly, alternate LLOCs seriously degraded the strategic effectiveness of many blockades and usually led to protraction, including in both world wars, Second Sino-Japanese, ROC-PRC, Korea, Vietnam, Rhodesia, and Iraq. Such alternate routes can also undermine diplomatic leverage.

In three pairs of cases, Japan against China, Britain against Germany, and the United States against Cuba, the blockading power used the same basic strategy twice, usually with greater success the first time. In part, this was because the blockaded country knew what to expect the second time and so made greater efforts to form outside coalitions and to find alternate supply lines. This suggests that countries should perhaps lower their expectations when employing essentially the exact same blockade strategy for a second time, since their enemies have had plenty of time to figure out better counter-strategies. Previous success should not be construed as an indicator of future victory; the enemy also has a learning curve.

When evaluating the efficacy of conducting a blockade strategy, it is important to consider all possible enemy responses. The intervention of third parties, such as the United States and UK in the Second Sino-Japanese War, or the United States in the PRC missile blockade, can effectively break a blockade. The nature of the theater determines whether land lines will become available. Certain theaters require the cooperation if not active support of third parties for blockades to be effective. The likelihood for strategic success plummeted for blockades that triggered major additions to the blockaded country's coalition. This is why strategic and operational effectiveness is so important.

STRATEGIC AND OPERATIONAL EFFECTIVENESS

Evaluating the effectiveness of a blockade is a three-part process: Did the blockade achieve its operational goal? Did this contribute to the achievement of strategic victory? Were the costs entailed worth the benefits delivered? Factors influencing effectiveness include blockade running and smuggling, the size of the area under blockade, and the availability of substitute markets or substitute products to overcome bottlenecks. Tight blockades do not let any prohibited items through, whereas porous blockades stop only a percentage of the contraband.

When evaluating effectiveness, of ten blockades where the blockading power emerged victorious, half were tight—Crimea, First Sino-Japanese, Spanish-American, Cuban Missile, and Falklands War. They generally involved small geographic areas—such as islands or peninsulas—or were focused on interdicting specific and crucial war materiel, such as coal or missiles. In four of the five cases, a decisive military victory was assured when the blockading force managed to defeat the enemy's navy. In the five porous blockades—Civil War, World War I, World War II, Korea, and Iraq—blockade runners, smuggling, and alternative land routes undermined the effectiveness of the blockade. However, in all ten cases, the blockaders managed to reduce the flow of goods, drive up costs, and impose unacceptable burdens on the enemy. Victory usually resulted not solely from the naval blockade, but from a combination of military efforts, including land operations.

Of the ten blockades that were part of successful wars, surprisingly only four were far blockades conducted by naval powers—Crimea, Korea, Falklands, and Iraq. Success rates increased for sea powers conducting near blockades, with five of this type succeeding; only Japan failed at a near blockade in the Second Sino-Japanese War, mainly due to the broadening of the war with the 1941 attack on Pearl Harbor to include other sea powers as its adversaries. As for blockades by land powers, really only the Union blockade of the South fully achieved its objective of halting the expansion of the Confederate Navy and eroding the export revenues of the South.

In the eight remaining blockades that either failed, or where the goal was to deter and so victory was difficult to ascertain, reasons for failure are often connected to the nature of the theater. In three cases—Napoleon, Second Sino-Japanese, and ROC-PRC—the area under blockade was enormous and so precluded effective enforcement. In the case of Vietnam and Rhodesia, both had long porous land borders, providing multiple alternate LLOCs. Finally, the ultimate outcome of two deterrent blockades—PRC missile and Australia—remains undecided.

Outside intervention by another great power was the most common reason for operational failure. For example, in the nineteenth century, Russia played an important role in opposing Napoleon, while in three cases during the twentieth century—including the Second Sino-Japanese, ROC-PRC, and Korean conflicts—the Soviet Union provided secure LLOCs to compensate China and Korea for lost SLOCs. Likewise, the United States intervened in the 1996 PRC missile blockade of Taiwan by sending two carrier battle groups to the Taiwan Strait. In the Vietnam case, mining Haiphong harbor did halt many of the Soviet ships from entering port, but this success came very late in the conflict. Assuming Washington's goal was to flip Beijing against Moscow, however, then it did win the war.

A blockade's effectiveness appears to be largely a function of the size of the blockaded area, the availability of alternative LLOCs, the ease with which SLOCs can be cut, and the interest of other powers intervening. The smaller and the less interconnected an enemy is, the tighter the blockade. In porous blockades that did not achieve a clear victory, enemy adaptations undercut the effectiveness of the blockades.

CONCLUSIONS

Naval blockades have often proven themselves to be both an effective offensive military strategy and a deterrent to halt undesired actions by an opponent. However, land powers have traditionally failed when applying blockades to sea powers or to island nations, with Napoleon's continental blockade and the

PRC missile blockade against Taiwan as two prime examples. This suggests that land powers might want to consider using methods other than blockade to obtain their political goals, such as diplomatic negotiations or economic sanctions. Meanwhile, sea powers blockading land powers must take into account the probability that new LLOCs can be created to avoid the greatest effects of the blockade; the three "nightmare" scenarios discussed under enemy adaptation were of this type. Interestingly, it was Russia/USSR that most often played this "spoiler" role by utilizing its central geographic position to open up new land lines.

The most obvious category of successful naval blockades involved sea powers blockading islands, such as Cuba or the Falklands, or isolated peninsulas such as the Crimea or Shandong, where blockade had the dual effect of halting trade and putting military pressure on the enemy. All five of the so-called dream scenarios fit this description. However, blockades of large peninsulas or coastal states that have adequate land transportation—in particular railways—and powerful allies—for example, Korea and Vietnam—were not nearly as effective.

Blockading powers that attempted to repeat a successful blockade often found themselves stymied the second time by enemy adaptation. Certainly, Imperial Japan failed to subdue China in the 1930s and 1940s, just as the World War II blockade of Germany was arguably less effective than in World War I. While, on the surface, the second U.S. blockade of Cuba appeared equally successful to the first, nuclear weapons and the threat of invasion were extenuating factors. This suggests that blockaded countries learn the lessons of history as well, if not better, than the blockaders. This has implications for any future PRC attempt to blockade Taiwan. Since 1996, Taiwan has endeavored to augment its naval forces and has worked hard to add potential coalition members—including most importantly Japan—to its side.

Finally, as technology has changed, so have blockades. The role of technology in naval blockades has been especially crucial, from the transition from wood to copper-hulled ships in the early nineteenth century, from coal to oil combustion in the early twentieth century, and then with the inclusion of airpower and submarines to assist surface ships to keep the blockade tight; perhaps in no other sphere of military activity have changes in technology had such an immediate and obvious impact on naval tactics. Good examples include the more dependable coal supplies of the U.S. Navy during the Spanish-American War, just as the modern and hi-tech ships of the 1990s gave the coalition in Iraq the leverage it needed to halt oil smuggling.

Over time, blockading countries have moved away from surface patrols and underwater mines and shifted more toward airpower and missiles. As a result, invasion of territory has become less common, while the threat of aerial attack more common. In "choke point" blockades, such as the PRC missile blockade of Taiwan, the target is not a particular navy or coastline, but disruption of trade routes or creation of exclusion zones; quite often, an important underlying goal has been to disrupt stock markets or raise insurance rates, thus making the cost of doing business too high. In Australia's "reverse blockade," the enemy was not even a country or a military force, but illegal immigrants and the smuggling groups transporting them.

Due to the very complexity of the international trading system, naval blockades by individual countries will probably decline, while coalitions of the willing or UN-sponsored interdiction programs will most likely increase. Container ships rarely have only one type of goods, or from just one country. Future blockades will not necessarily be close blockades far from the blockader's shores, but will probably include the blocking of specific goods in distant ports of debarkation, before the goods are inspected and sealed in containers for transport. This will avoid unduly impacting neutrals in the conflict. Finally, patrols by sea will probably diminish in favor of new forms of aerial and space-based weapons, communications, and highly accurate sensors. As before, sea power will continue to be essential for sustaining blockades, but the sensing tools that sea powers will use to aid in the enforcement of blockade operations will more often be located in the air and in outer space.

NOTES

1. The blockade cases referred to in this chapter include an essay on legal issues, Napoleon's Continental Blockade, the 1812 British blockade, Crimean War, Union blockade against the Confederacy, First Sino-Japanese War, Spanish-American War, World War I, Second Sino-Japanese War, World War II, Chinese Nationalist blockade of the PRC, Korean War, 1962 Cuban Missile Crisis, Vietnam War, British Beira Patrol against Rhodesia, 1982 Falklands War, 1990–2003 blockade of Iraq, the 1995–1996 Chinese "missile blockade" of Taiwan, and the Australia "reverse blockade" to keep unwanted immigrants out, in Bruce A. Elleman and S.C.M. Paine, eds., *Naval Blockades and Seapower: Strategies and Counter-strategies, 1805–2005* (London: Routledge, 2006).

2. Andrew D. Lambert, "The Crimean War Blockade, 1854–56," in *Ibid.*, 46–60.

3. See Paul G. Halpern, "World War I: The Blockade," in *Ibid.*, 91–103, and Geoffrey Till, "Naval Blockade and Economic Warfare in the European War, 1939–45," in *Ibid.*, 117–30.

4. David M. Stevens, "'To disrupt, deter and deny': Sealing Australia's Maritime Borders," in *Ibid.*, 225–35.

5. Bruce A. Elleman, "The Nationalists' Blockade of the PRC, 1949–58," in *Ibid.*, 133–43.

Chapter 3

Coalitions

For the last two centuries, navies have rarely gone to war alone; rather, they have usually operated within coalitions and in combination with ground forces. Since the advent of airpower, they have also operated with air forces. Many of the most important conflicts of the past two centuries have involved naval coalitions on at least one of the opposing sides. Interestingly, there has been a tendency for the side with the naval coalition to win and, in the case of wars between two naval coalitions, for the side with the most competent naval elements to persevere.[1]

Victory in this sense means not just operational but also strategic victory, measured by the achievement of the national goals for which the war was fought. Put simply, what factors have made naval coalitions strategically effective? In contrast to Alfred Thayer Mahan's nineteenth-century vision of navies fighting other navies for command of the sea, recent naval coalitions have often fought adversaries lacking navies entirely to deliver military forces—often through the use of sea-based airpower—far inland. In some cases, naval air has even obviated the need for basing on the territory under dispute.

During the nineteenth century, naval coalitions tended to be confined to the great powers of the day. Since the beginning of the Cold War, however, the membership of naval coalitions has become increasingly heterogeneous and inclusive, meaning the membership has broadened beyond the great powers to include a wide array of countries, which often bring niche capabilities rather than comprehensive military assets. This has brought to the fore issues of interoperability, communication, deconfliction, and rules of engagement (ROE).

HISTORICAL ORIGINS OF NAVAL COALITIONS

Throughout history naval coalitions have focused on conventional state interests, including national survival, territorial aggrandizement, economic interests, and the protection of nationals, whereas at the turn of the twenty-first
century some naval coalitions have focused on the prevention of genocide
not directly involving the nationals of any coalition member. Increasingly,
military effectiveness must be counterbalanced with the minimization of collateral damage to win the media war of hearts and minds to retain the support
of the electorate at home and of any coalition partners. There is even a whole
new category of military operations called humanitarian operations—such
as the U.S. Navy's Operation *Unified Assistance* in Indonesia, Thailand, and
Sri Lanka following the December 26, 2004, earthquake and tsunamis—that
focus on using naval forces not to take life but to preserve it.[2]

In the nineteenth century, monarchies controlled much of the world and
the media meant newspapers, which not everyone could afford to buy or
could even read. Over the course of the twentieth century, Europe, the United
States, and key countries in East Asia became increasingly democratic, with
the enfranchisement of the entire adult population. Meanwhile, their educational opportunities rapidly expanded, with the picture media becoming
increasingly globalized even in highly authoritarian countries through the
advent of television and the internet. The ongoing communications revolution, whose full implications are yet to be understood, forms one important
backdrop, but not the focus, of modern-day naval coalitions.

Unlike formal alliances, naval coalitions concern temporary groupings of
countries combining military forces that include naval assets in pursuit of a
common objective. By contrast, alliances pertain to permanent groupings of
states, formalized in treaties, also in pursuit of a common objective. Some
coalitions become formalized into alliances through treaties that regulate
the relationship. Other coalitions include alliances within them. But they all
share, at least at one point in time, the achievement of one or more unifying
goals.

In the past two centuries, as naval coalitions have become increasingly
global in their membership, they have simultaneously become more localized in their operations. Instead of global coalitions fighting global wars,
more recent naval coalitions have tended to focus on maximizing leverage to
restore order within a particular country, such as Afghanistan, and sometimes
only a portion of a country, such as Bosnia. Typically, modern naval coalitions concentrate the combined powers of many states against diplomatically
isolated adversaries, so that strategic victory requires at least two offensive
prongs: one military and the other diplomatic. To force a resolution, naval
coalitions often focus not just on their adversary's military and government,

but also on its commerce and economy, so a third common prong integrates an economic strategy.

Over the years, particularly since World War II when the United States has possessed overwhelming naval superiority over its coalition partners, coordinating strategy, making equipment interoperable, establishing communications, and balancing conflicting ROE have all become increasingly important. Many of the more intractable problems facing coalition members have derived not so much from differing national perspectives, as from tensions over command and control (C2).

For reasons of sovereignty, in the past nations rarely put their forces under the tactical let alone operational command of another power. In recent years, coalition partners have accepted tactical control by another coalition member, became more comfortable with operational control, and are now considering sharing combatant command authority. But full unity of command within a coalition remains difficult, and a former deputy secretary of defense in Australia has argued that the United States must involve its partners "in the coalition's decision making more than it has done so far."[3] Naval coalitions can be examined by coalition type, theater of operations, membership stability, duration, command relationships, naval strategy, operational and strategic objectives, and enemy response.

COALITION TYPES AND THEATER OF OPERATIONS

Up until the end of World War II, most naval coalitions were homogeneous but exclusive. This meant that the relatively few coalition members tended to have roughly equivalent populations and militaries and so could contribute fairly equally to the war effort. These tended to be great-power coalitions, often with ship-building capabilities. After World War II, however, coalitions have tended to include a far greater range of members in terms of size, capacity, and contributions. Thus, the membership has become increasingly inclusive as it has become more heterogeneous. This shift not only reflects the bipolar nature of the Cold War, where broader coalition membership gave greater legitimacy to each side, but also reflects a growing reliance on the niche capabilities of the different coalition members.

Since the end of the Cold War, naval coalitions have consistently opposed diplomatically isolated continental adversaries. Successful naval coalitions usually leveraged a wide variety of assets by being inclusive and heterogeneous. They based their cooperation on a set of solid goals and strategic objectives. In other words, many countries of differing capabilities cooperated and leveraged their asymmetrical naval assets against a largely nonnaval adversary.

The most successful naval coalitions, not surprisingly, have operated in theaters that allowed maritime powers to exert influence over land, either through dispatching expeditionary troops, shelling from the sea, or by using airpower, whether carrier-based aircraft or sea-based missiles. In the twentieth century, coalitions became increasingly global in scope but focused on regional problems—in other words, like a lens focusing light they assembled capabilities worldwide to concentrate on a comparatively small area.

Likewise, the costs of taking military action were distributed among the many members of the coalition, even while the combined assets concentrated the operational effect on a limited theater. This cost sharing has made taking military action politically feasible for the coalition members and strategically effective against a foe that could not hope to overcome the combined force of the coalition.

NAVAL COALITION MEMBERSHIP, CUMULATIVE OPERATIONS, AND UNITY OF COMMAND

The stability of coalition membership is of crucial importance. The intervention of a hostile third party, meaning an addition to the opposing coalition, strongly correlates with strategic failure. This was true for the Axis during World War II, the Nationalist defeat in the Civil War, and the U.S. Navy during the 1995–1996 missile "blockade" of Taiwan. Likewise, during many conflicts the defection of a coalition member—such as Italy during World War I—made an enormous difference, just as the late addition of members—including the United States in both world wars—helped turn the tide of battle. During the Cold War, for example, the United States proved willing to break one naval coalition in a peripheral operation—the conflict in Vietnam—in order to gain a new and even better coalition partner—the People's Republic of China—and thereby undermine the scope, unity, and capacity of the USSR's own coalitions in the long war.

Ever since World War I, naval coalition wars have relied on the cumulative or compounding effects of operations—also known as attrition warfare—rather than on a discrete sequence of operations—that is, until Operation *Desert Storm* against Iraq. It is unclear whether this war and those that followed in Afghanistan and Iraq will someday be seen as exceptional.[4] There were many that questioned the need for sending "boots on the ground" when sanctions appeared to be working, turning this minor theater into the nation's so-called longest war.[5]

Theorists often consider unity of command to be a coalition's COG. Unified command closely correlated with strategic victory, just as its absence greatly contributed to strategic defeat—the Axis powers being a prime example of the latter, since both the Nazis and the Japanese were racist regimes. Since the Cold War, the firepower of one country—the United States—has tended to dominate naval coalitions. This has made the interoperability of equipment and communications with the U.S. Navy of growing importance to many smaller navies. The PRC is the sole exception to this trend, as Beijing tries to attract smaller navies to work with China against the United States. So far, it has failed to find many takers.

NAVAL STRATEGY AND OPERATIONAL AND STRATEGIC OBJECTIVES

Many naval strategies have won command of the sea—with Britain's defeat of Napoleon and its victory in both world wars being good cases in point. But this is not always possible or is too costly, so sea denial or deterrence strategies have also been attempted. In only a handful of the case studies was a fleet-in-being strategy used—this showed itself most clearly when the Triple Intervention forced Japan to return Liaodong to China merely by the threat of a naval deployment, or when Chinese military forces stationed on the Paracel Islands helped stop Soviet intervention in the 1979 Sino-Vietnamese War.

Likewise, during the Cold War, the Soviet Navy was rarely committed to action, for fear that its value as a deterrent force would be undermined. Both sides also recognized that their navies had a one-shot use, meaning the anticipated nuclear response would annihilate the first to attack. One's adversary, on the other hand, can also use sea denial strategies and deterrence—for example, the Soviet naval coalition with the Chinese Communists to provide sea denial in post–World War II Manchuria provides a case in point.

When evaluating operational objectives, key missions include attacking an enemy's commerce and especially its logistics and merchant fleets through blockade, actual fires against shore targets, and interdiction at sea. Attacking an adversary's naval forces is also important, although in many of the attrition-based case studies—Boxers, Bosnia, Kosovo, and Afghanistan—the other side of the conflict did not possess either a navy or significant naval forces, so land forces and commerce became the prime target through fires ashore, blockades, and counter-blockades.

Another interesting change over the years has been the shift from primarily land or joint sea/land campaigns on the enemy's coastline, to large land wars supplied from the sea, to campaigns utilizing sea-based airpower to affect events on the land. With the exception of Operation *Desert Storm* in the early 1990s and with Operation *Iraqi Freedom* beginning in 2003, many of the major naval coalitions since the end of the Vietnam conflict have conducted primarily air or air/land campaigns, indicating the centrality of aircraft carriers. Meanwhile, sea lift has remained critical to transport and supply armies in distant theaters.

While coalition members tend to share a major strategic objective, competing interests help account for the short life of many naval coalitions that collapse once the primary strategic objective was achieved. The more concrete the goals and objectives the stronger the coalition. Throughout the nineteenth century, the primary objectives were the expansion of empire and balance of power. In recent years, promoting regional stability has become increasingly important. Typical naval coalition enemies—for example, Bosnia and Kosovo—have often valued the political objective more highly than did the naval coalition members. To compensate for this asymmetry, the combined power of numerous coalition members has been necessary to achieve strategic success over a recalcitrant adversary.

THE ADVERSARY'S RESPONSE

Generally speaking, successful naval coalitions do best when they face diplomatically isolated continental adversaries. The adversary is not a potted plant that will remain stationary, however, but can change the conditions of the conflict. Preferred anti-coalition strategy targets the weakest member—for example, Germany's attempt to defeat Russia in both world wars—but when the value of the object is high for all members such attempts have backfired, with the coalition strengthening as a result—the United States entered both wars on the sides of the Allies only after Russia came under dire threat.

One effective anti-coalition strategy has been to leverage competing economic interests and underlying rivalries—for example, Saddam Hussein used the "oil for food" program to convince a number of European and Middle Eastern countries not to support Operation *Iraqi Freedom*. In the past, coalitions repeatedly foundered on competing secondary objectives, most notably in the many unsuccessful coalitions to defeat revolutionary France and Napoleon.

In the case of coalitions composed of members that did not value the political objective equally, the member with the lowest value of the object would often be targeted first. During the Cold War, this sometimes included the United States. During both the Chinese Civil War and during the peripheral campaign in Vietnam, U.S. public opinion was persuaded—in part due to Communist propaganda—that the object was not worth the effort. In both cases, domestic opposition compelled Washington either not to intervene, in the case of China, or to withdraw, in the case of Vietnam, thereby granting the USSR what appeared to be a victory. However, appearances can be deceptive; in the first conflict, allowing the CCP to take all of Mainland China virtually guaranteed a rapid split in the Communist "camp," while in the second case Washington "traded up" by sacrificing South Vietnam—arguably considered lost already by many American leaders—for an even better coalition with China aimed at the USSR.

The success of any anti-coalition strategy depends on an underlying asymmetry in the value of the political objective, so that costs can be driven up to the point where they exceed a key member of the naval coalition's value of the object, causing a defection from the coalition, while not yet exceeding that of the adversary. Escalating costs, not operational failure, can often result in strategic failure.

In recent years, coalitions have not been successful when voters perceive that costs are beginning to outweigh the value of the political objective—Spain's decision to withdraw from the Iraq coalition following a terrorist bombing in 2004, or withdrawing American forces from Syria in 2019, are just two examples. Perhaps this is because so many nations now adhere to the increasingly comprehensive international legal order, so that the order is no longer in dispute, at least in the West, but the cost each nation is willing to expend to support it is still hotly contested.

Operational success was usually necessary but not always sufficient to achieve strategic victory. The Axis enjoyed stunning operational success at the beginning of World War II, only to meet with failure by turning the bulk of the world against it. In Vietnam, the U.S. military never lost a major engagement, yet it was accused later of losing the war. More recently, strategic success in Iraq has been called into question, not because of operational problems, but because of an inability to stop Iraqis from killing each other in the post-conflict period.

CONCLUSIONS

As many of these nineteenth, twentieth, and early twenty-first century naval cases demonstrate, fleet-on-fleet engagements have been the exception not the rule. Naval blockades, however, have been common. Since the advent of airpower, navies have become and remain an important means to get bombers and now cruise missiles within range of their intended targets. Throughout this entire period, navies have also performed crucial constabulary functions to keep the global commons open to maritime trade. Navies have often proven their operational effectiveness by following an enduring principle of warfare. To quote Sir Julian S. Corbett, the preeminent British naval theorist of the twentieth century, who was paraphrasing Carl von Clausewitz, the preeminent military theorist of the nineteenth century, wars, especially limited wars, do not necessarily turn on the "armed strength of the belligerents, but upon the amount of strength which they are able or willing to bring to bear at the decisive point."[6]

The extreme versatility of the power projection capabilities inherent in navies allows naval coalitions to choose from a broader array of potential decisive points than generally available to land powers, which are confined by the geography ashore. Naval coalitions leverage to their advantage both their own mobility and the homeland security and force protection that the vast maritime global commons provide, particularly from continental adversaries tied to the land. Thus, naval assets can provide greater flexibility as to the time and place to engage the enemy, and can help slow the speed and effectiveness of the enemy's response.

Naval attributes prove particularly useful in protracted conflicts, where long-term sustainability is a key to victory. In both the long war against revolutionary and Napoleonic France, and the long Cold War against the Soviet Union, while most of fighting took place on land, navies kept the global commons open to trade. This allowed wealth accumulation to continue apace for the winning coalition while the losing side became overextended on land, its economy became increasingly burdened by war, and its citizenry felt comparatively impoverished. In other words, navies played a key role for the winning side of maintaining business as usual for the home front, an advantage unattainable to non-naval powers. This disparity during long wars had enormous implications for the military balance, which over time shifted away from Revolutionary France and the Soviet Union. The Global War on Terror is another good example, since the economy in the West has continued to grow even as the military effort has intensified; avoiding a second costly 9-11 attack has been well worth the relatively meager military investment.

During the nineteenth century, and even in the early part of the twentieth century, gunboat diplomacy displayed naval power in order to intimidate the adversary. With the increasing power of the press, however, this would almost certainly be portrayed today as bullying and so politically backfire. By contrast, in today's world coalition naval forces possess the key advantage in their ability to influence the land while they "stand off" shore, using the water both to protect themselves from attack and to limit their visibility to the enemy and to the media. Most modern coalition forces are never seen by the enemy, even while their influence is more keenly felt than ever. The Taliban in land-locked Afghanistan probably never imagined that they would come under attack from aircraft carriers in the Indian Ocean. In the current long war—the "constrainment" effort to force the PRC to adopt global Western norms—it seems highly likely that naval coalitions—including the United States, Japan, Australia, and Indian "Quad"—will continue to play a significant role bolstering the United States; by contrast, the PRC has no reliable naval coalition partners to speak of.

NOTES

1. The case studies include an essay on international law, the Napoleonic Wars, Crimean War, Second Opium War, Bismarck, First Sino-Japanese War, the Boxer Uprising, World War I, World War II, the Chinese Civil War, Vietnam War, Cold War, first Gulf War, Bosnia, Kosovo, *Enduring Freedom*, and *Iraqi Freedom*, in Bruce A. Elleman and S.C.M. Paine, eds., *Naval Coalition Warfare: From the Napoleonic War to Operation Iraqi Freedom* (London: Routledge, 2008).

2. See Bruce A. Elleman, *Waves of Hope: The U.S. Navy's Response to the Tsunami in Northern Indonesia* (Newport, RI: Naval War College Press, 2007), Newport Papers No 28.

3. Paul Dibb, "The Future of International Coalitions: How Useful? How Manageable?" *The Washington Quarterly*, 25, no. 2 (2002): 143.

4. For a discussion of cumulative vs sequential operations, see J.C. Wylie, *Military Strategy: A General Theory of Power Control* (Annapolis, MD: Naval Institute Press, 1967), 117–21.

5. Pundits who say the conflict in Afghanistan is America's longest war tend to ignore the centuries-long insurgency between European colonists and aboriginals living on the North American continent, but this lengthy domestic conflict arguably seasoned Americans to fight long, protracted conflicts, with no immediate end in sight. In fact, Americans excel at protracted wars, like the Cold War and GWOT, and use protraction and attrition to favor their forces over the adversaries.

6. Julian S. Corbett, *Some Principles of Maritime Strategy with an Introduction and Notes by Eric J. Grove* (Annapolis: Naval Institute Press, 1988), 58.

Chapter 4

Piracy

Piracy, or "robbery on the high seas," has existed for as long as people and commodities have traversed the oceans. The ancient Greeks, Romans, and Chinese all complained of it, and all created naval forces to fight pirates. The word "piracy" comes from the Latin *piata*, "sea robber," and before that from the Greek *peirates*—"brigand" or "one who attacks." It has long been considered a scourge, undermining the common good. Since pirates rarely leave memoirs—"dead men tell no tales"—information about piracy typically comes from victims.[1]

Views of piracy have evolved over time, especially since 1608, when the Dutch jurist Hugo Grotius published his *Mare Liberum* [*The Freedom of the Seas, or the Right Which Belongs to the Dutch to Take Part in the East Indian Trade*]. As modern nation-states emerged from feudalism, privateering for both profit and war supplemented piracy at the margins of national sovereignty. More recently, an ocean enclosure movement under the aegis of the UNCLOS has granted states access to maritime resources far beyond their territorial limits. This in turn has given states more responsibility for providing safe passage through their waters, including conducting antipiracy patrols.

There are many different types of piracy: simple robbery at sea; absconding with a cargo; and even taking control over a ship, reflagging it, and then attempting to sell the vessel intact as a "phantom ship." Sometimes pirates actively seek out specific ships to attack, while in other instances they wait for unsuspecting vessels to approach within striking distance, usually at strategic choke points. There has been a long history of piracy.

MARITIME PIRACY IN HISTORICAL PERSPECTIVE

Throughout much of human history it was assumed that the seas could not be owned, occupied, or governed, so fighting pirates at sea, although desirable, was beyond the jurisdiction and ability of most states, whether feudal or national. As Grotius asserted in *Mare Liberum*, "the sea is common to all, because it is so limitless that it cannot become a possession of any one, and because it is adapted for the use of all, whether we consider it from the point of view of navigation or of fisheries."[2] Grotius's pro-Dutch view was developed to counter the activities of, in particular, Spain and Portugal, who were using their navies to assert their global maritime spheres of influence. In this fashion, Grotius's "freedom of the seas" doctrine became a widely accepted foundation of modern international law.

As commercial trade expanded, coastal communities evolved maritime practices to earn money from passing merchantmen. This was one advantage of liminal space, or the precise location where the land and the sea interact. These practices ranged from the piloting and provisioning of ships, to extortion, to outright pirating. In these early years, piracy was not just an enterprise of criminals but a widespread practice of entire seafaring communities, including the Bugis and Riau in the Malay world, Iban raiding and pirating communities on the west coast of Borneo, the Iranun around Jolo and the Sulu Sea, and other pirate gangs in Vietnamese and Chinese coastal areas.

Lured by the spice trade, and later by the tea and opium trade with China, Western European powers competed with each other to expand their trade networks and overseas colonies in these regions. Europe was the focus of economic development and growth in the eighteenth and early nineteenth centuries; the Barbary pirates, accordingly, preyed on Mediterranean shipping. Whether high-value sea robbery by organized criminal groups or low-value petty theft by impoverished seafarers, piracy was related both to changing economic conditions, such as poverty, industrialization, and urbanization, and political conditions, including a government's legitimacy and ability to maintain law and order.

Pirates in particular sought to exploit differences in the value of goods from one region to another. This especially happened during Britain's eighteenth-century attempts to regulate trade with its colonies in North America and during the nineteenth-century opium trade between India and China. Organized criminal groups resorted to piracy when it was more profitable than drug trafficking or smuggling. In the thirteen American colonies, for example, many people were eager to buy cheap goods from pirates. This was also the case among early Southeast Asian pirates, who preyed on the lucrative West–East opium trade and then sold the higher-quality Indian opium to local buyers.

Piracy thrives in waters off land areas where law and order is absent. Another causal factor is economic or political upheaval, such as the end of a war. This happened after the First Opium War, World Wars I and II, and the Cold War; in each case economic activity increased, but naval patrols by the major belligerents decreased. The end of the U.S. war in Vietnam led to another predatory form of piracy, aimed at preying on the mass migration of people fleeing from Vietnam. These pirate attacks were largely ignored by regional governments, which hoped to use piracy to stem the flow of unwanted refugees.

Piracy hot spots have included East Asia and the South China Sea, South and Southeast Asia, and along multiple coastlines of Africa. Some of these hot spots, such as the Sulu region, have long experience with local piracy; others, like the Gulf of Thailand, do not. This suggests that history and culture are not the only major determinants of piracy. In general, as targets of opportunity increase, piracy increases. Once opportunistic piracy has proven itself to be highly profitable, organized criminal groups often move in, push out the original perpetrators, and attempt to make even greater profits. Or, the opportunistic pirates and organized crime can adopt a symbiotic relationship where they divide up the spoils. Location is usually one of the most important factors.

GEOGRAPHIC FACTORS ENCOURAGING PIRACY AND MARITIME CRIME

The location of a criminal attack determines whether it is an act of piracy or simply a maritime crime within the jurisdiction of a particular country. This legal distinction, of course, is meaningless to the victim. Traditionally, piracy included almost any theft on the water, even along a country's coastline or on its rivers, which explains why many major medieval cities were located far inland up major river systems. From the eighteenth century onward, however, "maritime crime" was considered to take place in territorial waters out to 3 nautical miles, with piracy occurring beyond 3 nautical miles on what was by then called the "high seas." Territorial waters progressively extended outward to the current 12 nautical miles. With the 1994 entry into force of the UNCLOS, 12-nautical-mile territorial waters, 24-nautical-mile contiguous zone, and 200-nautical-mile "exclusive economic zones" were codified, with some countries arguing that international waters—or high seas—had decreased correspondingly.

Historically, pirates have most often operated from small islands or archipelagoes immediately adjacent to major shipping lanes. Pirates value the geographic importance of access to ports, straits, and the SLOCs through them. Although located close to shipping activity, pirate havens on land can be extremely hard to find and therefore difficult to police. One response of the international community to the problem of locating, identifying, and prosecuting pirates on land, especially if local governments decline to act, is to use navies to catch pirates in the act of committing crimes at sea. When pirates have been captured by international forces, it has usually been at sea, and most often during piratical raids gone wrong.

However, such a policy is expensive, and the most cost-effective approach remains improving police work ashore. Ports and their adjacent waters are the most likely places for maritime crime. For example, the widespread petty theft in the port of Chittagong, Bangladesh, is a case in point. Such acts might be perpetrated by a variety of individuals or groups on an opportunistic basis. Pirates may also scout target ships in ports. Especially in China during the 1920s, pirate leaders would select targets in port and even travel as passengers in the ships they planned to attack—often paying first-class fares—so they could observe their workings. Such detailed preparations could result in pirates' hijacking the entire ship, robbing the other passengers of their valuables, and eventually ransoming the ship and passengers for huge sums. This practice became so widespread that some ships were pirated many times.

Other dangerous areas are shipping lanes through international straits. Pirates take special advantage of narrows to attack ships, especially the Malacca Strait and the Strait of Gibraltar. Pirates also take advantage of ambiguities of jurisdiction, waters where boundaries have not been delimited, or where naval or maritime forces—such as coast guards or marine police—do not normally operate. The piracy attacks against the Vietnamese "boat people" during the 1970s and 1980s fit this category. Remote or peripheral waters between various Southeast Asian countries afford ripe opportunities for piracy. Gaps between island chains are a good example. For example, in early June 2008 there was an attempted pirate attack on a cattle transport steaming from the Philippines to Australia. It took place in Indonesian waters about 70 miles south of Balut Island, an area that was not routinely patrolled.

Motivations for piracy or maritime crime are most often related to economic deprivation, in the case of opportunistic crime, or a cultural or lifestyle choice, in the case of organized criminal gangs. Sudden and severe impoverishment, especially among marginal seafaring communities, can make piracy a viable means to meet basic needs. For example, the rapid increase in the number of piracy attacks in Indonesian waters and ports after 1997 may be attributed to that nation's sharp economic downturn and domestic instability in the wake of the regional currency crisis. A decline in global fisheries and encroachment on local grounds may also result in unemployment in the fisheries sector. Economic duress also makes impoverished fishermen more vulnerable to and available for recruitment by entrepreneurial criminal organizations. In some instances, captured sailors have been forced to become pirates.

Piracy can also flourish when maritime commerce grows faster than government's ability to protect it. This was dramatically shown in the early eighteenth century, when pirates ignored peace treaties to continue preying on Spanish and Portuguese "treasure ships" coming from the New World. In Southeast Asia, it was common for political leaders to hire mercenaries to raid shipping and enemy villages. Such raids were considered integral parts of warfare. In China, by contrast, pirates wanted the state to be strong enough to allow commerce to grow and yet weak enough to allow for opportunistic gaps in maritime security. During the 1990s, a similar phenomenon reoccurred in China, which became one of the largest markets for smuggled goods, at least until the government cracked down on piracy to retain its standing as a legitimate trading nation.

The evolution of the nation-state and the creation of a modern international legal system is also a factor. A law enforcement response to organized crime is warranted but requires political will to act, sufficient funding to staff law enforcement agencies with trained personnel, and an adequate legal system under which alleged perpetrators can be brought to justice. However, there will be situations where local governments do not wish to act or proposed solutions will require considerable time to take effect. The international community might then commit naval forces to assist local forces or act unilaterally in an attempt to "solve" the problem. Such interventions have generally occurred on land, destroying piracy bases and exterminating pirates. Such behavior now runs counter to international law limiting what external powers can do on another state's sovereign territory. Furthermore, it should be recognized that any action by external navies is by definition a response to the symptom and not the underlying cause. International regulation is necessary to fix the causes of piracy.

THE INTERNATIONAL REGULATORY REGIME

The preferred solutions to piracy and maritime crime are often land based and involve law enforcement agencies. This is because of the all too obvious fact that pirates and criminal gangs must operate, live, and sell their stolen goods on land. As the volume and velocity of world trade increase, the targets and opportunities for piracy and maritime crime also increase. Over 90 percent of the world's merchandise trade by volume now moves by sea, especially oil tankers and bulk container carriers. The regulatory regime relating to international shipping has evolved over time to match it, with a broad framework of six major stakeholders: (1) the International Maritime Organization (IMO),

(2) flag states, (3) the shipping industry moving to "flags of convenience," (4) port states, (5) coastal states, and (6) International Cooperation.

The IMO is a specialized agency of the United Nations responsible for maritime issues, in charge of conventions and binding treaties, codes, advisory resolutions—some countries, but by no means all, have adopted these into their domestic legislation—and nonbinding guidelines. The IMO provides regulatory oversight of international shipping in maritime safety, marine pollution, liability and compensation, cargoes, marine technology, marine environment, navigation, lifesaving, search and rescue, radio communications, and training and certification.

Prior to World War I, only maritime states granted flags to shipping, but article 273 of the Versailles Peace Treaty of 1919 allowed landlocked states to have "flags" as well, and this concession was carried on, through the Geneva Convention on the High Seas 1958, into the UNCLOS. The flag state is where the ship is registered, and it has primary responsibility for the conduct of the ship. The IMO requires flag states to check regularly all ships under their registries, ensuring that all carry appropriate charts and navigational instruments, and that their crews are adequately trained.

Over the past forty years there has been an increasing tendency for shipowners to move their ships to "open registries" (i.e., open to owners of any nationality) or "flags of convenience," rather than their own national flags, based on crewing levels and conditions as required by the flag state, the individual tax, commercial tax, and financial laws in the flag state, the flag state's enforcement of maritime safety conventions, and the level of naval protection it can offer. But poor enforcement of safety conventions by some flag states and a rise in the number of flags of convenience have led to increased control by port states.

Accordingly, in 1982 the European Economic Community, concerned about failure to comply with maritime conventions, developed and signed the Paris Memorandum of Understanding on Port State Control. UNCLOS allows coastal and port states to make laws for the good conduct of ships in their territorial seas. At the instigation of the United States, the international community adopted in December 2002, a set of amendments to the International Convention for the Safety of Life at Sea (SOLAS) 1974. A new chapter was added (SOLAS chapter XI-2, "Special Measures to Enhance Maritime Security"), and the International Ship and Port Facility Security (ISPS) Code was introduced, coming into effect on July 1, 2004. The ISPS Code established a framework of preventive security for ships and ports.

Finally, the coastal state, through whose waters vessels transit en route to destinations in other nations, is also a major stakeholder. At a minimum, a coastal state must provide for the safety of shipping in its waters by providing navigational aids and charts, but it is unclear whether it must also protect shipping transiting its EEZ. This is the nub of the argument over the "security" of the Malacca Strait between the littoral (coastal) states of Indonesia, Malaysia, and Singapore, on the one hand, and "user countries" like Japan and the United States on the other hand. In July 2004, after years of bilateral patrols, Malaysia, Singapore, and Indonesia began to coordinate antipiracy patrols in the Malacca Strait in an arrangement known by the acronym "MALSINDO." During September 2005, Malaysia, Singapore, and Indonesia initiated "Eyes in the Sky," coordinated air patrols over the strait.

On November 11, 2004, eight out of the ten members of the Association of Southeast Asian Nations, plus China, Japan, South Korea, India, Sri Lanka, and Bangladesh, adopted the Regional Cooperation Agreement on Combating Piracy and Armed Robbery against Ships in Asia (ReCAAP). This entity differs from the International Maritime Bureau's Piracy Reporting Center (PRC), in that it is not connected with shipping companies or insurance firms. ReCAAP allocated funds to set up an independent reporting agency in Singapore to monitor piracy attacks. Such multilateral initiatives require the fusing of information from diverse sources.

Efforts are already being made to create new tools. Beginning in 2006, for example, NATO Naval Forces Europe began creating together a network of shore-based sensors ringing the Mediterranean and the IMO's Automatic Identification System (or AIS), increasing tracking of dozens of ships on the Mediterranean to thousands, and to within an accuracy of 50 feet. By the end of 2007, thirty-two countries throughout the Mediterranean, the North Atlantic, along the west coast of Africa, around the Black Sea, and in the Pacific were sharing this information. A sea traffic control regime of this type can give local coast guards and naval patrols the information they need to monitor suspected pirates and deter them. However, it cannot possibly deter all pirate attacks; to do that, shipowners and shipmasters must also intensify their efforts.

THE ROLES OF SHIPOWNERS AND SHIPMASTERS

Most attacks in Southeast Asia, and in the Malacca Strait in particular, occur against ships that are berthed or at anchor. Hence, port authorities have a major responsibility to improve physical security in their ports. The ISPS Code also requires that all people working in a port undergo security vetting and carry special identification, to hinder pirates from scouting for targets. At sea, maintaining a constant watch is the most important method for keeping pirates from boarding unnoticed. Physical barriers, barbed wire, or even electric fencing can slow attackers down. Crew members can use water hoses or "sonic boom" guns to try to keep boats at bay or cut thrown grapnel lines to prevent pirates from boarding. In addition, simple weapons like ships' signal cartridges and light pistols can be useful, as well as household items like empty beer bottles filled with sand.

Shipmasters transiting pirate-infested waters, or entering ports where criminal activity was known to occur, should advise their crews before heading into dangerous waters and tell them what measures should be taken. Such steps might include lighting all blind spots and dark areas, patrolling the weather deck regularly and in pairs, adopting a timetable for reports, and exercising increased vigilance when watches changed. The IMO recommends that any ships noting suspicious activity increase speed, commence evasive maneuvers, and use bow wave and stern wash to stop small boats from approaching. Once a pirate mother ship was sighted, the vessel can quickly head out to sea, which makes it more difficult for small boats to come alongside and board.

If pirates succeed in getting on board, the next defense comprises double-locked doors, especially to the bridge, engine room, communications room, and steering machinery room. However, most ships have many doors and hallways leading to the most important areas of the ship, and it is hard to bar them all. Ordinary padlocks usually do not last long in salt air and can be easily cut open with a pair of wire cutters; electronic key-card systems are harder to break. If the pirates do gain access to the control areas, the master and crew are usually instructed by the owners not to resist further. This applies especially to the use of firearms, since pirates are probably better armed, and the crew might be injured or killed if they fight back. Shipowners are also concerned that if a pirate is killed during an attack, revenge attacks on that line might result.

As soon as pirates board the ship, the crew can also activate the ship's security alert system, a silent alarm that sends a message warning the shipowner and other authorities that something has happened. But the shipowner, after receiving the warning, must verify that an attack is under way before advising the flag state, and the flag state must then advise the coastal state, which would presumably take action. There may be long delays due to communication problems. More importantly, there is no guarantee that any relevant local authority will receive the alarm; or that if received it will be recognized as valid among thousands of false signals that are sent; or that if a signal is received and verified, the coastal state will respond with adequate naval forces.

One alternative is the use of private security guards. A number of firms, usually staffed by retired soldiers or seamen, offer security services. But putting guards on all merchant ships is very expensive. Captain Jayant Abhyankar, the former deputy director of IMB, sounded a cautionary note about security personnel, which he once observed can be well intentioned, but it is hard to make a living doing it. Shipowners just cannot afford them. And if someone gets shot and killed, it becomes a legal mess. Armed security forces are a nonstarter, therefore, except in extremely rare circumstances. That said, it is typically professional navies that must respond to the piracy threat.

PROFESSIONAL NAVY'S RESPONSES TO PIRACY

It is difficult for individual ships or even states to fight piracy effectively, as it is a transnational crime and so requires a united response of the international community. One recent case of bilateral naval cooperation was the short-term agreement in 2002 between the U.S. Navy and the Indian Navy to guard American merchant ships carrying "high value" goods through the Malacca Strait and the Indian Ocean. According to this bilateral treaty, U.S. Navy patrolled in Southeast Asia, while the Indian Navy focused on the Bay of Bengal and the Indian Ocean. However, it is extremely unlikely that such an arrangement against piracy could be maintained for very long over the objections of coastal states.

International naval cooperation is the best way to manage a piracy threat if it cannot be contained on land. This can be done in a variety of ways, from state building to international naval patrols to convoys. But international participation is critical, since pirates can otherwise exploit national and sea boundaries to evade pursuit and capture. Naval forces need first of all to coordinate their surveillance and patrol efforts to detect, hunt down, and capture pirates. But in practice shipmasters often do not report attacks rapidly enough. Sending a navy vessel to intercept the merchant ship long after the fact might just be a waste of time and resources.

If the coastal state learns of an attack in progress and is willing to respond, its vessels must get to the merchant ship in time. Unless the ship is being hijacked, the pirates will usually be on board only a short period, and sending a warship may achieve little. The coastal state would have to base its forces near piracy hot spots permanently, but if it did, it is more than likely that pirates would just attack shipping somewhere else. Keeping response vessels always at sea is very expensive.

Personnel of any response vessel must also operate under the domestic law of the coastal state, so that they can take the alleged pirates into custody and return them to shore to face legal action. This legal aspect is often forgotten in debates about external forces intervening in another state's waters—they have no legal jurisdiction there and may therefore be committing a crime themselves. Oddly enough, ships interfering with pirates can sometimes be called pirates themselves. Increased awareness of the full scope of the maritime domain is a prerequisite for effective piracy prevention.

INCREASING MARITIME DOMAIN
AWARENESS (MDA)

Global trade is predicted to increase over the next few decades, so there will be a need for greater levels of maritime safety and security. This especially applies to the rapidly growing seaborne trade of developing countries now joining the export-led industrial revolution in Asia. If the international community commits its collective navies to antipiracy operations, a number of operational issues will need to be considered first to ensure the response is up to the task. These issues include (1) an adequate surveillance system, (2) agreed ROE for intercepting and boarding suspect vessels, and (3) legal powers to apprehend suspected pirates for eventual court action.

Clearly, maritime surveillance is the key to gaining a better understanding of what is happening on the oceans, but, currently, systems are not integrated within each country, let alone at regional or global levels. A country's navy must have a "common operating picture" of where its forces are at sea, and, if tasked with the responsibility, must have an idea where its merchant ships are; if further tasked with coastal surveillance, it should know what other types of vessels are in its waters. Departments of transport should also know what international shipping is in their waters or proposes to enter their nations' ports. All flag states should know the full and accurate location of vessels in their registries.

To generate a comprehensive maritime surveillance picture, all these disparate "inputs" must be integrated. Such integration is not easy. Naval information is often classified, while international shipping data is often confidential. Reporting protocols invariably use different computer systems, with incompatible software. Canada and Australia operate joint intelligence centers that fuse information from a variety of sources into one comprehensive picture. Canada does this in two marine security operations centers, while in Australia the Border Protection Command's Australian Maritime Information Fusion Center creates a threat assessment of vessels operating in or approaching Australian waters. The center tracks ship identity, crew, cargo, location, course, speed, and intended port of call. Both the Canadian and Australian systems are constrained as to disclosure of information by national privacy legislation.

The United States has promulgated a MDA policy aiming to "wire" every ship so that it can be identified and tracked throughout its journey, as is done in global air traffic control. MDA aims to require each ship at sea to emit a signal identifying its name, country of origin, and route. This would permit surveillance at sea and intelligence gathering on the background of suspected ships. When a ship is attacked by pirates, an emergency signal would report its location and what kind of danger it was in. The 2005 U.S. National

Strategy for Maritime Security had as its stated goal to promote global economic stability, protect legitimate activities, and prevent hostile or illegal acts within the maritime domain.

Aside from MDA, this initiative also called for seven other plans to address threats from piracy, international criminal activities such as illegal immigration and drug trafficking, and environmental degradation. In 2007, all three U.S. sea services issued *A Cooperative Strategy for 21st Century Seapower*, which calls for significantly increased commitment to advance MDA, with the goal of countering piracy, terrorism, weapons proliferation, drug trafficking, and other illicit activities. While these statements concern domestic American national and maritime security issues, the long-term goal of MDA is to expand its capacities to numerous countries. This goal particularly applies to piracy hot spots like Somalia.

THE PIRACY SITUATION OFF SOMALIA

The piracy situation off Somalia shows just how complex antipiracy suppression operations can become. Hijackings were frequent in these waters, one of the world's busiest and most important sea-lanes. During 2008, Somali pirates reportedly attacked 111 ships and seized 42. In June 2008, the United Nations Security Council passed a resolution authorizing the use of force against pirates in Somalia's territorial waters. It gave warships the power to intervene in piracy attacks on the high seas under UNCLOS, but warships in theory must then work with local law enforcement—Somali authorities, in this case—for subsequent prosecution, trial, and imprisonment.

The need for this multinational force was dramatically illustrated in September 2008 when pirates hijacked the Ukrainian cargo ship *Faina* off the central coast of Somalia. What commanded international attention was the ship's cargo: thirty-three Russian battle tanks and other heavy weapons, nominally intended for the Kenyan army but probably really destined for southern Sudan. U.S., Russian, and British warships surrounded the Ukrainian vessel, and NATO antipiracy patrols escorted UN food aid shipments.

The Security Council resolutions took many years to become effective. Even as an international armada surrounded *Faina*, pirates attacked three other vessels in Somali waters. In particular, on November 16, 2008, pirates seized the very large crude carrier (VLCC) *Sirius Star*, releasing it only after receiving a three million dollar ransom. This incident caused quite a shock to the shipping industry since this was the first VLCC hijacked for ransom and was reportedly located by the pirates through its AIS signal. *Sirius Star* sat off the Somali coast surrounded by warships, but no navy had the authority to recapture the ship. The ship was released in January 2009, but only after the owners paid the ransom. The inadequacy of international laws regulating piracy means that many captured Somali pirates have either been set free or sent to Kenya for trial, since there is no legal system in Somalia that can try them.

In early January 2009 it was announced that Combined Task Force 151 would be created to conduct antipiracy operations. It was given authority to act in Somali waters by no fewer than four Security Council resolutions, plus agreements with Kenya to prosecute any pirates captured. Thus, Somali piracy created an unprecedented international response, including ships from the United States, Europe, India, Australia, Japan, Russia, China, and Malaysia.

On April 8, 2009, for example, Somali pirates hijacked the U.S.-flagged ship *Maersk Alabama* and took ship captain Richard Phillips hostage. Four days later, Navy SEAL sharpshooters from the USS *Bainbridge* killed three pirates in a successful nighttime rescue. The Somali pirates were clearly not deterred by the U.S. Navy, and on November 18, 2009, attacked *Maersk Alabama* again, but this time were fought off by private guards armed with guns and a high-decibel sonic emitter. China also sent two frigates and a supply ship to the Horn of Africa, and pledged to regain control of the cargo ship *De Xin Hai*, which was seized by Somali pirates on October 19, 2009; it was released two months later, reportedly after China paid a $4,000,000 ransom.

These developments off Somalia show the pressing need for greater MDA. While external powers are deciding on whether to commit navies to the Gulf of Aden, shipowners are reportedly negotiating ransoms. Most often, shipowners bargain with the pirates over their ransom demands and then eventually pay—meaning the pirates win. This success merely motivates others to join their ranks. The root problem is a lawless state, or in the case of Somalia a pariah state, which refuses to abide by international law.

CONCLUSIONS

Piracy has existed for as long as people have used the sea. National navies were initially created as one method for managing piracy. Today, coast guards and marine police are also intimately involved. Ultimately, successful antipiracy measures require flag states and coastal/port states to be willing and able to take action. A crime against a ship on the high seas is subject to the jurisdiction of the flag state, according to its own criminal laws. An attack on a ship exercising the right of passage in territorial seas, however, is a crime under the laws of the coastal state, which needs to seize the attacking vessel and arrest the offenders. Meanwhile, an attack against a ship in port, at anchor in port, or anchored in internal waters is within the jurisdiction of the port state, even if a foreign ship is involved.

Almost every country has made maritime piracy and sea robbery a crime, and numerous intergovernmental and industry initiatives have urged states to adopt antipiracy measures. Criminalization alone, however, has not solved the problem. States have been reluctant to hunt down and capture pirates for numerous reasons, including the cost of antipiracy patrols, the suspicions of neighboring countries, and the persistence of unsettled territorial claims. Modern pirates can be highly mobile, have access to small yet very fast boats, and can be equipped with sophisticated navigational equipment and powerful weapons.

Success in piracy suppression will ultimately require coordinated efforts by states and shipowners. The international community can increase cooperation in a number of areas to manage piracy. It can ensure that the ISPS Code is enforced by flag states and port states. It can create a global surveillance system for international shipping. It can ensure that ships can alert authorities if attacked. It can ensure that piracy alerts are promptly reported to the appropriate flag-state and port-state authorities. It can guarantee that maritime forces have the legal authority to respond and are prepared to do so when necessary. It can also encourage affected countries to enact domestic legislation to prosecute pirates. However, when all of these fail, as they did off Somalia, naval force will inevitably be called upon as the solution of last resort.

NOTES

1. The cases referred to in this chapter include a legal essay, South China Sea Piracy, Taiping Rebellion, post-WWII Piracy in the South China Sea, Political Economy of Piracy, Vietnamese Boat People, Malacca Strait, Bangladesh, Southeast Asia, Barbary Pirates, Riff Pirates, Gulf of Guinea, and Horn of Africa, in Bruce A. Elleman, Andrew Forbes, David Rosenberg, eds., *Piracy and Maritime Crime: Historical and Modern Case Studies* (Newport, RI: NWC Press, 2010).

2. Hugo Grotius, *The Free Sea* (Indianapolis: Liberty Fund, 2004). https://scholar .harvard.edu/files/armitage/files/free_sea_ebook.pdf

Chapter 5

Expeditionary Warfare

Expeditionary warfare entails the deployment of a disposal force—not to be confused with disposable force—far from their normal base of operations and, in the case of a peripheral campaign in an ongoing hot war, to a theater non-contiguous with the main theater. Execution requires enormous logistical capabilities to transport, land, and sustain forces, often at great distance, which usually only a great sea power can muster. D-Day, Inchon, and Gallipoli represent a spectrum of the most famous examples of expeditionary warfare, with outcomes ranging from strategic victory to operational success to both strategic and operational failure.[1]

Expeditionary warfare is the preferred method of warfare for naval powers, whose goals include keeping all fighting overseas and far from home territory. Naval dominance provides the luxury of fighting in so-called away games, rather than the costly home games that devastate one's own territory and, in doing so, degrade the ability to remain in the war. If a naval power can leverage the sanctuary provided by its oceanic moat to maintain the health of its civilian economy during hostilities, this positions it to outlast a continental adversary in a protracted war aiming at victory through the exhaustion of the enemy.

Sea powers often conduct naval expeditionary campaigns on peripheral fronts as an indirect but economical way to exert pressure on land powers, whose superior or more numerous land forces they do not wish to engage directly. Over time, as their unmolested economies continue to grow and as military operations increasingly interfere with the economies of their enemies or the allies of their enemies, the economic balance of power shifts toward the sea power. In other words, expeditionary warfare, the military operation, often works in tandem with an economic strategy. Sir Julian Corbett was the first to describe campaigns in peripheral theaters in ongoing hot wars. From

55

the Korean War onward, however, many peripheral campaigns took place within an overarching cold war: the East-West Cold War, the Sino-Soviet split, or the Muslim extremist-Western clash of civilizations.

Grand strategy includes all aspects of national power, including military, economic, diplomatic, and information warfare. Expeditionary case studies should be considered from both an operational and strategic level of analysis rather than just the tactical level. The operational level focuses on the deployment and coordination of multiple military units in a common theater in pursuit of a common military goal. The strategic level goes beyond military goals to focus on the achievement of the national objectives for which forces have been deployed. Attainment of the military objective should promote the achievement of the national objective, but in most cases the national objective requires the integration of operational success with many other non-military instruments of national power such as diplomacy, finance, intelligence, communications, transportation, production, food security, energy, and so on.

This combination is properly called grand strategy—"grand" because it integrates all the relevant military and non-military elements of national power and "strategy" because these elements of national power are marshaled within a coherent analytical framework to achieve specific national objectives. A national goal only very rarely is a military or operational objective—common national objectives concern the nature of the global or domestic order, or the global or regional balance of power.

Not all countries have a grand strategy. Many countries do not go beyond tactical training and operational plans and so can easily mistake operational victory for strategic victory. Yet operational victory at best is a necessary but insufficient condition for strategic victory. Counterintuitively, stunning operational success can prevent strategic victory if it conjures a counter-availing hostile coalition. For instance, Germany's and Japan's initial operational successes in World War II brought into being a superior hostile coalition that defeated them both operationally and strategically. Not understanding how operations and strategy interact is a major deterrent to victory. Timing is key.

TIME: EXECUTION AND DURATION

Both the speed of execution and the duration of an expeditionary operation can influence its effectiveness. Execution can be rapid or incremental, the introduction of different types of forces can be simultaneous or sequential, and the duration of the operation can range from short to protracted. For instance, the British expedition rapidly blockaded the White Sea during the Crimean War, but for a short period. In contrast, the Commonwealth forces arrived at Gallipoli incrementally and sequentially: the navy bombarded, paused, some army units arrived, paused, and more reinforcements arrived. At Inchon, forces from all services simultaneously converged and proceeded rapidly inland. In contrast, the New Guinea Campaign protracted over several years.

The simultaneous deployments of forces and rapid execution in the White Sea Campaign, the Inchon landing, the Paracels, the Falklands War, and in the 2003 invasion of Iraq all quickly achieved their operational goals. The White Sea Campaign was hardly a war-winning theater but, as intended, it imposed comparatively high costs on Russia, given the tiny British force deployed, the comparatively large Russian force pinned down, and the extent of the Russian trade it disrupted. In Korea, the Inchon landing was so successful that it led to an expansion of operational and strategic goals—reunification of the peninsula instead of a return to the 38th parallel; war protraction resulted from this expansion of objectives, not from the Inchon strategy. China rapidly took the Paracels and Britain rapidly retook the Falklands. In Iraq, the initial set of operational goals (overthrowing the conventional forces of Saddam Hussein) proved insufficient and the follow-on operational goals (eliminating the insurgency) were much more difficult to achieve than the initial set. Regardless of any subsequent complications, all five of these expeditions achieved the operational objectives they were designed to achieve.

During the opening days of the Pacific War, Japan's numerous simultaneous attacks throughout the Pacific in late 1941 all swiftly achieved their operational goals. But they brought disaster at the strategic level of warfare by alienating neutral powers, thereby transforming a regional war with China into a global war where Japan faced a great-power coalition of the main sea powers, now intent upon regime change in Tokyo. Thus, swift execution seems linked with operational, but not necessarily with strategic, success.

The Gallipoli Campaign followed a different trajectory. Forces arrived sequentially by service and over a long period of time. This gave the Ottoman forces ample time to prepare, with disastrous results for those of the British Commonwealth. The timing of the execution made failure at Gallipoli likely. The Allies and the Japanese also introduced their forces incrementally at both New Guinea and Guadalcanal, but with far less army-navy coordination on the Japanese side than on the Allied side. Both campaigns were protracted, but protraction is not necessarily bad, particularly if the goal is enemy attrition. The Peninsular War (six years), New Guinea (three years), and Guadalcanal (one year) were all protracted peripheral campaigns and designed to inflict disproportionate enemy casualties, which they did. However, the winning side in Guadalcanal and New Guinea, in contrast to the losing side in Gallipoli, had—and continued to leverage—its superior access to the theater, leaving the losing side undermanned and undersupplied, and putting time on the side with better access to the theater.

When considering the elements of time and duration, it is important, therefore, to distinguish between protraction by error, such as at Gallipoli, and by intent, such as in Iberia or Guadalcanal. Protraction worked well against an occupying force isolated by geography from the main force, thereby escalating the occupation costs and eventually forcing a withdrawal.

SPACE: THE NATURE OF THE THEATER

In most cases sea powers use expeditionary warfare against land powers, and most often on a peripheral front, since an opposed landing on a main front can be difficult if not impossible. Even the D-Day landing occurred in a theater peripheral to the Eastern Front where the overwhelming majority of German forces remained locked in combat against Russia—228 German divisions in the east compared to 58 divisions in the west[2]—and even on the Western Front the German forces were deceived into stationing troops so as to defend Calais, not at the actual landing site. Only rarely do either sea or land powers engage in expeditionary warfare against sea powers—Japan's peripheral strategy in World War II is the most famous sea vs sea case and it illustrates the dangers inherent in employing a peripheral strategy against another sea power. A great naval power attacked in this way will make use of the element of space to degrade the SLOCs of its adversary to render the peripheral strategy ineffective—and potentially disastrous—as Japan discovered. Some might argue, given Japan's massive deployments in China, that, despite its island geography, its leaders incorrectly perceived Japan to be a land power.

Expeditionary warfare by definition entails the deployment of non-essential troops, called a disposal force, far from their home bases. In virtually all of the case studies examined, distance meant the country under attack could not retaliate effectively against the home territory of its attacker. For the dominant naval power—generally the attacker in naval expeditionary warfare—distance afforded sanctuary. Not only did the oceans offer homeland security, but they also opened numerous potential avenues to attack the enemy. For the land power—generally the victim of naval expeditionary warfare—the oceans constituted both an insurmountable barrier against imposing costs on the enemy and a vulnerability to attack by sea. Although airpower and nuclear weapons have degraded the efficacy of the oceanic moat, they have not fully negated the comparative homeland security advantage of sea over land powers.

Naval expeditions work best for sea powers against land powers, against isolated islands or peninsulas, or against other lesser sea powers dependent on SLOCs. Land powers can render such attacks ineffective if their central geographic location provides alternate LLOCs or if they can draw the sea power forces inland to impose high military costs, as in the Mesopotamian Campaign for Britain. If the land power borders on key allies, these allies can provide critical military aid and sanctuary for military and other assets, causing the war to protract and costs for the expeditionary power to escalate. This was the communist strategy during the Cold War: their two Asian "hot wars" in Korea and Vietnam relied on resupply over land borders. In both cases, China and Russia armed the local forces, thereby precluding the reunification of the Korean Peninsula, under a non-communist government in the first case, and supporting the unification of North and South Vietnam, under a communist government in the second case.

Sea powers do particularly well when attacking an enemy position on an isolated island or peninsula, such as Guadalcanal, New Guinea, the Malayan Peninsula, or the Falklands; the People's Liberation Army Navy (PLAN) took the Paracel Islands away from South Vietnam in just one day. But this does not guarantee success, as Gallipoli has shown. When enemy supply lines must traverse the sea, the dominant naval power can win as much by cutting these lines at sea as by fighting the enemy on land. This was the case in New Guinea and Guadalcanal.

More than any other countries, in the examples that were investigated Britain appeared in ten case studies, Australia in seven, and the United States in five; sea powers figured prominently in multiple naval expeditionary operations. This is perhaps not too surprising since Britain was the preeminent sea power for the eighteenth and nineteenth centuries until supplanted by the United States in the twentieth century, while Australia has been a key maritime ally of both countries. By contrast, land powers have a very small chance of successfully attacking another power by sea, which perhaps explains China's highly selective use of naval expeditionary warfare in its relations with Vietnam, such as taking the Paracel Islands in 1974. This Chinese expedition was only possible because the U.S. Navy did not intervene, perhaps because Washington preferred these islands to be in Chinese hands rather than Hanoi's, which was closely allied with the USSR.

FORCE: JOINT AND COMBINED OPERATIONS

In addition to time and space, force also constitutes a critical operational dimension of expeditionary warfare. Execution of a naval expeditionary attack requires naval forces capable of overcoming an enemy's sea denial strategies. In most cases, this entailed amphibious landings, ongoing supply and reinforcement by sea, and the protection of these SLOCs and their denial to the enemy. The mere execution let alone success of expeditionary warfare requires enormous logistical capabilities. In the era of airpower, naval dominance and sea denial require air superiority and air denial. To make these effective, midair refueling is essential. Modern expeditionary campaigns are rarely conducted just by surface ships, therefore, but also rely heavily on submarines and airpower. Whereas jointness in the past focused on land-sea coordination, with the advent of airpower naval expeditionary warfare requires sea-air coordination as well.

Many naval expeditions included not only joint but also combined operations, both among services and with allies. For example, the Peninsular War, the campaigns of World Wars I and II, the Inchon landing, the Falklands War, and the initial invasions of Iraq and Afghanistan stand out as prime examples of joint operations. In all but rare cases like the White Sea Campaign, which was almost exclusively conducted at sea, naval expeditionary warfare requires joint operations. If the navy and army do not continuously coordinate then they risk, if not make certain, a Gallipoli.

Virtually all naval expeditions have also occurred within the context of coalitions, so that most have also entailed combined warfare. Naval coalitions have played key roles in the Peninsular War, the Crimean War, World War I, World War II, the Korean War, the Iraq War, and the conflict in Afghanistan. In the New Guinea campaign in World War II, the United States did not care about Japanese forces in New Guinea, but the Australians did. Thus, coalitions must support the needs of every member if they hope to be effective.

PERIPHERAL OPERATIONS

An important subset of expeditionary warfare concerns peripheral operations. A peripheral military operation occurs during an ongoing war in a theater that is secondary to the main front. In other words, a peripheral theater is a secondary theater. Peripheral operations figure prominently in strategy because among the most important decisions in wartime is the decision to open, not to open, to contest, or not to contest a new theater. The deployment of expeditionary forces to a peripheral theater rests on the decision to open that theater or to contest it if the enemy has acted first. Generally, such theaters sidestep the enemy main forces to take on a weaker subset.

Victory in a peripheral theater should not be confused with victory in the overarching war. The peripheral theater is valuable only in so far as it contributes to victory in the greater war and sets favorable conditions for peace. All the case studies examined from the Peninsular War through the Inchon landing in the Korean War occurred in peripheral theaters. The main theater was not Spain but Russia for Napoleon; not the White Sea but the Crimea for Russia; not Gallipoli or Mesopotamia but France for Germany; not Pearl Harbor but China for Japan; not Guadalcanal or New Guinea but the Japanese home islands for the United States; and not Inchon but Pusan for the United Nations.

Archival documents show that the conflict in Vietnam appears to have also been a peripheral campaign, with the strategic goal of dividing the USSR and China, and—as happened in 1972—flipping China from a Soviet to a U.S. ally. If true, then the goal of this war was never to win, per se, but to split the Sino-Soviet alliance and flip China. Like Vietnam, most peripheral campaigns included land invasions that were intended not for permanent conquest but to exert pressure and to sap the resources of the enemy.

SUCCESSFUL PERIPHERAL OPERATIONS

Successful peripheral operations—the Peninsular War, the White Sea Campaign, Guadalcanal and New Guinea for the Allies, and the Inchon landing—all entailed clearly linked operational and strategic outcomes. In addition, the winning sides in these five cases all gathered more accurate battlefield intelligence than did their enemies, and all demonstrated logistical superiority in both deploying and sustaining forces, as well as superiority in conducting joint operations.

Clear strategic links between the peripheral and main theaters meant that victory in the secondary theater contributed directly to victory on the main front. The war in Iberia, the model case on which Sir Julian Corbett based his naval theories, pinned and attrited French armies, making them unavailable for Napoleon's fatal Russian campaign. In the White Sea Campaign of the Crimean War, a tiny British force both pinned a much larger Russian force and cut trade, increasing the military and economic pressure on Russia to negotiate a settlement. In World War II, the Allies envisioned victory over Japan through an attrition strategy and so inflicted unsustainable Japanese losses, especially of scarce pilots, at Guadalcanal. In the Korean War, Inchon was the operational hammer for Pusan's anvil. UN forces landed at Inchon in order to encircle and annihilate enemy forces and fatally weaken the North Korean government.

Information superiority facilitated operational success. In the Peninsular War, Britain gleaned intelligence from the local population, which was generally hostile to France. During the Crimean War, Britain understood that Russia was singularly unprepared to fight in the White Sea theater. U.S. information superiority over Japan and Germany in World War II is perhaps the most famous case of code breaking; the ability to decipher Japanese diplomatic, naval, and eventually army codes minimized Allied losses while maximizing those of Japan. At Inchon, the North Korean leadership clearly did not expect a UN landing, a monumental failure in intelligence, while the UN correctly gauged the weakness of North Korean defenses there. In Vietnam, putting pressure on the Russian logistical line that ran through China exacerbated tensions so much that the two former allies went to war in 1969. According to many reports, the Sino-Soviet conflict almost went nuclear.

Finally, it is hard to imagine operations more joint than the Peninsular War or the Inchon landing. Throughout the campaign, Wellington's land forces remained in close communication with those at sea, while MacArthur's forces depended on naval superiority to land at an extraordinarily difficult location and to wall off the South Korean coastline from North Korean infiltration. Despite lapses in jointness at Guadalcanal and New Guinea, in comparative terms the Allies were far more joint than were the Japanese, whose land and sea services often treated each other as the main enemy. Most successful peripheral operations depended on clearly linked operational and strategic goals, plus comparative advantages in intelligence collection and analysis.

UNSUCCESSFUL PERIPHERAL OPERATIONS

Military operations must fit within the larger picture of national resources, goals, and non-military strategies. This sounds obvious, yet a remarkable number of belligerents have failed to go beyond the operational level of warfare. Many did not completely think out their operational choices to link the intended military effects to the desired political outcomes of the war, meaning the nature of the post-war peace.

In several of the cases examined, an unclear strategic relationship between the peripheral and the primary theaters resulted in a boomerang effect in the peripheral theater. British operations against the Ottoman Empire in World War I, Japanese operations in the Pacific during World War II, and U.S. operations in the Middle East transformed passive enemies into active belligerents. In World Wars I and II, these operations entailed fighting allies of the main enemy. In World War I, Germany was the main enemy for Britain; in World War II, China was the main enemy of Japan; and at the time of the decision to invade Iraq, al Qaeda and Taliban fighters in Afghanistan were the main enemies for the United States. In Vietnam, the main enemy was really the USSR.

Unfortunately, the secondary enemies—the Ottomans in World War I and the Western allies in World War II—whom Britain and Japan, respectively, chose to fight, were actually the dominant powers in the relevant peripheral theaters, meaning that while Britain and Japan had deployed their main forces elsewhere, their secondary enemy could focus its own forces in the peripheral theater or, in the case of the United States in World War II, was economically so much larger than Japan, that it could still bring more to the peripheral theater than could Japan. As a result, these peripheral theaters served to overextend the perpetrator rather than the victim. In the two world wars, peripheral operations engaged Britain and Japan in fighting secondary enemies, whom they could have sidestepped entirely if they had made wiser decisions.

British problems in Gallipoli and Mesopotamia; Japanese problems in Pearl Harbor, Guadalcanal, and New Guinea; and Argentine problems in the Falklands reflected, in part, another problem of strategy, a failure to identify the enemy's strategic or operational COG. The Ottoman army in World War I was neither an operational nor a strategic COG for the Central powers. Nor did the locations of Pearl Harbor, Guadalcanal, or New Guinea bring anything to bear on the China theater for Japan, quite the contrary, Pearl Harbor instantly conjured a great-power U.S-British alliance with China. In the Falklands, Argentina failed to focus on Britain's operational COG, its two aircraft carriers. Just damaging one might have escalated the costs of the war beyond what British voters were willing to pay. All of these issues—the irrelevance of the Ottoman armies to the outcome of the war in Europe and of the Pacific theater to victory in China, and the centrality of aircraft carriers to Britain's operational and political ability to continue hostilities in the Falklands—are actually obvious in hindsight. Yet recognizing the obvious often requires careful assessment.

In addition to problems of strategy, there were also problems of execution. The British-led forces at Gallipoli failed at the execution of joint operations. Indeed, Gallipoli is a negative example illustrating incredible logistical failures: naval and land forces were introduced sequentially and incrementally over many months. Rather than disorienting the Ottoman Empire with surprise, Britain gave it ample time to prepare. Proper execution would have required extensive advance naval and army coordination to pound the coast, land the men, and move up and out as fast as possible toward the Straits to open them to Entente traffic.

Superior intelligence is not simply valuable, but critical. Intelligence embraces a wide array of information obtained from a diversity of sources, whose utility depends on competent analysis. The information inferiority of Argentina in the Falklands and particularly of Japan in the Pacific proved fatal to both. In World War II, even with the ability to decrypt many Japanese communications, the United States found the fighting to be hard going.[3] Without information superiority, the United States could not have destroyed Japan's merchant marine, whose loss undermined Japan's ability to manufacture war materiel, feed the home islands, and shift troops and supplies among distant theaters. Without information superiority, the United States still might have won the island campaigns, but at greater cost, since it would not have known where to bypass Japanese troop concentrations or where to find Japanese carriers and convoys. Costs would have escalated to a level that might have caused the United States to downgrade its objectives. Japan still might have lost the war, but at the price of a negotiated rather than an unconditional surrender. Argentina's failure to understand either British critical vulnerabilities or London politics cost it the Falklands, which Britain became determined to retain only after Argentina had occupied them. Argentina would have done far better with a diplomatic rather than a military strategy, or, if determined to take military action, had done so only after, not before, Britain decommissioned key elements of its Cold War navy.

To summarize, peripheral operations failed when not carefully integrated into a greater grand strategy linking both the probable operational result in the peripheral theater to victory in the overarching war as well as linking the strategy of war with the achievement of national goals. Flexibility and adaptability were key. In some cases, battle in a peripheral theater impacted neutrals and so activated a formerly passive enemy, producing overextension, not—as intended—of the main enemy, but of the perpetrator of the peripheral operation, now spread thin over multiple theaters. A peripheral theater that was the main theater for an enemy ally exacerbated this outcome because the enemy's ally could focus all energies on an adversary with divided attention. Furthermore, it is amazing how many powers have found joint operations nearly impossible to execute. The coordination of land and naval forces for an amphibious landing and for coastal operations seems obvious. Yet navies and armies often work at cross-purposes. Likewise, successful contested landings depend not only on joint operations but also on superior intelligence for the invading forces to survive the vulnerable landing period, plus air superiority to protect them from enemy attack.

OPERATIONAL VS STRATEGIC RISK

Otto von Bismarck, the grand strategist of the succession of wars that transformed Prussia into a great power, famously said: "Only a fool learns from his own mistakes"; Bismarck, of course, learned from the mistakes of "others." Surprisingly few nations consistently focus on grand strategy, a term of British coinage reflecting their highly analytical approach to foreign policy.[4] This sin of omission has produced on occasion a corresponding failure to consider risk.

Both the Pearl Harbor and Inchon strategies entailed enormous operational risk. Navies have special reasons to be risk averse. This is because they depend on a comparatively small number of extremely expensive platforms that once lost cannot easily be reconstituted. Pearl Harbor and Inchon both put ships and men at risk. If the U.S. aircraft carriers had been in the vicinity of but not at Pearl Harbor, Japan might have lost capital ships. During the Korean War, under easily imaginable circumstances, the United States might have lost numerous ships and men at Inchon, where a sunk ship in the narrow approaches might have impeded land-sea access or where, given the massive tidal flows, delays might have left boats stranded by an outgoing tide on the mudflats to become easy marks for coastal gunfire. Even small operations, such as the Falklands War, can risk extremely expensive capital ships; damage to just one of the two British aircraft carriers might have easily changed the outcome of the conflict.

But sometimes the stakes warrant the risk. At Inchon, unlike at Pearl Harbor, operational success contributed directly to the defeat of the main enemy. Moreover, Inchon, unlike Pearl Harbor, did not guarantee the entry of new active belligerents on the enemy side. In other words, in addition to posing enormous operational risks, Pearl Harbor, unlike Inchon, also posed even greater strategic risks. In World War II, China lacked the capacity under any circumstances to threaten the Japanese home islands. But, as Japan quickly found out, the United States possessed and utilized this capacity to destroy virtually every Japanese city of any size and to demand unconditional surrender.

Japanese leaders, throughout the war with China and the ensuing war with the United States and the British Commonwealth, failed to tabulate the strategic risks of their operational strategies. Inchon was worth the operational risk because it promised the even higher reward of possibly terminating the war, which it might have done had the United States advanced only as far as the narrow waist of the Korean peninsula between Wonsan and Nampo and then traded back territory in return for peace.[5] In contrast, even under the best of circumstances, Pearl Harbor did not promise to end the quagmire in China, only to cut U.S. and British aid to Nationalist China. This outcome would not have made Japan any more capable of garrisoning all of China. Quite the contrary, the opening of new theaters and the proliferation of enemies dispersed Japanese forces far from China, compounding Japan's overextension. MacArthur's strategy in Korea ran into trouble when he ignored strategic risk to continue the offensive all the way to the Chinese border, triggering a costly third-party intervention by China.

The Falklands also posed high operational risks, but these occurred within the context of naval downsizing in Britain so that naval leaders saw the hostilities as an opportunity to demonstrate the value of the service to put a brake on the downsizing. The strategic risks were low, as the Cold War—the war on which British survival rested—seemed unlikely to heat up as a result of the Falklands War. Yet the prestige value for Britain from a victory against Argentina was high. Britain's success demonstrated that, contrary to the persistent trend of British decline after World War I, it remained a great military power if defined by the ability to project power far from home.

ALLEGIANCE OF THE LOCAL POPULATION

The Peninsular War is often considered the model for all subsequent peripheral operations, while Gallipoli is reviled, particularly in Australia and New Zealand, which lost so many for so little while under British command. In many ways the theaters were similar. They were far from the main front and isolated from the main adversary, which could not easily reach either theater. Both were in very strategic locations—the Iberian Peninsula controlled access to the Mediterranean while the Dardanelles controlled access to southern Russia and the Black Sea. Both theaters allowed Britain to leverage its naval dominance and engage its underutilized naval capacity in combat.

Clearly at the level of execution, however, the campaigns shared nothing in common. Keeping one's flank against the ocean is key. Both campaigns did so. But the Duke of Wellington, one of Britain's greatest generals, commanded his forces in Iberia with a clear understanding of the connection between his military operations there and the greater war in Europe. In contrast, the generals and admirals in charge of Gallipoli resented the diversion of their assets far from the main front and apparently resented each other as well as Sir Winston Churchill, first lord of the Admiralty, whose brainchild it was. So there was minimal army-navy cooperation, no visible civil-military coordination, and disastrous execution at every level but the tactical, where Commonwealth soldiers—in particular Australians and New Zealanders—fought bravely at horrendous cost.

There was another factor at work. The local population in Portugal and Spain supported Britain during the Napoleonic Wars or, more accurately, Britain supported the local population's fight against French domination. Together Wellington's conventional army and Spanish guerrilla forces put the French forces in the untenable position of having to concentrate to fight the conventional army while having to disperse to fight the insurgency. The Iberian geography impeded the arrival of French reinforcements with its high mountains and the provisioning of large armies with its arid landscape, while its long coastline greatly facilitating British operations by allowing efficient replenishment, deployment, and escape by sea. None of this would have been possible with a hostile local population.

Had the local population been equally friendly as Iberia, Gallipoli might have succeeded. Indeed, this possibility apparently occurred to the Ottomans. When countering Russia's simultaneous attack in the Caucasus, they massacred Armenians whom they perceived to be sympathetic to the Entente powers. The Ottomans did not want an internal hostile population assisting the British. Hundreds of thousands died. The tragic Armenian genocide may have been an unintended consequence of Gallipoli, just as the tragic sectarian violence in Iraq has been an unintended consequence of the Iraq War.

In the Pacific theater of World War II, Japan also faced increasingly hostile local populations. Local volunteers acting as coast watchers contributed to U.S. dominance in the information war by observing and reporting on Japanese deployments. This was crucial to the interpretation of other intelligence derived from decryptions of message traffic. Over time, rather than assisting, Vietnam's disillusioned populace began to oppose U.S. forces. Likewise, a hostile local population posed enormous problems for U.S. operations in Afghanistan and Iraq.

In other words, an outside power can comparatively easily stir up trouble in a peripheral theater for an occupation force facing a hostile local population. Arm that population and the ensuing insurgency becomes an expensive proposition for the army of occupation. Britain did this to the French in Spain, the Soviet Union and China did this to the United States in Korea, and this happened to the U.S.-led forces in Afghanistan and Iraq. The importance of intelligence gathering, in particular for establishing the location and timing for the opening of a new theater of operations, is clear. Often a sympathetic populace living in-theater provides key information, so an essential corollary to comprehensive intelligence gathering is the requirement not to alienate the local population, lest these local allegiances shift to the enemy.

CONCLUSIONS

Expeditionary warfare, especially in peripheral theaters, can win wars. Sir Julian Corbett, the greatest theorist of peripheral operations, isolated six strategic factors that must align for an optimal peripheral operation: the attacker (1) must be the dominant naval power in the theater; (2) must have command of the forces it deploys (rather than their being under allied command); (3) must coordinate with allies fighting in the main theater; and (4) must be physically separated by sea so that an oceanic moat provides homeland defense. (5) The peripheral theater must be accessible by sea but geographically isolated, affording the dominant sea power better access than the enemy (presumably a land power). (6) Finally, the perpetrator must deploy a "disposal" force, meaning not a "disposable" force on a suicide run, but a force that can be deployed at acceptable risk so that in the worst-case scenario, its loss will not compromise the main war effort or homeland defense.[6] Even given the presence of all of the above factors, Corbett cautioned that the effective execution of a peripheral operation at the beginning of the twentieth century required the continuous coordination of naval and ground forces, meaning exemplary joint operations.[7]

Based on the case studies examined here, Corbett's list could be expanded to include (1) a clear connection between operational and strategic goals; (2) intelligence superiority not only in theater but extending to a better understanding of enemy motivations than the enemy's understanding of you; (3) and entailing the correct identification of the enemy's operational and strategic centers of gravity or at least avoiding a gross misidentification; (4) an evaluation of both operational and especially strategic risk; (5) a careful examination of the likely allegiance of the local population—if hostile, much less can be achieved in theater than if friendly—and; (6) great caution before undertaking a peripheral operation that awakens a passive enemy; or (7) that opens a second theater for oneself against a one-theater enemy.

Since Corbett's time, the development of airpower has added a third dimension to jointness, so that if alive today he would undoubtedly add air dominance and satellites to sea dominance. Airpower has degraded the oceanic moat that still protects but at a reduced rate. For example, on 11 September 2001, al Qaeda attempted to jump America's oceanic moat without a navy or even any conventional forces, by using airpower in a most unconventional attack on a distant theater. Apparently, al Qaeda's leaders assumed invulnerability to reprisals given their inland location in Afghanistan but airpower in combination with precision munitions has also degraded the security of formerly remote locations. Like the Japanese attack on Pearl Harbor, the 9-11 attack had a transformative psychological effect on Americans, who immediately embarked on a previously inconceivable foreign policy objective of regime change, an objective antithetical to their attackers' interests in both cases. After 9-11, this entailed regime change not only in Afghanistan, but before long in Iraq as well.

Like the Japanese at Pearl Harbor, al Qaeda enjoyed remarkable operational success in imposing skewed costs. The 9-11 attacks caused a significant loss of lives and enormous economic damage at minimal cost. But it turned out that high-rent office buildings in New York City and a wing of the Pentagon did not constitute either operational or strategic centers of gravity for the United States. The choice of date, mimicking the common emergency telephone number in the United States of 911, and the choices of targets—the Pentagon and office buildings rather presumptuously called the "World Trade Center"—were all highly symbolic as if destroying symbols could defeat a country. Symbols can indeed animate people but often for battle, not for capitulation. So, from the point of view of al Qaeda, the attacks had a boomerang effect, bringing their activities under the hostile scrutiny of intelligence services worldwide.

NOTES

1. The case studies examined here include a chapter on legal issues, the Iberian campaign, Royal Navy's White Sea Campaign in the Crimean War, Gallipoli, World War I Mesopotamia campaign, Pearl Harbor, Guadalcanal, New Guinea, Korea, Malayan Emergency and Confrontation, China's 1974 Paracel Expedition, the Falklands War, first Iraq War, and the Global War on Terror, in Bruce A. Elleman and S.C.M. Paine, eds., *Naval Power and Expeditionary Warfare: Peripheral Campaigns and New Theatres of Naval Warfare* (London: Routledge, 2012).

2. Richard Overy, *Russia's War* (New York: Penguin, 1997), 236, 240.

3. Edward J. Drea, *MacArthur's ULTRA: Codebreaking and the War against Japan, 1942–1945* (Lawrence: University of Kansas Press, 1992).

4. B. H. Liddell Hart, *Strategy* (New York: Praeger, 1954), 335–36.

5. Bernard Brodie, *War & Politics* (New York: Macmillan, 1973), 92–95.

6. Julian S. Corbett, *Some Principles of Maritime Strategy* (New York: Longmans, Green, and Co. 19011), 52–55, 57–58, 61–63.

7. *Ibid.*, 60.

Chapter 6

Commerce Raiding

At its most basic, commerce raiding is a legal form of piracy. In the late nineteenth century, the French *Jeune École*, or "new school," of naval thinking promoted a commerce-raiding strategy for the weaker naval power to defeat the dominant naval power. France provided the vocabulary for the discussion—*Jeune École* and *guerre de course* (war of the chase)—and embodied the geopolitical predicament addressed: France had been a dominant land power, known for its large and proficient army and resentful of British imperial dominance and commercial preeminence. But its navy had rarely matched the Royal Navy in either quantity or quality, and its economy could not support both a preeminent army and navy. So its naval planners thought of an economical way out of their dilemma. They argued that a *guerre de course* allowed a weaker maritime power, such as France, to impose disproportionate costs on the stronger sea power in order to achieve its objectives. Sadly for France, the strategy did not work as anticipated, and British naval dominance and imperial primacy endured.[1]

The dynamic of rivalries is especially important between sea powers and land powers. This issue is an important one today in that from the heyday of the British Empire to the present, sea powers have set the global order and land powers have contested it. So the dynamic is still with us, and it is of vital national import to all countries that benefit from the present international order of freedom of navigation (FON), free trade, and the rule of international law. Commerce raiding, or *guerre de course*, is associated with major wars, such as the U.S. Civil War and the two world wars. Yet in many cases, if not most often, such operations have been conducted with relatively little public awareness. This does not indicate ineffectiveness, however. As a military tactic, commerce raiding has time after time proven itself a most efficient way

71

to exert subtle yet constant pressure on an opponent, similar to the vexation of having a tiny pebble stuck in your shoe.[2]

This section will focus on how and why *guerre de course* strategies have been adopted and conducted both in non-war and in wartime conflicts. Re-examining examples from the eighteenth, nineteenth, and twentieth centuries makes several factors apparent. First, while dominant sea powers have frequently conducted commerce raiding—most notably the American campaign against Japan in World War II—weak naval powers or continental powers have also attempted to cut off opponents' international trade, as the American revolutionaries did in the 1770s, and as Napoleon tried to do to Britain from 1803 to 1815. Second, *guerre de course* campaigns are often protracted, especially if the victim, particularly a continental one, opens alternate LLOCs. In attacks on sea powers, however, speed of execution is essential, as shown by Germany's failure to defeat Great Britain in either world war. The more time a sea power has to create the means to protect its sea trade, the less effective the *guerre de course* strategy will be. Third, changes in technology have greatly impacted commerce raiding—for example, the transition from wood to copper-sheathed ships in the early nineteenth century, the change from coal to oil combustion in the early twentieth century, and the development of airplanes and submarines. Most recently, Somali "pirates" have used small skiffs and handheld GPS devices to capture enormous oil tankers, bringing low-level but highly affordable and dependable technology to the fore of commerce raiding.

THE GROWTH OF PRIVATEERING

Privateering, as distinct from attacking shipping under letters of *marque*, was evident as early as the eleventh century, and by the early seventeenth century it was widespread in the evolving global economic system. By the end of the seventeenth century, the issuing of letters of *marque* was widely considered a belligerent act, and so they were used less often, replaced instead by commissions for privateering—in effect, *guerre de course* under contract. There were a number of reasons why a sovereign might commission privateers. Most importantly, it offered a way to destroy a rival state's shipping and create economic turmoil at virtually no cost to the issuing state. Large professional navies were expensive and often nonproductive. Therefore, privateering represented a cheaper form of naval warfare.

In England, numerous sets of "instructions to privateers" were issued between 1649 and 1780. It was through the regulation of prizes—how they were valued and who received shares—that the state placed strict controls on privateering. In 1563, the Lord High Admiral required inventories and bail for prizes so that the courts would know precisely what had been captured and its exact value. Privateers had to promise not to break up their prizes and sell them, to turn in all their prizes to the government, and to pay the Admiralty a tenth of their value. After 1603, any ship captured without proper letters was condemned and confiscated by the Lord High Admiral. This became a new precedent, whereby all prizes taken illegally would go to the Lord High Admiral, while the captor could be considered a pirate and treated as such.

A number of other regulations were issued to control the distribution of prizes. In 1692, the first Prize Act was passed, containing provisions for sharing proceeds. Before this act was adopted, shares had been apportioned by agreement, custom, or the Crown. The sale of prizes in neutral countries was now discouraged, probably due to the difficulty of the king and the Lord High Admiral in getting their shares—a tenth and fifteenth, respectively. The Prize Act gave captors a statutory right to their prizes, which had previously been at the pleasure of the Crown. Economic factors were also important to the spread of commerce raiding.

ECONOMIC FACTORS AND COMMERCE RAIDING

One major cause for the sudden rise in commerce raiding during the seventeenth and eighteenth centuries was the passage of the British Navigation Acts in 1651. These acts directed that goods could be brought into England or English possessions only by British ships or by ships of the countries where the goods originated. As a result, foreign tobacco and other agricultural products imported on British ships could be sold in England and its colonies at low prices. The same goods imported on non-British ships were charged with additional duties. Rejecting this monopoly, many merchants in the American colonies traded with privateers instead, often with the full knowledge and tacit support of local officials. In cities and towns all along the Atlantic coast, privateer loot was "imported" in defiance of the Navigation Acts: "Very often the same merchants and officials who furnished the illegal market for privateer plunder also outfitted expeditions in exchange for guaranteed shares in a ship's loot."[3]

This trade reached its climax in 1700, when there were so many pirates along New England's coastline that one official described the region as being in a "state of war." A second reason behind the upsurge in piracy was the War of the Spanish Succession (1702–1713), between England and Spain. During that conflict privateering was legal so long as the privateer had a valid commission. If it was lost, privateers could be treated as pirates. This was the cause of William Dampier's sojourn in a Dutch prison as an accused pirate.

In May 1720, Captain Shelvocke risked drowning to reboard his sinking ship *Speedwell* to retrieve his "commission scroll and the chest containing eleven hundred dollars of the owners' money."[4]

Spain and England signed a peace treaty in 1713, but thousands of privateers refused to quit and instead became full-time pirates. There was especially stiff competition to control the lucrative resources of the Caribbean. By 1715, an estimated two thousand pirates operated out of Nassau, preying on Spanish galleons carrying gold and silver back to Europe. The profits that could be made from even one successful attack were enormous. Piracy peaked during the ten years between 1716 and 1725, a period called "the Golden Age of Piracy." During this period, piracy reached new heights, including the infamous exploits of Edward Thatch (or Teach), alias Blackbeard the Pirate, who was finally killed in 1718, and Captain Bartholomew Roberts, who reportedly pirated some four hundred ships during just three years of looting and burning before he was finally captured and executed.

The Royal Navy responded to this threat by setting up convoys to protect merchant ships, or offering—for a hefty fee—to transport cargo on its own warships. It tried to stop piracy. Nevertheless, it proved extraordinarily difficult to track down and eliminate pirates. There was simply too much money involved and the enormous profits that could be made from convoying made many Royal Navy captains less than desirous of destroying the very threat which was the indirect source of their income. It took a concerted effort by naval authorities to suppress it; only by 1725 had the most infamous pirates been captured and hanged.

Meanwhile, competing colonial powers continued to use privateers to supplement their naval forces against enemies. Weak governments often turned to privateers. For example, during the American Revolution, the Continental Congress commissioned over 2,500 privateers, and the Americans captured 2,300 prizes from the British, losing less than half that number. Later still, during the War of 1812, American privateers played a major role; the "U.S. brig *Yankee*, for example, was credited with destroying or capturing some five million dollars' worth of English shipping and cargo during that time."[5] Sometimes privateering and blockade could work hand in hand: from 1793 to 1796, some 2,100 British ships were seized by French privateers even while the British fleet blockaded France.

Privateering, for its part, slowly petered out after the final defeat of Napoleon in 1815, as neutral countries took greater exception to the prospect of their own trade being attacked in war. By the mid-1800s, privateering was no longer practiced by the major naval powers in Europe. With the growth of the Industrial Revolution, colonial empires, and global trade, most states agreed that attacks on commerce should be a last resort and should not be undertaken at all by private individuals for personal profit. In the 1856

Declaration of Paris, the major naval powers—with the United States a notable exception—agreed that privateering should be outlawed.

Once a state could build up and maintain its own navy, it was very dangerous for the government to allow "independent" armed naval forces to persist. In such circumstances, as Lord Nelson put it, "all privateers are no better than pirates."[6] Governments also began to justify the use of professional naval forces against pirates. By this time, Western European countries had largely established their global spheres of influence, and suppressing piracy was now in their economic interest. By the nineteenth century, with superior firepower, better charts, and steam-powered ships, governments would be better able to police the seas and curb privateering.

COMMERCE RAIDING DURING THE TWENTIETH CENTURY

Commerce raiding has been a traditional mission for all major navies and has played a particularly important role in Western maritime history. Alfred Thayer Mahan highlighted the important role of commerce raiders in the American Revolution, the War of 1812, and the U.S. Civil War. Sir Julian Corbett, the unofficial Admiralty historian, emphasized the costs of interfering with international trade, writing in 1907: "The prolonged exercise of belligerent rights" over mercantile shipping, "even of the most undoubted kind, produces an interference with trade that becomes more and more oppressive."[7]

Only seven years after Corbett's book was published, Britain was at war, defending its very existence from a German campaign of unrestricted submarine warfare. Fortunately for London, Washington found German behavior threatening to the rights of neutral powers and eventually declared war on Berlin. In contrast, in World War II it was the U.S. Navy that carried out a thoroughly successful unrestricted submarine warfare campaign, this time against Japan. Post-war, however, the international community tended to band together whenever any country or regional war interfered with international trade, as best shown during the Iran-Iraq Tanker War of the 1980s and the recent piracy threat off Somalia.

Guerre de course—or more generically, commerce raiding—is a means to contribute to the achievement of national or nonstate-actor goals. Another factor influencing the ability of states to respond to commerce raiding comprised efforts to limit the freedom of the seas. This trend began in the late 1700s, when the newly founded United States of America became the first nation-state to extend its claim as sovereign territory to 3 miles offshore. Thomas Jefferson, as secretary of state, argued in 1793: "The greatest distance [of the outer boundary of territorial waters] to which any respectable assent among nations has at any time been given is the extent of human sight, estimated upward of twenty miles, and the smallest distance, I believe, claimed by any nation whatever, is the utmost range of a cannon ball, usually stated at one sea league."[8]

The "cannon-shot rule" declared that the ability to exert naval power over a coastal area was sufficient to establish a property interest in its marine resources, such as fish stocks or pearls. The area within the 3-nautical-mile limit, however, was not private property but would be administered by each state as a common natural resource under public stewardship. In these waters, acts of robbery would be considered maritime crime, not piracy. Many countries followed the American lead.

TYPES OF COMMERCE RAIDING

Commerce raiding types can be categorized in a number of ways: rapid, intermittent, tightening, or loosening (in terms of implementation); short, medium, and long (in terms of duration); close or distant (in terms of the distance of the theater from the territory of the victim); near or far (in terms of the distance of the theater from the territory of the perpetrator); joint (when different military services of one country cooperate) or combined (when militaries of allied countries coordinate); and partial or total (in terms of porosity). Over time technological breakthroughs have greatly influenced the cost, execution, and feasibility of all types of commerce raiding, as shown initially by the development of instruments to locate and target specific ships in World War II, and most recently by the ability of small Somali skiffs to hijack huge oil tankers with the aid of handheld GPS tracking devices.

Both the rate of implementation and duration of a commerce raiding campaign can influence its effectiveness. Implementation can be rapid, intermittent, tightening, or loosening, while the duration can be short, medium, or long. For instance, the French quickly adopted commerce raiding operations during Napoleon's French Wars, but over the long term they conducted them only intermittently; meanwhile, because of faulty torpedoes and poor leadership, American commerce raiding against Japan during World War II tightened only gradually over several years.

Five rapidly implemented commerce raiding campaigns comprise the Confederate side of the U.S. Civil War, the Jeune École (in theory, at least), the Japanese in the First Sino-Japanese War, the American campaign upon entry in World War I, and the Fascists in the Spanish Civil War. In all of these conflicts, rapid commerce raiding operations were relatively short (one to two years) to medium (three to four years) in duration and were usually waged by the victorious side—but not always, as the American Civil War showed. In the First Sino-Japanese War, the Chinese never contested Japanese command of the sea after suffering the loss of a troop transport and then defeat in one naval engagement. Once the United States entered World War I, its convoys and antisubmarine warfare campaign began rapidly and soon neutralized German commerce raiding. In line with the expectations of Jeune École theorists, the rapid introduction of commerce raiding seemed to force the Spanish Republic to capitulate. Nevertheless, commerce raiding was not the sole determining factor in the outcome of these wars.

Likewise, in all four cases of gradually tightening commerce raiding— Britain in the Seven Years' War, Germany in both world wars, and the United States against Japan in World War II—the raiding did not determine the outcome of the wars. Rather, the cumulative effects of commerce raiding worked in conjunction with other strategies: the attrition of ground forces, blockade, naval combat, alliance, and (in the World War II case of Japan) the American use of atomic bombs. The extensive size of these theaters perhaps explains why implementation was gradual versus rapid. Strategies of gradually tightening raiding worked best for the dominant sea power but not for land powers, or even for a secondary sea power such as Germany in both world wars. Britain and the United States successfully combined commerce raiding with other strategies to win, variously, the Seven Years' War and both world wars, while unrestricted submarine warfare by Germany in World War I cost that nation the war by transforming a great naval power, the United States, from a neutral into a belligerent.

Five cases of intermittent commerce raiding—the American Revolution, the French Wars, the War of 1812, the Tanker War, and Somalia—produced mixed results: loss, draw, or victory due partly to other factors (such as French intervention at Yorktown, in the case of the American Revolution). These campaigns were perhaps most strategically effective in what they prevented from happening—in other words, in their deterrent or diversionary effects. For example, U.S. commerce raiding in the War of 1812 tied down many Royal Navy ships that might otherwise have attacked conventional American targets. However, when intermittent commerce raiding negatively affected the international community, such as during the French Wars, the Tanker War, and Somalia, it spurred the intervention of neutral powers.

There were only two cases of loosening campaigns—Russia in the Russo-Japanese War and Japan in World War II—both powers whose attention turned to massive land battles that they were losing. In Russia's case, threats of neutral intervention convinced Russia to terminate commerce raiding from neutral Chinese ports. By contrast, huge Japanese naval and merchant ship losses after 1943 precluded effective countermeasures.

Six commerce raiding campaigns were long (five years or more)—the Seven Years' War, the American Revolution, the French Wars, Germany during World War II, the Tanker War, and Somali piracy. Two of these six gradually tightened over time, while the others were intermittent. Short and medium-length commerce raiding campaigns generally concentrated on an operational COG, such as the Japanese sinking of the Chinese troopship *Kowshing* or the Confederate focus on Union shipping.

Only six of the cases examined (not counting Jeune École theorists) ended in clear victories for the sides with the more robust commerce raiding campaigns. In the Seven Years' War, the American Revolution, the First Sino-Japanese War, the American campaigns during both World Wars I and II, and the Spanish Civil War, the ability to conduct a commerce raiding campaign or to protect vital imports by sea appears to have been crucial for victory. Even so, it was but one of multiple critical factors that together determined the outcome. In eight cases, however, a side engaging in commerce raiding either lost or the conflict ended in a draw. All were continental powers, with the exception of Japan in World War II, and Japan in that war chose a continental strategy rather than a purely maritime strategy that could have led to a more productive use of its navy and merchant marine.

In other words, generally commerce raiding seems more strategically effective for a naval power than a continental power. Land powers that pursue the strategy can often achieve the operational effect of imposing far greater financial losses on their enemy than their raiding operations cost. Although the ships sunk are not available for future passages and their replacement requires a vigorous shipbuilding capacity, dominant naval powers typically have such capacity, either domestically or through allies. So the costs from lost ships may be significant and cumulative but potentially disastrous only for a country lacking the capacity to replace lost ships and dependent on crucial war materiel delivered by sea. This means commerce raiding likely accelerated losses that eventually resulted in capitulation.

Moreover, commerce raiding can become a morale-enhancing catalyst for an angry victim. Although it might seem that overseas commerce would be a critical vulnerability for a maritime power, foreign trade has actually been most vulnerable when targeted by the dominant maritime power against a continental adversary. In fact, overseas commerce turns out to be an even more important critical vulnerability for continental powers, let alone secondary maritime powers, which lack the means to protect their trade. Dominant maritime powers tend to combine blockade with commerce raiding to cut off the victim's overseas trade virtually in its entirety—as exemplified by Germany's fate in both world wars. In large measure, Germany was trapped by its geography.

SPACE: THE NATURE OF THE THEATER

In most cases—ten of the sixteen studied—land powers adopted commerce raiding operations, and in eight they targeted sea powers. Only two of the campaigns were part of victorious wars: the American Revolution (targeting a sea power) and Spanish Civil War (targeting a land power). In each of these two cases the outcome depended in part on conventional military aid supplied by great-power allies—France for the decisive battle of Yorktown and the Axis powers for the Spanish Fascists. In half of the ten cases, the land powers engaged in commerce raiding had significant navies, and yet only one case resulted in victory—the Fascists in Spain, whose maritime assets included allied navies. The Spanish case was also the only one of the five in which the victim was a land, not a sea, power. In other words, commerce raiding conducted by land powers against sea powers has not generally resulted in a victorious war.

Five of the campaigns were conducted by sea powers, which won all but one of the wars. The only loss was Japan's in World War II, in which it took on the dominant naval powers, the United States and Great Britain. All the victorious campaigns save one took place in theaters distant from the victims and far from the perpetrators, the dominant sea power roaming the seas in search of targets. These were global wars—the Seven Years' War, World War I, and World War II—in which the global order was at stake and fighting took place around the planet. The exception, the First Sino-Japanese War, was a regional war between only two belligerents, not between global coalitions, and geography dictated a close-near theater.

The nature of the theater of operations can help determine success or failure. Similar to blockades, commerce raiding distances can vary greatly. The terms "close" (for roughly a hundred to 150 nautical miles) and "distant" (more than 150 nautical miles) refer to the distance of the theater from the victim country, while "near commerce raiding" and "far commerce raiding" refer to the distance of the theater from the commerce raiding country. Most cases included operations both distant from the shores of the victim and far from the shores of the perpetrator, such as in the Seven Years' War, the American Revolution, the French Wars, the War of 1812, the American Civil War, World War I for the United States, World War II for Japan and the United States, and more and more so in Somalia. Prior to technological improvements in the ability to locate hostile ships, nations engaged in far raids tended to pursue targets close to enemy shores.

Technological improvements, however, made raids adjacent to enemy shores increasingly dangerous, so close commerce raiding campaigns have become rare. For a limited time submarines changed this dynamic in World War II, when Germany sank numerous U.S. merchant ships along the Eastern Seaboard, but only until the United States implemented ASW countermeasures. In the case of the Spanish Civil War and the Tanker War, the belligerents lacked significant navies, permitting commerce raiding close to shore. Only three cases entailed commerce raiding near to the raider's shores—Japan in the First Sino-Japanese War, Russia in the Russo-Japanese War, and the Iran-Iraq Tanker War—cases where the belligerents bordered on each other or were separated by a narrow sea. Normally, merchant ships would not be sent close to enemies intent on raiding, unless geography offered no alternative.

In virtually all of these case studies, the country under attack by commerce raiders was too far away to retaliate effectively against the home territory of the perpetrator. The exclusively "distant" commerce raiding was also "far" commerce raiding. In one exceptional case, the Spanish Civil War, the commerce raiding occurred far from the perpetrator but close to the victim, mainly because the Republic lacked an adequate navy. Meanwhile, in the two cases of raiding exclusively close to the shores of the victim, the raiding was also near the shores of the perpetrator: the First Sino-Japanese War and the Tanker War. Both were regional, not global, wars, and the close-near factors reflected the constricted geography of the theater. In the Russo-Japanese War, which occurred in much the same theater as the First Sino-Japanese War, Russia took advantage of its geography to engage both in near commerce raiding, with its locally based naval assets, and also in far commerce raiding in the Red Sea, with its European-based naval assets. As for the situation in Somalia, as shipping companies ordered their vessels to sail farther away from Somalia, the "pirates" would also venture out onto the "high seas" to find prey.

Thus, history suggests that countries that are primarily land powers have a very small chance of successfully using commerce raiding operations, except perhaps for a deterrent effect or to improve leverage for a negotiated peace settlement in the rare case when the costs from commercial losses are sufficiently disproportionate to promote negotiations, such as U.S. commerce raiding operations during the American Revolution and the War of 1812. Commerce raiding has been most significant in global wars as one of many elements of national power necessary to defeat a great power, such as Germany in both world wars and Japan in World War II. These wars also utilized joint and combined operations.

FORCE: JOINT AND COMBINED OPERATIONS

After time and space, force constitutes a critical dimension of commerce raiding operations. Commerce raiding ignores the "commons," which under international law are open to the common use of all, by attempting to transform passage through the commons into a gauntlet that imposes heavy costs on the enemy by diverting, restricting, or eliminating traffic. With the advent of aircraft, submarines, and now missiles and satellites, the commons have expanded from the surface of the oceans to their depths and to the air and space above them. Prior to the development of aircraft and submarines, commerce raiding required mainly surface ships; in cases of raiding far from the raider's home territory it has also required "mother ships" or ports in friendly countries to service and replenish ships. With the development of new technology, commerce raiding has relied increasingly on submarine, air, satellite, and intelligence assets, especially to locate targets.

Over time, commerce raiding has moved away from purely naval operations to joint operations—entailing close cooperation among air, sea, and intelligence. In past eras, commerce raiding was often conducted by privateers and judged by prize courts. However, the 1856 Paris Declaration Respecting Maritime Law made privateering illegal, transforming privateers into pirates. In the era of modern international law, professional navies, not individuals, conduct commerce raiding, with the Somali pirates being the obvious exception of a pariah state. In practice, naval attacks on trade have been most effective for sea powers in global wars, which by their nature are coalition wars, so that coordinated—if not combined—operations have also figured prominently in these cases.

Surface patrols were crucial in virtually all of the case studies. The main exceptions are represented by the predominant roles played by submarines in Germany's commerce raiding operations during both world wars, plus the U.S. Navy's unrestricted submarine warfare campaign against Japan during World War II. Airpower, after its advent, also played a prominent role, particularly to locate German submarines in World War II. Land-based missiles became an important instrument of force in only one case study—the Tanker War—but their potential for use in future commerce raiding is great, especially in restricted waters like the Persian Gulf, the Malacca Strait, and the Taiwan Strait.

The most successful commerce raiding operations worked in combination with simultaneous land campaigns and often in combination with blockades. All three were evident in the American Civil War, the First Sino-Japanese War, the Entente strategy in World War I, the Spanish Civil War, and the Allied strategy in World War II. Commerce raiding was usually at best an important but secondary means to pressure an adversary to capitulate. Usually land campaigns exerted far more pressure than did commerce raiding. The only exception was the U.S. unrestricted submarine warfare against Japan, which targeted not only commerce but also the Imperial Japanese Navy, supply convoys, and army troop transports. Although the United States never invaded the Japanese home islands prior to its surrender, a devastating air campaign including two atomic bombs leveled Japan's cities, and a Soviet land invasion loomed had the war protracted further.

Commerce raiding was comparatively cheap to execute at the operational level, for all sides, and eventually it imposed greatly disproportionate costs on the enemy, both from trade losses and from countermeasures to end the raiding. U.S. submarines in the Pacific theater of World War II inflicted by far more damage against Japanese forces per dollar of American investment than any other military service or branch.[9] These disproportionate costs were evident in the Seven Years' War, the American Revolution, the War of 1812, the U.S. Civil War, the Russo-Japanese War, World War I for all sides, the Spanish Civil War, World War II for all sides, the Tanker War, and Somalia. The only exception might be Napoleon's continental blockade during the French Wars, where France might have suffered more than Britain did, not just because of the privateering, but because of the British blockade of French ports and the British policy of warehousing thousands of detained commerce raiders in prison hulks.

At the strategic level, however, the costs could also become enormous, as Germany discovered with its unrestricted submarine warfare campaign that brought the United States into World War I. Commerce raiding that threatens neutral shipping risks escalation and retaliation. Russia recognized these costs and cut short its campaign in the Russo-Japanese War rather than suffer British and American intervention. Conversely, however large the economic costs, they may be insufficient to alter the outcome of the war—for example, the American Revolution or the U.S. Civil War.

Finally, commerce raiding can be executed unilaterally or in combination with allies. Combined operations have figured prominently in commerce raiding. Global wars usually depend on allies—the Seven Years' War, the French Wars, and both world wars. Weak powers also often depend on strong allies— the colonists in the American Revolution and the Fascists in Spain. However, commerce raiding of neutral shipping is not to be undertaken lightly, since it is likely to produce an opposing alliance. The conduct of diplomacy was made complicated thereby for the American colonists targeting British trade, for revolutionary France, for the Confederates targeting Union trade, for Russia in the Russo-Japanese War, for Germany in World War I, for the Fascists in Spain, and for both sides in the Tanker War. The United States largely escaped political ramifications from destroying Japanese trade in World War II because Japan's simultaneous attacks on all of the neutral powers had left it with absolutely zero friends in Asia.

OPERATIONAL AND STRATEGIC GOALS

Commerce raiding is a means to an end. At the operational level, it provides a means to impede enemy trade, transportation, and communications through such actions as the destruction of merchant ships, the elimination of land forces while on shipboard, and the destruction of enemy naval forces;

strategic effects can range from sanction enforcement, cost escalation, and bottleneck creation to full economic strangulation, if applied in combination with blockade. At the strategic level it can contribute—sometimes alone, but more often in combination with other strategies—to the achievement of war aims, whether limited or unlimited. Since it tends to work slowly, commerce raiding has been most important in protracted coalition wars, which are often fought for unlimited objectives. World War I, for example, left Germany blockaded and hungry, its trade from the sea cut; World War II left Japan in even worse shape.

Commerce raiding can be total or partial. Total commerce raiding operations are designed to halt prohibited traffic completely, while partial campaigns, by intent or by default, allow either a percentage or certain categories of trade to continue. Commerce raiding strategies that are effective at sea but fail to cut alternative land routes are still partial, even though they may make critical contributions to victory. In practice total campaigns are rare, because they require specific circumstances to become feasible—for instance, China's unwitting cooperation with Japanese designs by failing to contest command of the sea in the First Sino-Japanese War, or the unusual oceanic theater of the World War II Pacific, marked by widely scattered islands and long distances separating Japan from key resources. Such factors allow a dominant naval power to cut off a secondary naval power by sea.

Finally, the commerce raider's goals can be unlimited, meaning the overthrow of the enemy government, or something less, such as a negotiated peace achieved by diplomats. Hence the terms "unlimited" and "limited" commerce raiding, defined in terms of strategic objective, not the quantity of resources devoted to the operation. In seven of the sixteen cases, the original strategic objectives were unlimited, and in at least one case—the German attack on Great Britain during World War II—the original, limited goal escalated to an unlimited goal for at least a time. These were mainly global wars.

Limited strategic objectives include U.S. goals in both the American Revolution and the War of 1812, neither of which involved seeking regime change in London. Likewise, the Confederacy in the Civil War did not seek to destroy the North and reunite the country under its own government but merely to achieve a negotiated settlement establishing its own independence. Other limited wars include the First Sino-Japanese War, which ended in a negotiated settlement, and the current situation off Somalia, which is more about maximizing revenue rather than overthrowing any particular country or challenging the global trade system. Japan tried to fight a limited war against the United States in World War II but became the object of an unlimited counterattack that overthrew the imperial government in Tokyo.

Not surprisingly, most commerce raiding operations focus on an enemy's trade, although the enemy's military force—including both naval vessels and troop transports (for instance, Japan's sinking of the Chinese troopship *Kowshing*)—can also be targeted. Wars for unlimited objectives always targeted both civilian and military vessels, and many (but not all) wars for limited objectives also targeted both.

ADAPTATIONS AND COUNTERMEASURES

Countermeasures against commerce raiding include reconnaissance, patrols, and interdiction of the raiders from the surface, under water, from the air, and now even from space. In the Age of Sail, surface ships conducted mainly search-and-destroy operations and such defensive measures as sailing in convoys. As submarines and aircraft became more available and dependable, they too were used for patrol and search-and-destroy duty. Thus, joint operations have played an increasingly important role, with joint sea-air operations substituting for joint land-sea operations in the modern period.

Enemies can make commerce raiding extraordinarily expensive in terms of money, personnel, prestige, and strategic effect, so much so that the costs can ultimately outweigh the benefits. For instance, Napoleon's strategy of commerce raiding hurt France more than Britain, because Britain was far better positioned to cut off French overseas trade than the reverse. Germany's unrestricted submarine campaign eventually cost it World War I by spurring the entry of the United States. The Tanker War, which sank nearly half the merchant tonnage lost in all of World War II, produced crippling economic and political effects for both sides. Moreover, the Tanker War ushered in an era of intrusive great-power intervention in the Middle East, which continues to this day.

Such outcomes can easily become nightmare scenarios for countries engaged in commerce raiding operations. However, if the victim either lacks effective countermeasures or does not incorporate them in time (such as Republican Spain or Japan in the Pacific theater of World War II) and the victim requires goods delivered by sea (critical war materiel, in the cases of Spain and Japan), commerce raiding can have critical "dream scenario" effects. But these situations are rare. Most commerce raiding operations fall somewhere between these extremes.

There are arguably five nightmare scenarios for the country first to adopt commerce raiding operations—Russia in the Russo-Japanese War, Germany in both World Wars I and II, Japan in World War II, and both parties in the Tanker War. In the first case, Russian naval vessels attempted to capture all commercial ships supplying Japan, but in the process prompted an opposing neutral reaction by Britain and to a lesser degree the United States, which was an emerging sea power at the time. German attacks on neutral commerce in

World War I triggered a U.S. third-party intervention. Initially, Germany's U-boat campaign in World War I was operationally successful, but once the Allies ramped up production, especially of new ships, organized convoys, and fine-tuned intelligence assets to locate the raiders, the long-term tonnage trends worked against Germany. Japan met a similar fate in World War II, when it underestimated the damage American submarines could do to its commercial fleet and all attempts to reform its shipping system proved too little too late. Likewise, both Iran and Iraq experienced huge financial losses and intrusive third-party interventions in the Tanker War.

In the first of the two dream scenarios—the First Sino-Japanese War and the U.S. unrestricted submarine campaign in World War II—the theater of hostilities was small and the victim (China) took no countermeasures, while in the second the theater was huge and the victim (Japan) took few countermeasures. In both cases, the theater ideally suited the capabilities of the commerce raider. In the first war, the Japanese had a navy with regional capabilities facing a Chinese navy under incompetent command. In the second war, Japan's reliance on numerous overseas resources in combination with the dispersion of its troops in China and over multiple scattered islands allowed the dominant naval power, the United States, to freeze the movements of Japan's goods and troops. In the dream scenarios, the victims largely followed the scripts anticipated by the commerce raiders, effectively becoming "cooperative" adversaries that could have imposed far higher costs on their enemies had they taken countermeasures and, in World War II, had Japan realized that its military codes had been compromised. Indeed, China could have won the First Sino-Japanese War had it targeted Japanese troop transports, contested their landings, and drawn any remaining Japanese forces inland for a long winter on low rations before delivering on them an annihilating counterattack during the spring.

Most of the commerce raiding case studies involved neither dream nor nightmare scenarios. Usually both sides adapted to the other's strategies. For example, in the U.S. Civil War the Union merchant marine companies quickly sold their ships to foreign countries, mainly Great Britain, to protect them from Confederate attack. Likewise, France sold off much of its merchant marine during the Seven Years' War. During the Russo-Japanese War, the Japanese quickly halted Russian attempts to use neutral Chinese ports to conduct commerce raiding attacks. But not all adaptations were effective. For example, in the American Revolution the U.S. government initially formed its own fleet of ships to attack the British, before belatedly deciding to grant letters of *marque* to private commerce raiders instead.

In one set of paired cases—the German U-boat campaigns in the two world wars—the commerce raiding country used the same basic strategy twice, with greater initial success the second time. However, in World War II not only did the Allies eventually obtain an Enigma machine and break the German codes, but the introduction of new technologies, including radar and aerial antisubmarine patrols, offset the greater capabilities of the German U-boats. Just as the war was ending, however, the Germans were about to introduce a new class of submarines that might have in turn offset these Allied advantages. Thus, the speed of adaptation can be crucial.

Over the years, the countermeasures to commerce raiding have become more effective as the technology for locating and targeting has improved. Search-and-destroy missions undermined commerce raiding in the Seven Years' War, the French Wars, the U.S. Civil War, World War I, the Battle of the Atlantic in World War II, and the Tanker War. The targeting of bases proved most effective by Britain in the French Wars, by the Union in the U.S. Civil War, and by the United States in World War II. Convoys greatly reduced the damage in the Seven Years' War, the French Wars, the War of 1812, World War I, World War II (Europe), and the Tanker War. Note that these countermeasures of search-and-destroy, base raids, and convoys are more accessible to the dominant than to the secondary naval power, and more accessible to maritime than continental powers generally. Base raids are rarely feasible for a secondary naval power, let alone a continental power.

When evaluating the efficacy of commerce raiding, it is important to consider all possible enemy responses, as well as the intervention of third parties. For example, French assistance during the American Revolution and the American intervention in both World Wars I and II cut short what might have otherwise been promising commerce raiding campaigns. In addition, geography determines the availability of alternate land lines. In theaters with alternative land routes available to replace trade by sea, effective commerce raiding requires the cooperation, if not the active support, of the third parties that control the alternative land routes, in order to sever them. The likelihood of operational and strategic effectiveness plummeted for commerce raiders that triggered major additions to the victim's coalition; hence the relatively cautious commerce raiding conducted by the Confederacy in the Civil War, Japan in the First Sino-Japanese War, Russia in the Russo-Japanese War, and the Fascists in the Spanish Civil War. Such precedents did not bode well for Somalia, which as a pariah state had no allies.

OPERATIONAL AND STRATEGIC EFFECTIVENESS

Evaluating the effectiveness of a commerce raiding campaign is a three-part process. Did the commerce raiding operation achieve its operational goals? Did this contribute to the achievement of strategic success? Were the costs entailed worth the benefits delivered? Factors influencing effectiveness include the number of commerce raiders, the size of the theater, the economic or military importance of the targeted goods, and the availability of substitutes to offset bottlenecks. Tight commerce raiding operations do not in theory let any prohibited items through, whereas porous operations stop only a percentage of the traffic.

Rather than a binary choice of targets—naval ship or merchantman—the case studies reveal a wide spectrum of potential targets, ranging from neutral merchantmen to enemy-commandeered merchantmen, enemy merchantmen, enemy-allied naval vessels, and finally enemy naval vessels. Each type of target entailed a different level of operational risk of the attacker surviving the engagement and a different level of strategic risk of precipitating a third-party intervention. For this reason, strategic effectiveness can be difficult to measure with any certainty. Of the six commerce raiding operations conducted by victorious powers (excluding the Jeune École), half were porous—Seven Years' War, the American Revolution, and the Spanish Civil War—and the other half tight—the First Sino-Japanese War, the Entente's destruction of German trade in World War I, and the U.S. destruction of Japanese trade in World War II.

With the exceptions of the First Sino-Japanese War and Spanish Civil War, the other four involved large geographic areas, and the tight commerce raiding campaigns focused on interdicting specific war materiel, such as petroleum, or in halting the enemy's commerce raiding efforts. By contrast, all cases resulting in a loss or a draw were porous. Nevertheless, in all eight of these cases commerce raiders managed to reduce the flow of goods, drive up costs, and impose burdens on the enemy. In all cases the outcome of the war turned not solely on commerce raiding but rather on the integration of sequential operations.

Of the eight commerce raiding campaigns that were either victorious or a draw (excluding the Jeune École), only four were conducted by naval powers, while in the four others—the American Revolution, the War of 1812, the Spanish Civil War, and the Tanker War—the perpetrator hardly had a navy, which was also the case for Somalia. This suggests that selected land powers can successfully use commerce raiding operations to further their objectives, in particular if a draw leading to a negotiated settlement is an acceptable outcome. On the operational level, commerce raiding provides a means to inflict disproportionately high costs on the enemy. For this to translate favorably at the strategic level requires avoidance of hostile third-party intervention and the absence of cost-effective countermeasures.

Of the six cases studied that ended in defeat for the side engaged in commerce raiding, four involved land powers targeting the dominant maritime power—France targeting Britain in the Napoleonic Wars, Germany targeting Britain and the United States in both world wars, and Japan also targeting the

United States in World War II. Similarly, in the U.S. Civil War the Confederate Navy was inferior to that of the Union. Not surprisingly, maritime dominance positions a country to minimize the impact of commerce raiding.

Outside intervention by another great power was the most common reason for strategic failure. For example, in the eighteenth and nineteenth centuries France played a major role in opposing Britain—most successfully in the American Revolution—while in the twentieth century the United States twice came to Great Britain's assistance against Germany. Whenever commerce raiding has affected the global trade system, such as in the Tanker War or in Somalia, great-power diplomatic if not military intervention becomes more likely. Affected third parties actively engaged in diplomacy in the Seven Years' War, the Napoleonic Wars, the American Civil War, the First Sino-Japanese War, the Russo-Japanese War, both world wars, the Spanish Civil War, and the Tanker War. Thus, commerce raiding can entail significant strategic risk.

CONCLUSIONS

As naval theorist Alfred Thayer Mahan observed over a century ago in the concluding paragraphs of his classic *The Influence of Sea Power upon History*, commerce raiding has been "a most important secondary operation of naval warfare." Mahan predicted that it was "not likely to be abandoned till war itself has ceased." But he warned against regarding it as the cheap silver bullet, sufficient on its own "to crush an enemy." He called such optimism "a most dangerous delusion," particularly when aimed at a strong sea power with a "widespread healthy commerce and a powerful navy." As he argued and this work has shown, far-flung commerce "can stand many a cruel shock."[10]

Mahan wrote these lines a generation before World War I, when commerce raiding figured more prominently than he imagined it might, let alone World War II, when commerce raiding brought imperial Japan to its knees. Particularly in global wars, commerce raiding in combination with other military strategies and other instruments of national power can produce outcomes lethal to the victims. Although the Jeune École presented commerce raiding as a weapon of the weaker maritime power to defeat the dominant maritime power, in practice it has most often offered a strategically effective way for the dominant naval power to set the conditions for the economic decline of a continental adversary and thereby to put time on its side in a high-stakes attrition war.

Commerce raiding was not strategically decisive but tended to work in combination with other strategies, such as blockade, embargo, invasion, and bombing, and together these strategies were strategically effective. The maritime powers were more financially able to conduct these strategies than their continental adversaries were to endure them. Over time the cumulative effects changed the balance of forces in the favor of the maritime powers by inducing the financial and military exhaustion of the continental adversaries. The British victory in the Seven Years' War, the Entente victory in World War I, and the Allied victory in World War II illustrate this pattern.

Certain geographic conditions are particularly favorable to the strategy. Peninsular or island adversaries dependent on trade to conduct military operations in conflicts against more powerful foes proved particularly vulnerable to commerce raiding. For example, the Spanish Republic did not survive the Spanish Civil War, nor did Imperial Japan survive World War II. For them, when commerce raiding cut military supply lines, defeat loomed.

In most of the case studies examined, the weaker naval power, not the stronger, adopted a commerce-raiding strategy, since the stronger power, often the guarantor of the international order, was more likely to impose a blockade rather than to put international commerce at risk. This suggests that a weaker naval power could not effectively blockade a stronger power and so fell back on commerce raiding as the only feasible way to attack the enemy's trade, disperse it, and impose costs on the enemy's navy seeking to protect endangered trade. Weaker maritime powers engaging in commerce raiding have included the American colonies in the American Revolution, France in the French Wars, the United States in 1812, the Confederacy in the U.S. Civil War, Russia in the Russo-Japanese War, and Germany in both world wars. All lost or drew except for the American colonies, and in that war a costly insurgency in combination with the French-supported victory at Yorktown, not simply commerce raiding, accounted for the British change of heart.

Commerce raiding seemed to impose disproportionate costs on the adversary in the cases studied, mainly because it was far cheaper to conduct than to eradicate, but this was insufficient to change the wars' outcomes. In fact, with the possible exception of the Seven Years' War, through the end of World War I commerce raiding actually had only a minor impact on commerce. In the American Revolution, the French Wars, the U.S. Civil War, the Russo-Japanese War, and World War I, most of the traffic arrived safely. Only with the development of technology capable of efficiently locating merchant ships at sea and accurately targeting them did commerce raiding become a potentially lethal strategy for the dominant maritime power. In the Pacific theater, this American strategy sank so many Japanese commercial ships so quickly that it virtually froze Japan's expeditionary forces in place, strangled its economy, and immobilized its fleet for lack of fuel.

The most strategically effective *guerre de course* operations included the Entente elimination of German trade in World War I and the Allied elimination of German, Italian, and Japanese trade in World War II. In these cases the victors combined commerce raiding with blockade. The dominant naval powers allied themselves and wiped out the commerce of their enemies. It was most effective against the one maritime enemy, Japan, that had no internal land-locked trade routes. Key conditions for these examples were, first, the technology to find and destroy targets—in World War II, a combination of cryptography and torpedoes. Second, commerce raiding in conjunction with blockade to minimize seepage. Third, a global war with no powerful neutrals to ally with the victim and resist the raiding.

In regional wars with powerful neutral nations sitting on the sidelines, commerce raiding is likely to prejudice their interests. Keeping neutrals out of the conflict is key. Second-order effects against neutrals can trigger a war-changing third-party intervention. For example, British commerce raiding in the Seven Years' War threatened Dutch interests. In the Russo-Japanese War, Russia abandoned its commerce raiding lest Britain and the United States intervene. This can protract the war, thereby putting time on the side of the opponent.

Because commerce raiding is inexpensive to conduct but costly to stop, theoretically the strategy would work best in a low-stakes war, to work in combination with other strategies to impose high enough costs on the adversary to induce a negotiated settlement. But the case studies in this book do not support this conclusion. For the dominant maritime power, naval attacks on commerce threaten the very global commercial order it is intent on preserving; any sustained restriction on commerce quickly ups the stakes from commercial loss to the survival of the global system. Also, such attacks can affect neutral shipping, through higher insurance and freight rates, bringing other interested parties into the conflict. Counterintuitively, then, in limited wars where belligerents seek to minimize escalation, commerce raiding actually turns out to be extremely expensive to conduct, given its potentially alienating effect on others.

As technology has changed, so have commerce raiding operations. Attacking countries have turned to smaller boats, which depend on speed and darkness to succeed. The deployment of large naval ships to oppose these efforts has become increasingly expensive and often ineffective. In "choke point" commerce raiding, such as the Tanker War or Russian commerce raiding in the Red Sea during the Russo-Japanese War, the disruption of trade can impact stock, commodity, and insurance markets, causing numerous second-order effects with potentially global reach.

Owing to the interconnections of the international trading system, commerce raiding by developed countries will probably decline, since these nations have ever larger stakes in the global economy, but commerce raiding operations by failed or pariah states could increase, as they perceive them to be a lucrative business in lands of little economic opportunity. The wide-spread use of GPS, AIS, and other modern technologies suggests that future commerce raiding attacks may take place hundreds, or even thousands, of miles from shore. Countermeasures will thus extend farther out to sea as well, which means they will increasingly rely on new forms of aerial and space-based surveillance and even interdiction. As before, navies will remain essential for countering commerce raiding, but the necessary sensing tools will increasingly require the integration of naval, air, and space assets.

NOTES

1. The case studies considered here include the Seven Years War, American Revolution, Napoleonic Wars, War of 1812, U.S. Civil War, the Jeune École, the First Sino-Japanese War, Russo-Japanese War, World War I from the German side, and then from the Anglo-British side, Spanish Civil War, World War II in German, Japan's Shipping Challenge in the Pacific War, the U.S. Unrestricted Submarine Warfare Campaign, the Tanker War, and Somalia, in Bruce A. Elleman and S.C.M. Paine, eds., *Commerce Raiding: Historical Case Studies* (Newport, RI: NWC Press, 2013).

2. Wanling Tung's elective EL 751 paper on Commerce Raiding, 19 January 2020; by permission of the author.

3. Frank Sherry, *Raiders and Rebels: The Golden Age of Piracy* (New York: Hearst Marine Books, 1986), 24–25.

4. Kenneth Poolman, *The Speedwell Voyage: A Tale of Piracy and Mutiny in the Eighteenth Century* (Annapolis, MD: Naval Institute Press, 1999), 82.

5. Sherry, *Raiders and Rebels,* 216.

6. A. G. Course, *Pirates of the Western Seas* (London: Frederick Muller, 1969), 2.

7. Sir Julian Corbett, *England in the Seven Years' War* (London: Longmans, Green, 1907 [repr. 1918]), 2: 5.

8. Ram P. Anand, *Origin and Development of the Law of the Sea* (The Hague: Nijhoff, 1983), 139.

9. Ronald H. Spector, *Eagle Against the Sun* (New York: Free Press, 1985), 487; Sadao Asada, *From Mahan to Pearl Harbor: The Imperial Japanese Navy and the United States* (Annapolis, MD: Naval Institute Press, 2006), 181; George W. Baer, *One Hundred Years of Sea Power: The U.S. Navy, 1890–1990* (Stanford, CA: Stanford Univ. Press, 1993), 233–34.

10. Alfred Thayer Mahan, *The Influence of Sea Power upon History 1660–1783* (1890; repr. New York: Wang and Hill, 1957), 481.

Chapter 7

Non-military Naval Operations

Navies are most commonly thought of in terms of warfare. Naval blockades, commerce raiding, and expeditionary warfare are the meat-and-potatoes of most wartime stories. However, since almost the very beginning of professional navies they have been asked to conduct many operations that are not strictly war related; antipiracy patrols are just one example of this, dating back at least to the Roman empire, if not before. In more modern times, patrols against the transportation of African slaves—and in contemporary times the trafficking of many kinds of disadvantaged peoples, and especially women—have become more common. In addition, navies can be tasked to respond to a wide range of both man-made and natural disasters, including oil spills, hurricanes, and tsunamis.[1]

After the end of the Cold War, many of the military's missions no longer fit the standard warfighting paradigm. A new term "military operations other than war" or MOOTWA was coined to discuss these missions. Many officers did not like this shift, since it seemed to be diminishing the military's role. General John Shalikashvili expressed this widely held sentiment, one that he later stated he did not share, by saying: "Real men don't do mootwa."[2] Of course, while the term might be new, the missions are not. A RAND study identified no fewer than 846 MOOTWA between 1916 and 1996 in which just the U.S. Air Force, or its Army predecessor, played a role.[3] Such operations allow a navy to "punch above its weight," by providing essential services beyond its typical capabilities.

For well over a century and a half, the U.S. Navy has also engaged in many non-military missions, dating back to the antislavery patrols of the 1840s. Navies can also play a major role in diplomacy, economics, fisheries, humanitarian relief, pure scientific research, and disaster relief, to name just a few. Often, the goal of the U.S. Navy mission was not strictly focused on aiding U.S. citizens, but on assisting allies or simply helping those in need by making available much-needed materiel. These missions affected numerous audiences, ranging from individuals to interest groups to entire nations. Thus, it is important to consider both the targets of these missions as well as the wide range of audiences observing from the sidelines and to consider how direct and indirect effects impact all stakeholders.

TARGETS OF NON-MILITARY OPERATIONS

Whereas during wartime the target of a naval force is typically either an enemy or an ally of the enemy, in non-military operations the "target" is quite often one's own citizens or friends; also the goal is rarely destruction, more often assistance. Examples include freeing slaves, feeding noncombatants in wartime, shutting down one's own commerce by embargo, protecting marine life through research and pollutant containment, and defending shipping from piracy. If these activities occurred on land, they would be considered matters of law enforcement, not military action, but on the high seas professional navies are often tasked to carry them out; in littoral waters coast guards generally assume these responsibilities.

Counterintuitively, the indirect, secondary target is often more important than the direct target—for example, domestic voters, who can determine whether politicians remain in office, and the members of the press, which often interprets news items and influences voters. Thus, voters and the media are often the indirect targets of operations to protect the environment and help refugees. For example, after an oil spill the initial environmental cleanup is the direct target, but press and voter perceptions of the cleanup are often secondary targets. In the case of Britain's "starvation blockade" against Germany in World War I, the blockade strategy might have become unsustainable if it had alienated American and British voters by causing the mass starvation of innocent neutrals in Belgium and in occupied France. Herbert Hoover's humanitarian mission to provide food to those caught in the midst of war avoided this dilemma.

Likewise, if the U.S. Navy can show—by conducting research on sonar and whales—that its activities do not damage marine life, or better yet, if it can improve conditions for marine life—by building artificial reefs—voters might view the navy in an ever more positive light. Although the immediate target of Coast Guard operations following the BP Gulf of Mexico oil spill was the rescue of workers and pressing BP to cap the well, the secondary target of preventing the infiltration of oil into marshlands, which would have outraged conservationists, the fishing industry, and tourists, was even more important for the recovery of the ecosystem. In the case of the Chinese navy's recent antipiracy efforts, the primary target might be the pirates, but the maritime proficiency and intelligence it is gaining, in combination with the pride that Chinese citizens derive from these new power projection capabilities, are arguably far more important to the PLAN and the Chinese government.

In contrast to these successful operations, it is possible to reach the intended target but in unanticipated and undesired ways. American attempts to pressure Japan to withdraw from China in the 1930s failed; Washington's public ultimatums hardened rather than softened Japanese attitudes. When the United States attempted to deter Japan from further escalation in China, it imposed a succession of sanctions, with great fanfare in the press. Sanctions broadly targeted the Japanese government and people, on the assumption that finance was a central consideration of Tokyo's decision making. Apparently, the sanctions did in fact convince Japan's finance minister that war with the United States was untenable; he, at least, received the intended message loud and clear. But Japan's naval and, particularly, army leaders did not wish to accept such a conclusion. They became desperate instead to deter the United States and concluded that attacks across the Pacific constituted their best, albeit remote, hope. So the American strategy boomeranged with regard to Japan's military leaders and delivered an outcome opposite to what was intended. In this case, the U.S. government correctly gauged Japan's civilian leaders but failed to anticipate the adverse reaction of its military.

Primary targets are often individuals in distress. Non-military operations can assist victims of slavery or disaster survivors or help refugees flee a war zone. The number of individuals included can be small or in the tens of thousands, if not more. For example, the navy's Operation *Frequent Wind*, helping thirty thousand refugees flee Vietnam for the Philippines, melded later into Operation *New Life*, which moved them to Guam for processing before permanent resettlement in the United States and other nations. An important secondary target was the victorious North Vietnamese government, which was denied the South Vietnamese naval ships, as well as its officers and their families. Sometimes the secondary targets are audiences—people who are witnessing events and whose subsequent actions may be influenced by the non-military operation.

AUDIENCES OF NON-MILITARY OPERATIONS

In a world connected by instantaneous mass communication, onlookers are far more numerous than participants. Observers can be subdivided into specific audiences with differentiating interests and agendas. In the past, the professional press provided the lens through which viewers interpreted events; now, with bloggers and the social media, isolated individuals can unexpectedly attract mass followings. Audiences include voters and political parties at home and in allied and enemy nations, the press at home and abroad, nonstate actors, foreign governments or foreign militaries or foreign intelligence agencies, and also a range of foreign and domestic nongovernmental interest groups, such as environmentalists. In fact, audiences can include any group that has an interest in maritime affairs. The problem for naval strategists becomes reaching the targeted audience without alienating other, unintended audiences.

Publicity is not necessarily an effective method to exert pressure, particularly in societies concerned with preserving "face," so a navy's ability to stay out of the headlines is valuable. Because naval forces operate far out to sea, their actions generally remain invisible and become public only when a government decides to make them public. The "negative space" ability to limit the number of audiences is one of the greatest strengths of this "secret service." As Adm. Joseph Prueher, Jr., U.S. ambassador in China during the 2001 EP-3 negotiations, later explained in connection with the success of his efforts to get the aircraft's crew home, negotiating with China often requires building "ladders for the Chinese to climb down" from untenable diplomatic positions.[4] Naval deployments in proximity to the shore but far enough away to be out of the public eye can provide critical leverage during diplomatic talks without subjecting leaders to public humiliation, let alone to the domestic backlash that such humiliation would entail.

During the Venezuelan crisis, for example, President Theodore Roosevelt's fleet-in-being had no immediate target; rather, its primary audience comprised the highest levels of the German and British governments, whom Roosevelt sought to deter from naval action against Venezuela. A secondary but critical audience was that of South American leaders, whom Roosevelt did not wish to alienate lest they seek outside assistance to counterbalance the United States. In 1906, after forcing Germany to back down, Roosevelt sent Secretary of State Elihu Root on a "goodwill tour" to South America to make it clear that the United States desired only to guarantee the independence and sovereignty of the Latin American republics.[5]

But there were other audiences too, especially those audiences that Roosevelt wanted to keep in ignorance. He did not wish American voters or the Democratic Party to stir up an anti-British or anti-German crusade that might have strengthened British and German determination to send military forces to the Caribbean. A fourth potential audience was the international press. The mobilization of the entire U.S. fleet was kept secret to everyone but the American, British, and German governments, that is, it never reached the attention of the press or through them the public. In the absence of an evident crisis, the American and European press never became an important audience, a fact that avoided unwanted public opinion or outside pressure. Thus, secrecy allowed Roosevelt to reach just his intended audiences without setting off the others.

Even nonhumans can be the targets of naval operations and navy-funded research, with humans the intended audience. In particular, environmentalists are a major, and quickly growing, audience for such issues as marine mammals subjected to intense sound from naval sonar. Navy-sponsored research programs have greatly expanded fundamental knowledge about marine mammal hearing and have produced innovations in underwater acoustic propagation models, tags for monitoring animals at depth, and increasingly sophisticated operational aids for detecting and predicting movements of individual animals at sea. Such information assists not only the navy but also a wide range of other audiences in the fields of shipping, fisheries, marine biology, and research to reduce by-catch and ship strikes and to monitor migration patterns, essential behaviors, and population trends. This will become even more critical as global warming progresses.

There is a wide array of audiences associated with environmental disasters. The U.S. Coast Guard, for instance, acted quickly after the *Deepwater Horizon* explosion. The initial target was the rescue of the missing crew members on the oil rig. But the more important audiences of this operation were American voters and Congress, the former wishing to assess the damage and determine which political party to praise or blame, and the latter, in combination with U.S. courts, determining appropriate punishment for BP, with extensive follow-on effects for oil exploration and exploitation in U.S. territorial waters. Restoration of fisheries and coastal economies depended on the efficacy of the environmental cleanup, which affected a number of other audiences, including fishermen, sportsmen, and tourists, to name just a few. Indeed, in the long term, these tertiary audiences may well be the most important politically and restoration of the coastal environment the most important issue economically.

Not all audiences are sympathetic to naval missions conducted during peacetime. For example, most Secretaries of the Navy who served during the antislavery squadron's existence hailed from southern states. Because a primary unintended audience comprised southern plantation owners, who depended on the slave economy, the secretaries were not inclined to suppress the trade. For virtually the entire history of the squadron, the Secretary of the Navy instructed commanders to prioritize the protection of legal American commerce over the suppression of slave trade. Only when a northerner, Isaac Toucey (1859–1861), assumed the post did the primary audience shift to northern abolitionists and the patrols start aggressively targeting the slave trade.

POSITIVE AND NEGATIVE OBJECTIVES AND
THEIR DIRECT AND INDIRECT EFFECTS

The objectives of naval missions can be positive or negative. Positive objectives make something happen and so are usually obvious to everyone. These can include facilitating the movement of people or cargo, convoying ships through pirate-infested waters, or promoting research and development to study specific problems. Early in the history of the U.S. Navy, the U.S. Naval Observatory was tasked to become the world's timekeeper and principal authority for navigational astronomical data—a useful, positive objective. A non-military humanitarian-aid mission, such as the Belgian relief effort in aid of neutrals during World War I, can also contribute to a military operation, in such ways as strengthening the impact of a starvation blockade against the enemy.

While positive objectives are usually easy to document, negative objectives are more difficult to discern because they seek to prevent undesired actions or situations. Who can prove that anything was prevented or that any attempt was even made? Such "nonevents" are virtually impossible to measure and so are often difficult to notice, let alone document. President Roosevelt's "whisper diplomacy," which deterred German and British military intervention in Venezuela, is a rare but well-documented instance of the achievement of a negative objective. His fleet-in-being had a direct effect of deterring European military intervention in the Americas—a very high-value national security objective for the United States.

An equally important indirect effect in that case was the British prime minister's reaction to the crisis. Afterward, he chose to cultivate close ties with Washington, an approach that promoted the creation of the Anglo-American "special relationship." While this indirect result was not necessarily sought by Roosevelt at the outset of the crisis, it helped set up the framework of the Anglo-American cooperation that coalesced in World War I, continued through World War II and the Cold War, and arguably remains at the center of American and British foreign policies to this day. Therefore, counterintuitively, indirect effects of negative objectives can be just as important as, if not more important in the long run than, the direct effects from the positive objectives that catch people's attention.

Antipiracy missions also concern the negative objective of deterrence. Faced with a growing piracy threat off the coast of Somalia, China's PLAN began to conduct convoys to achieve the negative objective of deterring Somali pirates from attack. While the primary audience was the commercial shipping, which was directly affected by the success of the convoys, an indirect audience—especially once non-Chinese-flagged ships joined the convoys—was the rest of the world. The international press praised Chinese naval contributions to fighting piracy and China's international image benefited. Increasingly, the PLAN's antipiracy mandate has focused on broad international security objectives in order to maximize this indirect effect.

Deterrence is not always feasible, however. In the early 1940s, an American oil embargo backed up by a fleet-in-being based at Pearl Harbor did not, as had been intended, result in a Japanese withdrawal from China. Rather, it prompted a massive escalation on December 7, 1941—Japan's bombing of Pearl Harbor—along with attacks on British and Dutch interests throughout the Pacific. As one scholar reflects, "It is interesting to speculate whether continuing the oil shipments would have kept Japan out of the war long enough for the deterrent force in the Philippines and in the British Far Eastern Fleet to become completely effective, or whether Japan would have reacted regardless of the oil policy."[6] Ultimately, securing the maritime commons turned out to be key to victory.

SECURING THE MARITIME COMMONS

One of the navy's primary missions entails the negative objective of preventing disruption of the global economic order by stopping interference with oceanic transportation. Freedom of Navigation Operations are a major U.S. Navy activity. Given that 90 percent of world trade travels by sea, this mission supports economic prosperity globally. The global commons is often kept open to legal traffic by such non-military missions as elimination of piracy, interdiction of human trafficking, seizure of banned cargos, prevention of dumping or leaking of pollutants, and research on the maritime environment and other issues.

Focusing on global problems is not new; for the U.S. Navy this mission dates back to at least the early nineteenth century. Initiatives by Matthew Fontaine Maury, appointed in 1842 as the first superintendent of the Naval Observatory, transformed that institution from a repository for navigational gear and charts to a center for astronomical and oceanographic observation and for data mining of charts and logbooks on currents, winds, and climate. Much of the U.S. Navy's early research in such areas as hull design, navigational aids, and weaponry was specific to its missions, but modern-day research and development encompasses communications, climate, modeling, deep-sea mapping, visualization of battle spaces, creation of virtual training environments, and physical and cyberspace probes. Many of these research projects provide benefits well beyond war fighting, indeed well beyond the maritime world writ large, to benefit the civilian economy.

Oil spills of the magnitude of *Deepwater Horizon* threaten, if not contained expeditiously, negative environmental effects for decades to come.

According to the World Health Organization, dependence on marine resources doubled in a period of about forty years in the twentieth century: "The average apparent per capita fish consumption increased from about 9 kg per year in the early 1960s to 16 kg in 1997."[7] With the oceans already under stress from overfishing and overuse, especially by China, the maritime environment may already be damaged beyond repair by permanent ecological changes. Therefore, the protection of the seas from further pollution and from overfishing is not a trivial mission.

The sinking of navy ships provides an alternative to natural reefs for fish habitats plus for recreational diving, which can damage the latter. Environmental groups such as the Sierra Club and Base Action Network are concerned, however, that the use of the ships for artificial reefs might injure the ecosystem by introducing pollutants and spurring the migration of fish from natural to artificial reefs. But surveys conducted on *Spiegel Grove* off Key Largo, Florida, and anecdotal information from such longer-established artificial reefs as the ex–Coast Guard cutters *Duane* and *Bibb* off Key Largo indicate that the vessels have not diminished marine life on existing reef systems. In fact, artificial reefs can relieve the pressure on the surrounding natural reefs from recreational use and stimulate new populations of reef fish.

In the waters off Somalia, Chinese commanding officers and sailors have worked closely with other navies to secure the maritime commons, through frequent bilateral exchanges as well as multi-stakeholder settings. The PLAN has carefully crafted its antipiracy missions to portray abroad its blue-water operations positively. Initially, China's navy escorted only Chinese-flagged ships through the Gulf of Aden, but later approximately 70 percent of ships in a given Chinese escort flotilla have been foreign flagged. PLAN antipiracy task forces have called in dozens of foreign ports for a variety of purposes, from core needs, such as replenishment, to diplomatic and friendly initiatives ranging from military parades in Seychelles to opening warships for public visits in Malta. In March 2011, the PLAN assisted Chinese citizens fleeing Libya by conducting a Noncombatant Evacuation Operation. As part of the operation, the PLAN frigate *Xuzhou* was sent to Libya, described as "a demonstration of the widening spectrum of China's military operations, with a growing role played by 'military operations other than war.'"[8] Thus, non-military missions can become win-win scenarios for all parties involved.

WIN-WIN, LOSE-LOSE, AND MIXED-OUTCOME OPERATIONS

Most non-military naval operations benefited not only the particular nations carrying them out, but also many other stakeholders supporting the peaceful use of the global maritime commons. Thus, they were win-win operations for all parties adhering to international law. Humanitarian relief, fundamental research, and antipiracy missions all fall into this category. Such non-military operations can further a country's larger strategic goals.

One of the most important humanitarian missions conducted by the U.S. Navy was the post-tsunami Operation *Unified Assistance* in Southeast Asia of 2004–2005, in which over thirteen thousand service members on twenty-five U.S. Navy ships delivered essential food, water, and medicine to tens of thousands of desperate survivors.[9] On a much smaller scale, in June 2013 the PLAN deployed hospital ship *Peace Ark* from Zhejiang Province's Zhoushan Port on *Harmonious Mission 2013*, in which the vessel visited Brunei, Maldives, Pakistan, India, Bangladesh, Myanmar, Indonesia, and Cambodia over four months. This ship also participated in a combined medical tour with naval ships from Indonesia and Singapore in Labuan Bajo, Indonesia, on September 12, 2013.

Marine research is another win-win. The Navy's Office of Naval Research has supported research for fifty-eight Nobel Prize winners, spanning the fields of chemistry, economics, medicine, and physics. Among the first winners were Felix Bloch (physics, 1952), for measurement of magnetic resonance imaging and atomic nuclei, and Georg von Bekesy (medicine, 1961), for the biomechanics of hearing, studies seminal to unraveling underwater sound impacts. The Office of Naval Research assisted the *Trieste* deep-sea dives, the development of the deep-diving submersible *Alvin* and experimental underwater habitat Sea Lab, and it funded the remotely operated sea floor vehicle *Jason* and the hunt for *Titanic*. Finally, it has a growing program in unmanned undersea and aerial vehicles deployed for basic research, as well as military uses.

Antipiracy patrols are a win-win both for those conducting the mission and for shipping companies globally—although they are, of course, a "lose" for the pirates. The *Liberation Army Daily*, the PLA's mouthpiece, has described the PLAN as having created by cooperation in the Gulf of Aden an "effective information network with over 50 warships from more than 20 countries and organizations through information resource sharing in the Gulf of Aden and the waters off the Somali coast."[10] There are both realist and idealist reasons behind China's antipiracy operations. The former includes the "desire to protect Chinese shipping, expand China's influence, and to provide opportunities for realistic training that will enhance the PLAN's capabilities in military operations other than war." But the latter involves China's desire to contribute meaningfully to regional security.[11]

Naval operations can be an economic sparkplug. Financial win-win scenarios include using naval vessels to create reefs, thereby disposing of old ships cheaply while promoting marine life and recreation. There can be socioeconomic benefits from tourism for communities that host artificial reefs. For example, with the *Vandenberg* and the *Spiegel Grove* sinkings, the U.S. Navy, the Maritime Administration, state and local governments, local business organizations like chambers of commerce and tourism boards, and advocacy groups were all involved. The *Spiegel Grove* project has recovered most of its costs significantly ahead of schedule, owing in large part to increased tourism from the new diving destination.

Not all win-win scenarios are perceived as such at the time, particularly if there are competing audiences. For example, during the early nineteenth century, the U.S. Navy and Royal Navy shared the goal of eliminating the oceanic transport of slaves. The Royal Navy had an active and well-established West African Squadron. But the U.S. government, because of political sensitivities from British searches during the War of 1812, would not allow the British to search American-flagged vessels. Commodore William Edmonstone of the Royal Navy West African Squadron noted, "As vessels engaged in the Slave Trade almost invariably fly the American flag, and our cruisers are prohibited from in any way interfering with them, of course we are to a very serious extent powerless in putting a check on the trade."[12] Thus, American political sensitivity about ship searches undermined what would otherwise have been a clear win for both countries.

Some operations produce public win-win scenarios that are in fact, behind the scenes, win-lose in nature. Herbert Hoover used the fact that his humanitarian relief efforts covertly assisted the blockade of the Central Powers to leverage British support for his efforts, including the free use of British shipping. He also convinced the Germans that if they did not let him feed the neutrals, Germany would be required by international law to do so itself. Thus, Hoover presented the humanitarian aid for Belgium and northern France as a win for both parties. However, his private papers show quite clearly that the humanitarian aid allowed Britain to fine-tune its blockade against the Central Powers so as to affect just their populations, without starving the civilians of occupied countries. The so-called starvation blockade by the Royal Navy proved highly effective: "By the end of World War I there is no question that the German and Austrian populations were suffering as a result of the blockade."[13] In reality, the Belgian relief effort was really a win-lose scenario, where the Belgians won big but the Germans and especially the Poles lost, since it assisted the blockaders to starve out the Central Powers.

A win-lose scenario resulted from the rescue of refugees during the final days of the Vietnam War, when thirty-two South Vietnamese naval ships, some in barely seaworthy condition and carrying more than thirty thousand refugees, crossed the South China Sea to the Philippines. The naval escort not only saved the South Vietnamese naval officers and their families from possible persecution but prevented the remaining naval vessels from falling into the hands of the conquering North Vietnamese forces, a clear strategic win for the United States and loss for North Vietnam. For the Philippines it was a win as well: to obtain permission for the ships to land, Ambassador William Sullivan convinced a reluctant President Ferdinand Marcos to give the refugees safe haven in return for the transfer of many of the South Vietnamese naval ships to the Philippine navy. China also won during the 1979 war.

There is only one lose-lose case study in this collection—the 1930's American oil embargo against Japan. Rather than deescalate the war in China or deter war against the West, the embargo precipitated the escalation of regional wars in Europe and China into a global war. The costs were catastrophic for all sides and produced an outcome antithetical to both American and Japanese interests. By war's end the Japanese had eviscerated the Nationalist forces in China, positioning the communists to win the long Chinese civil war. If there is a lesson to be learned concerning deterrent measures, it would be the requirement for a careful calculation of the value of the undesired behavior to the opponent. Rightly or wrongly, the Japanese government considered prosecution of the war in China to be a matter of regime survival and so felt that it was on "death ground" in late 1941.

DUAL-USE NAVAL EQUIPMENT AND COST EFFICIENCY

Given that navies can serve wartime and peacetime missions, the ability to do both promotes cost efficiency, allowing a relatively small navy to punch above its weight class. The naval capabilities associated with embargo enforcement, reduction of collateral damage from blockades, mitigation of environmental disasters, and fleet-level deterrence enable cost-effective strategies for the United States. Beyond the economies associated with dual use with respect to wartime and peacetime missions, its war-fighting capabilities and non-military missions allow the U.S. Navy to put a combined hard-power and soft-power squeeze on potential enemies, either to predispose or to deter action.

Naval ships are particularly well suited to non-military operations by virtue of their dual-use capabilities. The same naval equipment that can support a war can also support humanitarian missions, patrol operations, or search and rescue. A proficient navy represents a spectrum of capabilities that can be applied both in war and peace. For instance, following the *Deepwater Horizon* disaster the shortage of booms to retain the drifting oil was so severe that military aircraft flew in extra booms from Alaska. In recent years, policy and planning work at the federal level has made an important leap from scenario-based planning for each potential type of event (resulting in reams of planning documents for particular scenarios ranging from pandemics to terrorism) to capabilities-based planning, wherein capabilities are examined and refined to deliver what is needed as circumstances arise. Capabilities-based planning has resulted in the more economical integration of much-needed Department of Defense (DOD) capabilities into the existing domestic response structure, all the while observing the constitutional limitations on domestic use of the military.

Many non-military missions involve saving lives and so are extremely time sensitive. Either people are reached in time and saved, or they perish. Such missions involve refugees at sea, people blown overboard from oil rigs, hungry neutrals, and innocents threatened by pirates. Such problems are solved either quickly or not at all, so speed can be essential. The early nineteenth-century antislavery patrols were such a mission; they constituted law enforcement, not war fighting, but warships conducted them quite effectively, especially as steam-driven units became available. Similarly, off the coast of Somalia, *Qingdao*, a Type 052 Luhu-class destroyer commissioned in 1996, has served as the Chinese antipiracy task force's command ship.

Hi-tech vessels can be assigned relatively easily to non-military missions, thus allowing governments to get the most effective and efficient use out of modern navies. If wartime is supposed to be the exception and peacetime the rule, non-military uses of navies might actually be the most frequently called upon missions and therefore deserving of budgeting attention. Even more importantly, having overpowering naval force on call in times of state-to-state tension can provide sea powers enormous diplomatic leverage to deescalate crises, even while remaining largely outside public view. Both of these points argue for retaining a large navy composed of many capable ships rather than downsizing or building ships with lesser capabilities. Given the cost of warfare, the ability to avoid war is worth an expensive military force structure. World War II made clear the false economy of failing to maintain military forces in Europe and Asia sufficient to deter expansionist ambitions.

The military use of navies remains their primary purpose, because of the horrendous stakes involved in wars, which one enters with the navy one has, not with the navy one wishes one had. As a former chief of Naval Operations, Adm. Gary Roughead, has made clear, "I am also a firm believer that the hard power can soften up, but the soft power normally cannot harden up."[14] In wartime, naval coalitions will fail if they lack the naval capabilities to get soldiers and supplies into the theater, to protect overseas trade, or to shut down the commons for enemy use. In peacetime, these naval assets can inspect ships for contraband, act as fleets-in-being to dissuade attack, and conduct a wide range of humanitarian missions. Non-military operations are excellent practice for war.

Many non-military operations involving naval task forces or fleets-in-being can help keep ships in readiness for war. Even while performing useful missions of a non-military nature, crews continue to train for duties essential to warfare. If these humanitarian missions can supplement training exercises, and in particular if some activities turn out to be even more useful than training exercises, they will be viewed in a different financial light—that is, as maximizing tax dollars by incorporating dual-use missions and training.

CONCLUSIONS

While the term "Mootwa" dates only to the 1990s, the U.S. Navy has a nearly two-hundred-year history of sponsoring non-military missions that affect many aspects of our lives. After the Cold War ended, the U.S. military developed the "3/1" strategy, in which a big Venn diagram circle called "major combat operations" encompassed several smaller inner circles—stability operations, the global war on terrorism, and homeland defense. This framework was an important first step in the creation of a new maritime strategy. These smaller circles also included counterterrorism, peacekeeping, antipiracy operations, and even humanitarian assistance and disaster relief.

The navy's October 2007 maritime strategy *A Cooperative Strategy for 21st Century Seapower* specifically provided for humanitarian missions: "Human suffering moves us to act, and the expeditionary character of maritime forces uniquely positions them to provide assistance. Our ability to conduct rapid and sustained noncombatant evacuation operations is critical to relieving the plight of our citizens and others when their safety is in jeopardy." Working with allies and coalition partners is key to success. The navy hopes to "foster and sustain cooperative relationships with an expanding set of allies and international partners to enhance global security . . . by countering piracy, terrorism, weapons proliferation, drug trafficking, and other illicit activities."[15]

Modern navies should be envisioned not as comprising either military or non-military capabilities but rather as extraordinarily flexible "hard power" platforms with an infinite array of "hard" and "soft" extension packages at their disposal. While in the past the U.S. Navy has taken the lead in many soft-power missions, in recent years other global navies, such as China's, have performed a wide range of non-military operations as well, such as patrolling sea-lanes against pirates or most recently searching for a missing airliner. These activities break the traditional mold of what most people think of as primary naval missions. In fact, both large and small navies can punch above their weight class by providing soft-power solutions across a spectrum of natural and man-made threat scenarios ranging from environmental disasters to the outbreak of war.

NOTES

1. The case studies discussed here include U.S. Navy Anti-slavery Patrols, the 1902–1903 Venezuelan Crisis, Commission for Relief of Belgium, Embargo of Japan, post-Vietnam War Humanitarian Assistance, Using Sunken Ships as Reefs, Whale Stranding, the *Deepwater Horizon* Oil Spill, and China's Anti-Piracy Patrols, in Bruce A. Elleman and S.C.M. Paine, *Navies and Soft Power: Historical Case Studies of Naval Power and the Nonuse of Military Force* (Newport, RI: NWC Press, 2015).

2. www.wordsense.eu/Citations:mootwa/

3. Allen Vick, et al, *Preparing the U.S. Air Force for Operations Other Than War*, Appendix A "USAF MOOTWA Operations, 1916–1996," RAND, 1997, 79–162; www.rand.org/pubs/monograph_reports/MR842/MR842.appa.pdf

4. See John B. Hattendorf and Bruce A. Elleman, eds., *Nineteen-Gun Salute: Case Studies of Operational, Strategic, and Diplomatic Naval Leadership during the 20th and Early 21st Centuries* (Newport, RI: Naval War College Press/U.S. Government Printing Office, 2010), 242.

5. James R. Holmes, *Theodore Roosevelt and the World Order* (Washington, DC: Potomac Books, 2007), 190–91.

6. James H. Herzog, *Closing the Open Door: American-Japanese Diplomatic Negotiations, 1936–1941* (Annapolis, MD: Naval Institute Press, 1973), 238.

7. "Global and Regional Food Consumption Patterns and Trends: Availability and Consumption of Fish," *World Health Organization*, www.who.int/.

8. Simone Dossi, "The EU, China, and Nontraditional Security: Prospects for Cooperation in the Mediterranean Region," *Mediterranean Quarterly* 26, no 1 (2015): 91–92, cited by Geoffrey F. Gresh, *To Rule Eurasia's Waves: The Great Power Competition at Sea* (New Haven, CT: Yale University Press, 2020), 60.

9. See Bruce A. Elleman, *Waves of Hope: The U.S. Navy's Response to the Tsunami in Northern Indonesia*, Newport Paper 28 (Newport, RI: Naval War College Press, 2007).

10. Cao Jinping and Wu Dengfeng, "PLA Navy Deepens Cooperation with Naval Escort Forces of Various Countries," *Liberation Army Daily*, 26 December 2012, www.chnarmy.com/.

11. Erik Lin-Greenberg, "Dragon Boats: Assessing China's Anti-Piracy Operations in the Gulf of Aden," *Defense and Security Analysis* 6, no. 26 (2010): 213–30.

12. Quoted in Christopher Lloyd, *The Navy and the Slave Trade: The Suppression of the African Slave Trade in the Nineteenth Century* (London: Frank Cass, 1968), 179.

13. Paul Halpern, "World War I: The Blockade," in Bruce A. Elleman and S. C. M. Paine (eds.), *Naval Blockades and Seapower: Strategies and Counter-strategies, 1805–2005* (London: Routledge, 2006), 103.

14. Gary Roughead, telephone Interview, 14 December 2012.

15. J. T. Conway, G. Roughead, and T. W. Allen, "A Cooperative Strategy for 21st Century Seapower," 17 October 2007, available at www.navy.mil/; repr. *Naval War College Review* 61, no. 1 (Winter 2008): 7–19.

Chapter 8

Sea Control

The rapid growth of China's navy, in conjunction with Beijing's aggressive actions in both the East China Sea and South China Sea, has raised the possibility that sea control throughout East Asia might soon be contested. In peacetime, the rules of international law apply and traffic proceeds over an uncommanded and uncontested sea. Because the sea is uncontested, there is no need to seek command. However, according to Sir Julian S. Corbett (1854–1922), in wartime command of the sea is normally in dispute. He wrote:

> The object of naval warfare must always be directly or indirectly either to secure the command of the sea or to prevent the enemy from securing it. . . . [T]he most common situation in naval war is that neither side has the command; that the normal position is not a commanded sea but an uncommanded sea.[1]

Often the notion of oceanic sea control is a mirage. As long as the enemy fleet can deploy and contest, oceanic sea control is not feasible in peacetime or wartime. Local sea control, if only for a brief window, and sometimes just local sea dominance, is attainable and a prerequisite for landing expeditionary forces and/or preventing the movement of hostile forces.

The terms *sea power* and *land power* will be used below as follows: A sea power refers to a country with unimpeded access to the sea, a superior navy, and a vibrant commercial sector, while a land power refers to a country hemmed in by closed seas and often hostile neighbors, and whose dominant military service has historically been the army both to fend off neighbors and to keep the ruling regime in power. This section will highlight the consequences from and prerequisites for attempting to exercise sea control, including: (1) the promise of access to land, (2) the transformation of neutrals

107

into belligerents, (3) the importance of partners, (4) the connection between partners and sanctions, (5) the geographic limitations for land powers, and (6) the geographic possibilities for sea powers.

ACCESS TO THE LAND

Sea powers are better positioned than land powers to cut off a land power's access to oceanic trade and to choose the time and place to fight. In the Napoleonic Wars, Napoleon attempted to impose a continental blockade to sever British trade links with the Continent. This entailed pressure on land and sea to discourage the littoral states from trading with Britain, but the strategy was ineffective. Contraband got through. Britain not only blockaded France by sea but also sought out and destroyed the enemy fleet at Trafalgar (1805). The battle did not end the war, but without a navy France no longer could credibly threaten to invade Britain, a sea power protected by an oceanic moat. This meant Britain no longer could be defeated militarily. Therefore, with Trafalgar, Britain had a prevent-defeat strategy in place, but not yet a deliver-victory strategy, which required the defeat of Napoleon's land forces.

In addition, with Trafalgar, Britain now could safely deploy its expeditionary forces to locations of its choosing to impose disproportionate costs on the enemy. It chose to support its allies by fighting on the Iberian Peninsula, where France struggled to supply its troops by land whereas Britain could easily support its allies by sea. The attrition from the Iberian, Russian, and other European campaigns together constituted a war-winning, deliver-victory strategy that destroyed France's ability to fight.[2]

During the long Napoleonic Wars, the land powers never had access to Britain, whereas Britain always had access to its enemies and so could hobble their trade. This advantage, while small at first, compounded over time, making Britain's victory assured. This belies the general assumption that protracted wars are always bad. In fact, during protracted wars neutral powers can often become belligerents, thereby shifting the balance of power.

TRANSFORMATION OF NEUTRALS
INTO BELLIGERENTS

Attempts to assume sea control over vast oceans in violation of the interests of neutrals tend to produce a strong opposing alliance and even introduce new belligerents. In other words, the goal of oceanic sea control can be self-defeating when it creates the very counterbalance that precludes sea control.

For this reason, keeping neutral powers from joining the enemy is critical to success.

During World War I, Germany's adoption of unrestricted submarine warfare against Britain rapidly brought U.S. entry into the war. Until then, the United States had profited from trade with both sides. Once it joined the war, it severed trade with Germany, continued to trade with the Entente, and sent large expeditionary forces to France, transforming a stalemate, with Germany in occupation of French territory, into a German rout.

Germany failed again, for many of the same reasons, during World War II. The Nazi desire for control on land and sea posed such a dire threat to other nations that the Nazi's actions conjured a lethal but unlikely enemy alliance of the leading imperial power (Britain), the leading Communist power (Russia), and the leading anti-colonial power (the United States). Only the Nazi threat could have forced such diverse countries to cooperate with each other.

Like Nazi Germany's expanding enemy list, Imperial Japan's own expanding enemy list also produced overextension and defeat in a war of attrition.[3] While attempting to cut Western assistance to Chiang Kai-shek's China, Tokyo unwisely made the United States, Britain, the Netherlands, Australia, and New Zealand new enemies. With zero neutral powers to worry about, the U.S. Navy immediately adopted unrestricted submarine warfare, which soon crippled Japan's supply lines. If the Japanese had retained even one neutral power in East Asia they might have avoided this worst-case outcome.

IMPORTANCE OF PARTNERS

U.S. unrestricted warfare against Imperial Japanese shipping in World War II avoided the debilitating effect of conjuring a lethal opposing alliance because of Japan's own flawed strategy. On December 7–8, 1941, Japan simultaneously attacked British, Dutch, and U.S. interests throughout the Pacific, and before long had invaded the Philippines, Indochina, Malaya, Thailand, the Dutch East Indies, and New Guinea. This immediately produced an anti-Japanese alliance of the United States, the Netherlands, Britain, Australia, and New Zealand—all the major non-Axis maritime powers concerned about shipping in Asian waters. Japan's occupation policies then alienated the local populations, so that there were no neutral states angry at the U.S. wholesale destruction of the Japanese merchant marine.

Policy objectives or strategies that run roughshod over the interests of others tend to produce a hostile opposing coalition antithetical to the goal of sea control. Rather than command of the sea, voluntary compliance with generally accepted rules of navigation is the more feasible and affordable goal, but this depends on a multitude of friends, who agree on the rules and whose sheer numbers can overwhelm those who would overturn the rules.

Even local sea control can be difficult. Local sea control became critical to the progress of the Pacific Ocean war in the contest for the island stepping-stones en route to the Japanese home islands. Although Japan initially exerted local command at night, while the United States exerted local control during the day, Allied materiel and logistical superiority allowed them to win the war of attrition, most notably at Guadalcanal and on New Guinea.[4] Thus, even in the Pacific Ocean war, which Americans perceive as the epitome of U.S. naval prowess, local sea control accorded to Corbett's normal wartime state: it was bitterly contested. Because it can be so hard to exert sea control, one alternative is to adopt sanctions and embargoes instead.

ADOPTING SANCTIONS AND EMBARGOES

Sea powers have preferred to fight their wars as cost effectively as possible, by minimizing expensive land campaigns and maximizing indirect economic pressure to undermine an adversary's ability to fight over time. During the Cold War, sanctions, embargoes, and trade restrictions were often employed as a cost-effective way to impose disproportionate costs on the enemy. Their effectiveness depended on allies willing to enforce them.

Viewed as one long conflict, the U.S. Navy's multiple operations against Iraq between 1990 and 2003 depended on the cooperation of allies to exert constant and reliable sea control in the Persian Gulf, the Red Sea, and the Mediterranean. As a result, the sanctions undermined Iraqi military effectiveness and helped prevent the development of weapons of mass destruction, although this impact was not fully appreciated until afterward.

The two sides eventually went to war. Local sea control by the coalition forces contributed to the rapid defeat of Iraq in 2003. It also contributed to the protection of the critical offshore oil terminals, the prevention of sea mining, and the sustainment of coalition forces.[5] These successes merely emphasize the importance of geography, and the limits that continental powers face when compared to sea powers.

GEOGRAPHIC LIMITATIONS FOR LAND POWERS

Closed seas can hem in land powers. In the Crimean War, Britain and France took advantage of the narrow egress to the Black and Baltic Seas to blockade the Imperial Russian Fleet, whereas their own fleets ranged the high seas and supported their land forces, which fought and won far from home in the

Crimea.[6] In the First Sino-Japanese War, Imperial Japan did one better. It not only trapped, but also destroyed, the Qing dynasty fleet in port.[7] Geography made China's ship movements obvious since there are only so many pathways through seas cluttered with islands. These land powers could not establish local sea control even on their own coastline at major ports.

Geography also opened the possibility of blockade in the 1950s. Immediately upon losing the civil war in 1949, the Nationalist navy blockaded the PRC. Narrow seas made merchant marine movements near its shores predictable, facilitating interception. Initially the blockade covered most of the coastline, but by the early 1950s it focused mainly on the southeast coast. The economic impact was significant: Without seaborne trade, the PRC turned increasingly to the Soviet Union for economic and technical assistance. Whereas prior to World War II, the Soviet Union accounted for only 1 percent of China's foreign trade, by 1957 its share increased to 50 percent.[8] This over-dependence then exacerbated pre-existing diplomatic tensions.

The Nationalist blockade ended in 1958, just as the first signs of the Sino-Soviet split emerged. Soon Soviet military pressure on the PRC by land more than compensated for previous Nationalist pressure by sea. In other words, by geography certain countries—almost always land powers—are inherently vulnerable to sea dominance by other powers, almost always sea powers. This gives sea powers a distinct geographic advantage.

GEOGRAPHIC ADVANTAGES FOR SEA POWERS

Peninsulas and islands offer particularly promising locations for sea powers to fight. In modern warfare, the combination of sea and air control is lethal to land forces. In the Korean War, the land power allies of North Korea lacked both the naval capacity and geographic position to contest U.S. sea control over the South Korean coastline. They could not even control the waters outside their own ports but at best could mine their own harbors—for example, the mining of Wonson after the Inchon landing—thereby denying the use of their ports to themselves and others. During the war, the United States established not only sea control but also air control. Soviet fears of escalation limited their contributions to the North Korean air force.[9] However, sea and air control did not produce decisive results as the war stalemated until Stalin's death produced a change in Communist strategy and a new willingness to end the war.

Land powers have even more difficulty supporting allies separated from them by the sea. The Soviet Union backed down during the Cuban Missile Crisis because it lacked the overwhelming naval superiority necessary to dominate, let alone to control, the seas so close to the U.S. coastline.

Although called a "quarantine," the United States actually imposed a blockade on Cuba. While the surface fleets were crucial, the largely unseen and
highly effective submarine confrontations were arguably even more important. The U.S. Navy's aggressive antisubmarine warfare operations made
clear to the Soviet Union the strength of U.S. resolve without reaching the
newspapers and stirring national passions or, in the case of the Soviet Union,
the passions of the ruling elite that could have reduced the Soviet ability to
back down.[10]

Unlike the Soviet Union during the missile crisis, Great Britain retained
the naval superiority necessary to prosecute the Falklands War. The islands,
although much closer to Argentina than to Great Britain, lay over 400 miles
off Argentine shores. British success required both sea and air dominance,
although they never attained full control of either. Brought out of retirement,
the carriers *Invincible* and *Hermes* provided much needed air cover with Sea
Harriers, proving that the Royal Navy retained the reach to contest command
of the sea and air, and project power far from home.[11] However, politically, if
even one of these carriers had been damaged, the British government would
have felt obliged to abandon the entire operation; they were the true COG of
the operation. Fortunately for them this did not happen. The British maintained temporary local sea control sufficient to impose a partial blockade of
Argentina and total blockade of the Falklands, producing a British victory.[12]
In other words, sea powers are more likely to succeed at expeditionary warfare than land powers, especially when exerting any type of sea control is at
stake.

CONCLUSIONS

What does this all mean for the PRC? A country without clear egress to the
sea tends to lose or cannot use its navy in wartime because of the narrow
seas it must transit in order to leave or reach home port: historical examples
include Russia in the Russo-Japanese War (1904–1905), which lost virtually
its entire fleet at the Battle of Tsushima, and Germany in both world wars.
The seas within the first island chain are cluttered with islands that preclude
safe transit. These islands make the South and East China Seas deathtraps not
so much for the U.S. Navy, which can choose not to deploy there, but for the
PLAN, which cannot avoid these waters.

Sea control tends to be a mirage at best and an enemy-coalition-building
mechanism at worst. Any state that attempts to exercise oceanic sea control
in defiance of the wishes of others can experience overextension. Imperial
Japan attempted to wall off Asia behind the first and second island chains—
geographic terminology developed in Imperial Japan and later used by the

PRC. Japan's actions created a hostile global coalition fatal to its imperial ambitions.

International legal rules, applying to both state and nonstate actors, and the institutions that develop, amend, and administer these rules, together constitute a global order. States defying the rules, by the very act of doing so, contest the global order, and so pose a global threat and not simply a regional threat. Global prosperity depends on many issues, including the FON that allows global commerce—over 90 percent of which travels by sea—to reach its destination.

Major trade routes traverse the South China Sea and East China Sea. If the PRC were not only to claim the South China Sea but also to attempt to control it, for instance, by excluding others, these actions could produce an opposing coalition, composed initially of those whose immediate territorial interests were most directly threatened, but eventually expanding to include those nations most deeply interested in the continuation of the present global order. The animating issues would be FON, territorial integrity, and sovereignty— all big-ticket items in the current global order. Those nations concerned about such issues constitute a long list of U.S. allies and coalition partners. In contrast, what countries can the PRC count as allies?

Each PRC attempt to exercise and expand sea control in defiance of others would create an additional impetus for anti-PRC coalition building. As a result, such coercion of neighbors opens an historic opportunity to draw these neighbors more deeply into the existing global order. Ironically, PRC defiance of global norms offers a rare opportunity to strengthen the regional security architecture through the growing participation of its neighbors. Ultimately, the goal would be for the PRC to become a full member of the global order and to abandon its long-standing ambition, dating to the Qing dynasty, to overturn the Western order based on international law and international institutions, and to reclaim for China the central position among nations that it occupied prior to the Industrial Revolution. These age-old ambitions are a nonstarter for anyone but the Han majority of the PRC.

In the meantime, the PRC apparently seeks the unattainable goal of dominating the seas in the same way that a land power dominates land—closing the commons to exclude others in a modern-day, maritime enclosure movement. The United States worries about the costs of preventing the PRC from closing its near seas to others. Since sea control on this scale is not feasible, rather than the U.S. Navy's assuming risks and costs to pressure the PLAN and its proxies to behave according to international norms, why not let the PRC assume the costs of attempting the impossible? If environmental groups interested in rising seas, fish stocks, and pollution and/or the coast guards of the neighboring littoral countries were simultaneously to monitor the many islands in the South China Sea, no single navy could feasibly control all their movements. States need not even be directly involved; nongovernmental organizations could demonstrate the impossibility of this type of sea control.

Blowback from any resulting confrontations need not escalate, but could provide the opportunity to strengthen international institutions by making recourse to them. Such incidents might well damage the PRC's expanding trading relations on which its continuing prosperity depends. Given the importance in East Asia of keeping face and avoiding the political costs of losing face, effective diplomacy and U.S. naval actions would need to stay out of the newspapers. As mentioned above, U.S. ambassador to the PRC Admiral Joseph W. Prueher once observed that negotiating with the PRC requires "building ladders" for the Chinese to "climb down" without losing face.[13] Although the PRC might respond to increasing blowback from its actions by building an even bigger navy, its constrained geography would remain and the likelihood of that navy surviving a war would be slim.

Meanwhile, continuing PRC attempts to control the seas in defiance of others could produce a boomerang effect detrimental to its long-term interests and undermine even its operational objective to attain sea control. Like Germany and Russia, the PRC is not geographically positioned to become a sea power, regardless of the size of its navy. Like Japan, it depends on numerous resources that can arrive in sufficient quantities only by sea. Any PRC attempt to shut down access by sea will undermine the very goals it seeks. In the long run, the leadership of the PRC should think about the fact that their maritime strategy is self-defeating and, more importantly, that the PRC would profit more by becoming a full member of the global order on which its recent prosperity rests. In the meantime, it will be essential for the U.S. Seventh Fleet to coordinate the maritime cooperation among the PRC's many neighbors, in particular Japan, India, and Australia, so that the accumulating precedents strengthen, rather than weaken, the security architecture of Asia.

NOTES

1. Sir Julian S. Corbett, *Some Principles of Maritime Strategy*, new edition (New York: Longmans, Green and Co., 1918), Part II, Chapter 1, 77.

2. Silvia Marzagalli, "Napoleon's Continental Blockade," in Bruce A. Elleman and S.C.M. Paine, eds., *Naval Blockades and Seapower: Strategies and Counter-Strategies, 1805–2005* (London: Routledge Press, 2006), 33; Michael Duffy, "Festering the Spanish ulcer: The Royal Navy and the Peninsular War, 1808–1814," in Bruce A. Elleman and S.C.M. Paine, *Naval Power and Expeditionary Warfare: Peripheral Campaigns and New Theatres of Naval Warfare* (London: Routledge Press, 2011), 15.

3. "Conclusions," in Bruce A. Elleman and S.C.M. Paine, eds., *Commerce Raiding: Historical Case Studies, 1755–2009* (Newport, RI: NWC Press, 2013), 279, 280, 282, 283.

4. Bradford A. Lee, "A Pivotal Campaign in a Peripheral Theatre: Guadalcanal and World War II in the Pacific," in Elleman and Paine, *Naval Power and Expeditionary Warfare*, 85, 92–93; David Stevens, "The New Guinea campaign during World War II," in Elleman and Paine, *Naval Power and Expeditionary Warfare*, 110–111.

5. James Goldrick, "Maritime Sanctions Enforcement against Iraq," in Elleman and Paine, *Naval Blockades and Seapower*, 213; Peter Jones, "The Maritime Campaign in Iraq," in Elleman and Paine, *Naval Power and Expeditionary Warfare*, 179.

6. Andrew Lambert, "The Crimean War Blockade," in Elleman and Paine, *Naval Blockades and Seapower*, 58.

7. "Conclusions," in Bruce A. Elleman and S.C.M. Paine, eds., *Commerce Raiding: Historical Case Studies, 1755–2009*, 273.

8. Bruce A. Elleman, "The Nationalists' Blockade of the PRC," in Elleman and Paine, *Naval Blockades and Seapower*, 142.

9. Donald Chisholm, "Amphibious Assault as Decisive Maneuver in Korea," in Elleman and Paine, *Naval Power and Expeditionary Warfare*, 114, 126; Malcolm Muir, Jr., "Air and Sea Power in Korea," in Elleman and Paine, *Naval Blockades and Seapower*, 155.

10. Jeffrey G. Barlow, "The Cuban Missile Crisis," in Elleman and Paine, *Naval Blockades and Seapower*, 166.

11. Eric Grove, "'Expect the Unexpected,'" in Elleman and Paine, *Naval Power and Expeditionary Warfare*, 161.

12. Charles W. Koburger, Jr., "The 1982 Falklands War," in Elleman and Paine, *Naval Blockades and Seapower*, 200.

13. Bruce A. Elleman, "The Right Skill Set: Joseph Wilson Prueher (1941–)" in John B. Hattendorf and Bruce A. Elleman, eds., *Nineteen Gun Salute* (Newport, RI: Naval War College Press, 2010), 242.

Chapter 9

Sea Denial

Recent PRC actions suggest that the PLAN is developing the capacity to bar others from its surrounding near seas. Whereas sea control is generally an illusion, sea denial is both possible and probable in wartime. Sea denial entails closing down part of the maritime commons to the traffic of others. Absent an internationally sanctioned embargo or measures limited to one's own territorial waters, active sea denial can constitute an act of war.

Unlike sea control (the mastery of a defined area), which is a positive objective, sea denial (preventing access by others) is a negative objective. The attainment of negative objectives is inherently difficult to quantify since it requires the tabulation of all failed attempts to traverse forbidden waters plus all decisions not to try to contest them. This is generally unknowable information. Yet the power to stop something that otherwise would have occurred and do so undetected—not by the enemy government necessarily but by everyone else—constitute great potential strengths of the strategy. It can force the target state to back down without its leaders bearing the public relations cost of having done so—this may make it more politically feasible to get the target government to act in desired ways.

Secrecy is far easier to retain on sea than on land. In the past, many sea denial operations received little attention in the press because initially no one but those on the impacted ships knew what had happened. If all the ships involved were naval ships, their respective governments could decline to go public. For example, during the Cold War, entire submarines disappeared with no public disclosures until many years after the fact. Families were told about an accident, not necessarily about hostile fire. This avoided escalatory pressure from enraged public opinion. The feasibility of sea denial depends on the geography of the theater and the specific domain. Each presents different challenges. The following is an overview of sea denial strategies organized by geography followed by domain: (1) sea denial from shorelines, (2) sea denial from ports, and (3) sea denial from islands, and then also (4) sea denial from the sea, (5) sea denial from the air, and (6) sea denial from under the sea. The ability to fine-tune sea denial is also important.

SEA DENIAL FROM SHORELINES

During the Napoleonic Wars, France could not deny the entire European coastline to British smuggling and the attempt to do so hurt French more than British commercial interests and alienated French allies.[1] In World War I, German gun emplacements and offshore mining closed its near seas to Britain, so Britain executed a distant blockade rather than a close blockade, locking the German navy in port and severing its commercial traffic. In both cases, the sea denial strategy injured the land power perpetrator more than the sea power, whose access to the high seas and, therefore, to global trade, could not so easily be blocked. In World War I, the economic effects of the blockade were slow and not decisive on their own, but proved successful in combination with land campaigns in cooperation with allies.

In the First Iraq War, Saddam Hussein attempted to prevent a U.S. amphibious landing on the Kuwaiti coastline by mining the surrounding waters. Ironically, his foray into sea denial coupled with a U.S. feint toward the shore pinned his own troops on the coast. The United States had already concluded the sea mines made that approach too risky and apparently surprised Saddam by coming at Kuwait from the land. Likewise, in the First Sino-Japanese War (1894–1895) and in the Russo-Japanese War (1904–1905), Japan took key Chinese and Russian naval bases from the land not from the sea.

Because denial entails a negative objective, the importance of the strategy can often be overlooked. During the First Sino-Japanese War, even though China's navy was technically superior to Japan's, the Qing dynasty feared losing its expensive, foreign-built ships and so kept them in port or on convoy duty. This allowed the Japanese to deploy and supply at will. China did not attempt to deny Japan access to major Korean ports or to Manchurian harbors to land and supply its expeditionary forces, even though Japan had no counterparts for China's largest battleships. China never tried to sink Japanese troop transports, which were often indefensible merchant ships. Instead China wound up losing its own navy mostly at anchor, blockaded in port.[2]

Sea denial against China has been in the news recently. A 2013 RAND study has suggested that the United States and its allies incorporate a far-blockade strategy by encouraging the PRC's neighbors to position short-range (100–200 kilometers), land-based, anti-ship missiles at a variety of choke points throughout East Asia, such as the Straits of Malacca, Sunda, and

Lombok. According to RAND, this choke point strategy would "shut down China's naval movements," undermine its ability to project power, and vastly complicate its problems should it initiate a conflict with its neighbors.[3] Sea denial can also be conducted effectively from ports.

SEA DENIAL FROM PORTS

During the Chinese Civil War, the USSR denied the Chinese Nationalists the use of Manchuria's ports for supporting military operations on land. This left them a single coastal railway line from the south to reach the theater of operations. The Nationalists then followed the Communist script by deploying their best armies to Manchuria, a theater surrounded by Communists on three sides, and then allowing their armies to be defeated in detail, rather than withdrawing from a theater in which the enemy had all the advantages. The Chinese Communists had no navy, yet the Soviet sea denial strategy neutralized the Nationalist navy. The strategy made Nationalist troop movements predictable, letting the Communists choose the time and place to cut the one railway line. The battles in Manchuria were decisive: during four years of bitter fighting, the Nationalists lost their best armies and the Communists then used Manchuria as their base to take the rest of the country the following year.[4]

The sea denial strategy of blockade can target key naval bases, such as the British blockade of the French bases at Brest and Toulon during the American Revolution; the Japanese blockade of the Qing dynasty fleet at Weihaiwei during the First Sino-Japanese War; and the Japanese blockade of the Imperial Russian naval base at Lüshun (Port Arthur plus Dalian), Manchuria, during the Russo-Japanese War. In the first instance, the British impeded rather than cut off French naval deployments, while in the second and third instances, the army of the blockading navy used artillery to sink the blockaded fleet in port. Key factors in determining the outcome were the ability to launch a joint attack and the presence of a cooperative adversary. Britain lacked the capacity to launch a successful joint operation against Brest or Toulon and France would have resisted a British attempt to land troops. In contrast, Japan successfully coordinated army and navy actions first against China and then against Russia. Yet its success also depended on the unwitting cooperation of its adversaries, which failed to coordinate land and naval forces.

Another example was Indonesia's failure to secure the port facilities at Dili. This oversight made possible Australia's intervention on behalf of East Timor's independence in 1999, when Australia undertook the International Force for East Timor. The Royal Australian Navy had only one heavy lift amphibious ship and so required port facilities to land troops. Dili harbor had one wharf and crane, which the Indonesians opposing East Timorese independence could have destroyed but did not. Prior to the ship's arrival, Australia flew its troops in on a C-130 transport to secure the harbor. Once the port facilities were under their control, the RAN ships could dock.[5] In addition to ports, sea denial can be exerted from island bases.

SEA DENIAL FROM ISLANDS

World War II in the Pacific can be seen as a succession of battles with the operational goal to close off the waters around island airbases in order to deny Japan key SLOCs. The Battle of the Coral Sea and the New Guinea Campaign concerned the supply lines to Australia. If Japan had consolidated control over New Guinea, thereby taking possession of the airfields at Port Moresby, it could have disrupted Allied supply lines to the south, threatened the Australian homeland, and denied the United States the use of Australia as a staging area for men and supplies. Once the Allies achieved logistical dominance through sea denial, however, Japanese expeditionary forces eventually surrendered.[6]

Japan successfully exercised sea denial around Truk (Micronesia), its most important naval base in the Pacific. Rather than challenging Japan over this one island, however, Allied naval ships simply bypassed Truk to occupy and build airbases on other less well-defended islands on the way to the Japanese home islands. This island-hopping approach neutralized the utility of Japan's significant investments in Truk's defenses and transformed the surrounding seas into a graveyard for Japanese ships. In the end, the Allies denied Japan the use of the surrounding waters, which meant it could not resupply and defend far-flung island bases.

The control of key islands potentially positions a country to deny passage to others. In January 1974, the PLAN wrested control of the Paracel Islands in the South China Sea from the collapsing South Vietnamese government. The United States did not intervene to aid its ally. Control of the Paracels positioned the PRC to blockade the North Vietnamese port of Haiphong. During the 1979 Sino-Vietnamese War, the Soviet Union did not honor its mutual defense treaty with Vietnam and declined to ship weapons to Haiphong.[7] Although more labor intensive and potentially costly than island bases, sea denial can also be exerted by ships at sea.

SEA DENIAL FROM SHIPS AT SEA

The presence of surface ships can deter actions without ever firing a shot. During the Venezuelan Crisis (1902–1903), when Germany and Britain threatened to intervene militarily, President Theodore Roosevelt deployed practically the entire U.S. Navy Atlantic Fleet to conduct "winter exercises" in the Caribbean. Germany and Britain reconsidered invading and settled the debt disagreement through arbitration instead. Although Carl von Clausewitz questioned the concept of "war by algebra"—sheer numerical superiority as the determining factor in land warfare—in this naval case the presence in the Caribbean of fifty-three American ships trumped twenty-nine British and German ships. The U.S. "fleet-in-being" backed up by U.S. Marines stationed strategically on island bases throughout the theater not only secured Roosevelt his objective, but did so in secret. The British and German governments, but not the rest of the world, were aware of the deployments, facilitating their ability to back down and revert to arbitration.[8]

Likewise the effects of Britain's sea denial effort in the 1950's Malayan Emergency went largely unnoticed. Periodic coastal patrols by the Royal Navy prevented the communist insurgents from infiltrating the long Malayan coastline. Because this sea denial strategy succeeded, insurgents were unable to move by sea, so there was nothing to see or report in the newspapers. The actual efficacy of such a "negative space" operations is difficult to measure since nobody can say what might have happened had the patrols not occurred.[9]

One of the longest sea denial operations ever carried out by the U.S. Navy was the Taiwan Patrol, conducted for twenty-nine years between 1950 and 1979. The United States sent destroyers up and down the Taiwan Strait, often two at a time and going in opposite directions, in order to dissuade both the PRC and Taiwan from invading each other and potentially triggering a third world war. The destroyers served not only as a buffer but also as a tripwire to bring in the Seventh Fleet if either country attempted to invade. Later the United States used the reduction of sea denial operations as a signaling device to reach out to the PRC: in 1969, at the height of the Sino-Soviet border conflict, the United States publicly downgraded the Taiwan Patrol from a permanent to an intermittent patrol as a first step in the process of opening U.S. relations with the PRC in order to cooperate against the Soviet Union.[10]

More recently, in the Tanker War and in the Second Iraq War, the U.S. Navy denied Iraq access to its offshore oil terminals and the ability to place mines.[11] The long years of the containment of Iraq from 1990 to 2003 yielded the additional benefit of denying transnational terrorist groups the use of these waters to spread elsewhere.[12] These cases of sea denial by surface ships required overwhelming naval dominance. But sea denial can also be conducted from the air.

SEA DENIAL FROM THE AIR

In World War II, the Battle for Britain revolved around control of the skies over the English Channel. German missiles could not be stopped, but so long as Britain's Royal Air Force dominated its skies the Royal Navy was well positioned to deny Germany access to its waters. Together this joint British denial by air and sea precluded a deadly German invasion of England. Once the United States got into the war, then third-party intervention doomed Germany.

Similarly, during the Falklands War, Britain used aircraft carriers and Harrier jets with VSTOL to deny Argentina the use of the airspace around the Falkland Islands. This made the naval blockade complete, leaving Britain in control of the islands, although if even one British aircraft carrier had been damaged the operation would have failed.[13] This example shows how precarious sea denial operations can be.

During the mid-1990s, the PRC tried—and failed—in its so-called missile blockade to use missiles for a sea denial strategy against Taiwan. On July 18, 1995, the PRC announced that ballistic missile tests would take place between July 21 and 28. In violation of the FON on the high seas, the PRC declared an exclusion zone 85 miles north of Taiwan, a 10-nautical-mile circle, which it warned ships and planes not to enter. Unlike similar missile tests conducted by Taiwan in the mid-1960s that were generally ignored since few outsiders were adversely affected, PRC actions diverted hundreds of commercial flights heading for Taipei.[14] Additional PRC missile tests carried out in 1996 prompted the United States to deploy not one but two aircraft carriers to the Taiwan region. This constituted the largest act of U.S. naval diplomacy against the PRC since the two strait crises in the 1950s.[15]

Thus, like the German use of missiles in World War II, Beijing's sea denial strategy against Taiwan using missiles ultimately failed due to U.S. intervention. Two U.S. Navy aircraft carriers—*Nimitz* and *Independence*—successfully "broke" the blockade. Undersea sea denial can be a bit trickier.

SEA DENIAL FROM UNDER THE SEA

Sea denial has been a key mission for submarines since their invention, most famously in Germany's U-boat campaigns in both world wars and more successfully in the U.S. campaign against Japan in World War II. In all three cases, logistical superiority was a prerequisite for success. Underlying material superiority provided greater capacity for production to outpace losses. By war's end, U.S. submarines sank 1,113 Japanese merchant ships and 201 warships, accounting for 55 percent of all lost Japanese ships.[16]

During the Korean War, UN forces faced possible sea denial operations by the 70–80 Soviet submarines based at Vladivostok. Initially two dozen of the approximately seventy-five reported sightings of unidentified submarines were confirmed as Soviet. This Soviet presence forced U.S. aircraft carriers to keep their distance, rendering them less effective. Soon fears on all sides of the escalation of a regional war into a nuclear global war reduced Soviet submarine actions so that UN naval forces dominated the Korean littoral.[17]

In the Cold War, Soviet naval strategy rested on naval bastions, heavily defended seas where only they could safely operate. The Soviet Northern Fleet bastion was the Barents Sea and that of the Soviet Pacific Fleet was the Sea of Okhotsk. Although the USSR tried to deny access to what it claimed were internal waters, U.S. submarines operated with relative impunity, tracking its submarine movements and potentially positioning U.S. nuclear weapons along its maritime borders. In 1987, Marshal Sergei F. Akhromeev, chief of the General Staff, told his U.S. counterparts of the effectiveness of their strategy. To find his own submarines, he said "All I have to do is look and see where your [surveillance] airplanes are flying."[18] Sea denial operations can be fine-tuned to focus on just one target, or perhaps just one strategic commodity.

FINE-TUNING SEA DENIAL

The ability to fine-tune sea denial in order to affect only the intended target and not innocent neutrals is extremely important. During the "starvation" blockade in World War I, the British government imposed carefully crafted contraband lists on neutral countries to minimize seepage of strategic goods to Germany without antagonizing it into occupying additional small neighbors, such as the Netherlands or Denmark, or encouraging these smaller neighbors to throw in their lot with Germany.[19]

American humanitarian aid to neutral countries was likewise important for fine-tuning the blockade. With British support, the United States organized the delivery of food aid to occupied Belgium and Northern France. This humanitarian program, known as the Commission for the Relief of Belgium, prevented press stories of starving civilians in occupied countries from forcing Britain to relax the blockade against Germany.[20] In the end, Britain's naval blockade combined with the U.S. humanitarian relief effort allowed a more precise targeting of the blockade just against Germany and, in the process, kept neutral powers from falling into the enemy camp.

Sea denial strategies do not necessarily have to sever all sea communications but can deny only certain types of traffic or can halt movement in one direction but not the other. For example, in early 1953, the United States tried to put additional pressure on the PRC to end the Korean War by threatening to "unleash" Chiang Kai-shek's troops on Taiwan to invade the mainland. The Taiwan Patrol continued to deny any PRC sea invasion of Taiwan, but new instructions ordered U.S. Navy vessels not to halt a future Nationalist attack on the PRC. As anticipated, Mao Zedong responded to this new threat far to the south by diverting his troops from Korea. Once Joseph Stalin died in March 1953, all remaining opposition to an armistice disappeared and a treaty was signed that summer.[21] Thus, counterintuitively, the United States put additional military pressure directly on the PRC by easing its sea denial operations aimed at containing Taiwan.

CONCLUSIONS

What are the implications of sea denial for the PRC? The geography of the theater is perhaps the most important single factor in undertaking or withstanding sea denial. Only certain geographic situations allow a country to impose a denial strategy in the event of war. Countries hemmed in by islands can fortify such islands to close their near seas to others. Conversely, a distant sea power can take advantage of such restricted geography to deny the enemy the use of its merchant marine and navy. For example, the islands in the East and South China Seas open the possibility for the PLAN to interdict and destroy sea traffic that dares cross westward of the First Island Chain. But even more significantly, this geography allows other countries to retaliate by cutting off PRC military and commercial traffic through a combination of submarine attacks on merchant shipping and of blockading and cutting off entirely more distant choke points such as the Malacca Strait.

Global warming may also complicate attempts to use a sea denial strategy to dominate the South China Sea. Many of the smaller formations throughout the sea are already partially or completely submerged at high tide. With rising seas due to global warming, some may become totally submerged and low-lying islands may face an increased risk of inundation. Those countries trying to claim these features by building structures on them assume the expensive proposition of possibly rebuilding these islands from scratch every time a major typhoon hits. Nature, in the form of severe weather and rising seas, may take care of sea denial attempts dependent on inhabiting the uninhabitable.

Given the PRC's dependence on trade to maintain its economic growth rates, it should in theory be hurt more than any other country by a strategy of sea denial. The strategy carries the additional risk of second-order effects such as skyrocketing insurance rates that might effectively halt not just targeted but all commercial traffic through contested waters, adverse risk assessments that might foreclose investments in maritime resource development, or lopsided press coverage that might feed xenophobic nationalism at home while alienating neighbors abroad.

In any future dispute, it will be important not to set off PRC nationalism, which could make the PRC inflexible. Given the political costs in Chinese culture of a "loss of face," naval operations conducted far from shore offer the United States the advantage of "communicating" directly with PRC leaders in secrecy, thus minimizing any loss of face should the PRC back down. A strong naval presence can provide significant diplomatic leverage, often in the form of negative incentives, even while remaining outside of public view.

Should the PRC adopt sea denial strategies, whether its objectives are mainly defensive or offensive may not necessarily be clear. Might the Communist government be paranoid about an invasion or attack by sea? Or, might it plan to use sea denial to pressure and dominate its smaller neighbors? Although PRC scholars present their country's 1974 seizure of the Paracels in the Vietnam War as a defensive action, the islands' occupation also provided the offensive capability to deny Soviet access to Haiphong during the 1979 Sino-Vietnamese War.

By contrast, the seizure of the many small islands in the South China Sea would not necessarily provide equivalent leverage over Malaysia, Indonesia, or the Philippines, which have lengthy coastlines on other seas. Vietnam, Brunei, and Cambodia are the only countries totally hemmed in by the choke points granting access to the South China Sea. Vietnam has already responded to perceived PRC aggression by rapidly expanding its air and naval forces, including amphibious planes and diesel submarines, plus building a number of fortified island bases, presumably with sea denial plans of its own.

Finally, PRC threats to close its coastal waters to merchant traffic resemble a bank robber claiming to have a hostage, but actually holding the gun to his own head. The PRC cannot escape its constrained maritime geography. Its immediate coastline is littered with thousands of small islands. While these islands provide certain sea denial capabilities to China, foreign ships do not have to go there. By contrast, Chinese ships must. Like a two-edged sword, sea denial can work both ways. So long as Beijing abides by international laws, however, escape is unnecessary as Chinese sea traffic would proceed peacefully.

NOTES

1. Silvia Marzagalli, "Napoleon's Continental Blockade," in Bruce A. Elleman and S.C.M. Paine (eds.), *Naval Blockades and Seapower: Strategies and Counter-Strategies, 1805–2005* (London: Routledge Press, 2006), 33.

2. "Conclusions," in Bruce A. Elleman and S.C.M. Paine, eds., *Commerce Raiding: Historical Case Studies, 1755–2009* (Newport, RI: NWC Press, 2013), 273.

3. Wendell Minnick, "RAND Suggests Using Land-based ASMs Against China," *Defense News*, 7 November 2013.

4. Bruce A. Elleman, "Soviet Sea Denial and the KMT-CCP Civil War in Manchuria, 1945–1949," in Bruce A. Elleman and S.C.M. Paine, eds., *Naval*

Coalition Warfare: From the Napoleonic War to Operation Iraqi Freedom (London: Routledge Press, 2008), 127.

5. Peter J. Dean, "Amphibious Warfare and the Evolution of the Australian Defence Policy, *Naval War College Review*, Vol. 67, no 4, 20–39.

6. David Stevens, "The New Guinea Campaign During World War II," in Bruce A. Elleman and S.C.M. Paine (eds.), *Naval Power and Expeditionary Warfare: Peripheral campaigns and new theatres of naval warfare* (London: Routledge Press, 2011),100, 110–11.

7. Bruce A. Elleman, "China's 1974 Expedition to the Paracel Islands," in Elleman and Paine, *Naval Power and Expeditionary Warfare*, 149.

8. See "Overwhelming Force and the Venezuelan Crisis of 1902–1903," in Henry J. Hendrix (ed.), *Theodore Roosevelt's Naval Diplomacy: the U.S. Navy and the Birth of the American Century* (Annapolis, MD: Naval Institute Press, 2009), 25–53.

9. Jeffrey Grey, "Naval Operations in Peripheral Conflict," in Elleman and Paine, *Naval Power and Expeditionary Warfare*, 133.

10. Bruce A. Elleman, *High Seas Buffer: The Taiwan Patrol Force, 1950–1979* (Newport, RI: NWC Press, 2012).

11. Peter Jones, "The Maritime Campaign in Iraq," in Elleman and Paine, *Naval Power and Expeditionary Warfare*, 179.

12. R. J. Schneller, "Operation *Enduring Freedom*," in Elleman and Paine, *Naval Coalition Warfare*, 205.

13. Eric Grove, "'Expect the Unexpected,'" in Elleman and Paine, *Naval Power and Expeditionary Warfare*, 161; Charles W. Koburger, Jr., "The 1982 Falklands War," in Elleman and Paine, *Naval Blockades*, 200.

14. Chris Rahman, "Ballistic Missiles in China's Anti-Taiwan Blockade Strategy," in Elleman and Paine, *Naval Blockades*, 215–23.

15. Elleman, *High Seas Buffer*.

16. Joel Holwitt, "Unrestricted Submarine Warfare: The U.S. Submarine Campaign against Japan," in Elleman and Paine, *Commerce Raiding*, 225–38.

17. Donald Chisholm, "Amphibious Assault as Decisive Maneuver in Korea," in Elleman and Paine, *Naval Power and Expeditionary Warfare*, 114, 117–18.

18. Edgar F. Puryear, Jr., "Readiness: Carlisle Albert Herman Trost (1930–)," in John B. Hattendorf and Bruce A. Elleman (eds.), *Nineteen-gun Salute: Case Studies of Operational, Strategic, and Diplomatic Naval Leadership during the 20th and Early 21st Centuries* (Newport, RI: U.S. Naval War College Press, 2010), 203.

19. Paul Halpern, "The Blockade of World War I," in Elleman and Paine, *Naval Blockades*, 99.

20. Herbert Hoover to British Foreign Minister Eustace Percy, 16 February 1916, CRB, Box 24, File 2, Hoover Institution Archives, cited in Bruce A. Elleman, "Herbert Hoover's Commission for the Relief of Belgium, 1914–1918."

21. Elleman, *High Seas Buffer*.

Chapter 10

Conclusions

Sea Powers vs Land Powers

Twenty-five centuries ago the ancient Greeks had already identified key problems complicating wars between sea and land powers. Thucydides's (c. 460–c. 395 BCE) *History of the Peloponnesian War* illustrates the enduring asymmetries that make wars between sea and land powers so difficult to win at an acceptable cost. Such conflicts tend to protract, making relative costs, comparative economic growth rates, alliances, and national resilience in many areas crucial for victory.

Great sea powers have large navies and their economies depend on commercial connections with lands across the seas. Over a century ago, Alfred Thayer Mahan laid out six prerequisites for great sea powers: (1) secure borders provided by an oceanic moat in combination with non-existent landward threats, (2) a dense internal transportation grid, (3) reliable egress by sea precluding blockade in wartime, (4) a dense coastal population, (5) a commerce-driven economy, and (6) stable government institutions promoting both commerce and a consistent foreign policy.[1]

In contrast, great land powers have large armies, not only to defend against landward threats, but often to keep the incumbent regime in power and, historically, also to expand outward. They usually border on their most lethal adversaries. Strategic stalemates among land powers can be especially dangerous because by geographic proximity the land powers can invade across land borders, the size of their armies usually pose a credible threat, and they often have the intent to resort to war. Since land powers face such immediate threats on their borders, they must focus on national security, whereas sea powers have the comparative security provided by the moat to focus on national prosperity and oceanic trade as a means to that end.

In modern history, land powers have sought national security by accumulating spheres of influence and exclusion zones in concentric rings around their borders. If possible, they have tried to prevent the rise, or even sought the dismemberment, of bordering great powers. They have tended to prefer weak neighbors and often assumed responsibility for their neighbors' foreign policies. By comparison, sea powers have desired a world order based on juridically equal sovereign states. They have tried to expand the reach of international law and international institutions in order to share the oceanic commons in the pursuit of trade. This has required laws regulating commerce and diplomacy. As it turns out, differing security concerns between land and sea powers underlie two mutually exclusive visions of the global order.

Germany became the most problematic land power confronting Britain during the century-long *Pax Britannica* (peace under British guarantee) between the Napoleonic Wars and World War II. Neither the German Empire nor the British Empire ultimately survived that confrontation. Post–World War II, Russia became the land power nightmare for the United States during the *Pax Americana* (peace under U.S. guarantee) during the Cold War. Both Germany and Russia are large countries, with borders deep in the Eurasian land mass and comparatively constricted access to the navigable seas. The peoples of each nation had a firm belief in their country's historical greatness and destiny to rule. The governments of each resented the wealth and influence of the dominant sea power of their time. They tried to overthrow the sea power's influence to become the guarantor of a new global order suited to a land power's preferences for surrounding exclusionary zones, not the FON and global commerce preferred by the sea powers. Both Germany and Russia lost not just one war to the sea powers, but many.

The terms *sea power* and *land power* will be used as follows: A sea power refers to a country with unimpeded access to the sea, a large navy, and a vibrant commercial sector, while a land power refers to a country hemmed in by closed seas and often hostile neighbors, and whose dominant military service has historically been the army, both to fend off neighbors and to keep the ruling regime in power. Land powers with two or more maritime access points will be discussed first, followed by those land powers with only one, often constricted, coastline.

SEA POWER VS LAND POWER WITH TWO OR MORE COASTLINES: FRANCE

France has significant access to multiple oceans and seas. Counter-clockwise these are the North Sea, Atlantic Ocean, and Mediterranean Sea. Ports on two or more coastlines make an enemy blockade more difficult and provide access to a greater array of theaters. Prior to the unification of the Germanic states in

1871, Britain was France's primary opponent: Britain was the dominant naval power bordering on the narrowest points of French access to the North Sea and Atlantic Ocean, and also controlling Gibraltar, the cork blocking transit to and from the Mediterranean.

Between 1689 and 1815, France was constantly at war. France maintained a large army to protect itself from its immediate neighbors, which likewise had large standing armies. Yet it also maintained a large navy that became increasingly important as France acquired overseas colonies in the seventeenth century and fought to defend these overseas territories and economic interests. France won few of these wars. In the American Revolution, France supported the American colonists at great expense to itself in the misguided belief that their independence would gravely injure post-war British economic interests. It turned out that Britain did not require occupation (the land power view) in order to continue to reap commercial profits (the sea power view).

In the ensuing Napoleonic Wars, in particular after the 1805 Battle of Trafalgar, so long as Great Britain held Gibraltar it could prevent France from combining its fleets. Meanwhile, the Royal Navy maintained full freedom of movement and so could choose the optimal location to land troops and supply allies on the Continent. Britain chose the Iberian Peninsula, where the relative ease of access and ability to support its own and allied troops greatly favored Britain over France.[2] Meanwhile, Napoleon's eternal quest for territorial expansion brought overextension and defeat by an increasingly competent and determined succession of opposing coalitions. Napoleon's own actions, which were lethal to the survival of his neighbors, created the glue that held together the final and fatal (for him) coalition.

Although France's gambit for continental control ultimately failed, the succession of wars went on for many generations and each individual war often consumed a decade. In other words, wars between land and sea powers tend to protract since neither can easily eliminate the primary military service of the other in order to enforce its desired peace terms. After the Napoleonic Wars, France focused on expansion not in Europe but overseas. It no longer fought Britain, but rather combined with Britain to fight Russia in the Crimean War, China in the Second Opium War and in the Boxer Uprising, and Germany in both world wars. With post-war decolonization, France combined with the West against Russia in the Cold War. France has fully joined the institutional and legal framework favored by Britain and has acted as a responsible veto-wielding member of the UN Security Council, unlike the Soviet Union and the People's Republic of China. Thus, after many years of fighting and the removal of Germany as a lethal neighboring threat, France finally accepted and joined the maritime global order.

SEA POWER VS LAND POWER WITH TWO
OR MORE COASTLINES: RUSSIA

Russia has access to the White Sea, Baltic Sea, Black Sea, Sea of Japan, Sea of Okhotsk, Bering Sea, and Arctic Ocean. For Russia the seas with population centers—the Baltic and Black Seas—were narrow and vulnerable to blockade, while those with broad access to open waters had no population centers for reasons of severe climate and many of the most important anchorages were iced in for months.

For the last three centuries, Russia has engaged in a continuous succession of wars. According to General Aleksei Kuropatkin, Russia's war minister (1898–1904), from 1700 to 1900 his country fought thirty-two foreign and two internal wars for 128 ⅓ years, leaving only 71 ⅔ years of peace. Twenty-two wars lasting a total of 101 years expanded the empire, while four, lasting a total of 4 ½ years, defended the empire. Seven wars and two campaigns lasting a total of ten years concerned European political issues.[3] Prior to the Crimean War, Russia won most of its wars, which were predominantly wars of continental expansion. Even so, Kuropatkin's account emphasizes their economic and human costs. From the Crimean War onward, however, Russia has lost most of its wars. Kuropatkin's account stops with the disastrous Russo-Japanese War and so does not cover Russia's even more catastrophic wars of the twentieth century.

During the Crimean War, France and Britain combined to put maritime pressure on Russia from the Black, Baltic, and White Seas.[4] German armies defeated Russia in World War I. In World War II, Russia's maritime allies did a much better job supplying Russia's armies so that the Allies prevailed but the alliance did not. With the defeat of the common lethal threat, the sea powers set about institutionalizing their preferred international order through the United Nations, the International Monetary Fund, World Bank, and the General Agreement on Tariffs and Trade, while Russia set about institutionalizing its preferred international order of communist states ringing its borders, most particularly in Eastern Europe occupied by the Red Army and in China and Korea.

These differing global orders produced a Cold War and a variety of costly regional hot wars. The regional wars occurred in China (1945–1949), where Russia helped the communists take power;[5] Korea (1950–1953), where a sea power coalition opposed a coalition of communist land powers;[6] Cuba (1962), where the U.S. Navy pressured the Soviet Navy to back down;[7] and Vietnam (1945–1975), where the communist land power coalition finally prevailed.[8] Like the anti-Nazi alliance of World War II, the communist alliance lasted only so long as its members shared the same primary enemy, the United States.

Once their primary enemy became each other, China and Russia engaged in border conflict in 1969 and China and Vietnam went to war in 1979, just four years after the reunification of Vietnam.[9] Russia, China, and Vietnam, as well as most of their other landward neighbors, all had territorial disputes with each other. Therefore, even while some of them teamed up some of the time, the territorial disputes and the fears of territorial encroachment by landward neighbors always lurked in the background. Sea powers do not usually have this problem since trade, not territory, is their main goal.

There is no consensus on exactly why the Cold War ended. The gap in Russia's per capita standard of living compared to that in the West continued to widen after the Industrial Revolution, which began to spread globally with the end of the Napoleonic Wars. Over time, this difference in wealth better positioned the West to outlast the Soviet Union in a protracted war. It is also the case that the wealth of the West depends on a global system of maritime trade, a system in which Russia has historically been only a marginal participant.

SEA POWER VS LAND POWERS WITH ONE CONSTRICTED COASTLINE

Germany and the PRC are land powers with access to only one coast and it is hemmed in by islands and straits. They have had great difficulty defeating sea powers. In Europe, Germany fought and lost two world wars against sea power alliances. In both cases, the sea powers took advantage of Germany's restricted access to the high seas to blockade its surface ships in port, to cut its access to maritime trade, and eventually to hunt its submarines to extinction. While Germany allied with Italy and Japan in World War II, they had different primary adversaries, failed to cooperate, and overextended in different theaters.[10] Over time, Germany succumbed to a fatal combination of land powers, whose armies destroyed the preponderance of its land forces, and sea powers, which supplied their land power allies while prosecuting blockades, commerce raiding, and expeditionary warfare. Post-war, the sea powers drew West Germany into their preferred maritime world order based on international law and international institutions.

Like Germany, the PRC also has access to a single, albeit much longer, coastline. Even though on the map the PRC seems to enjoy an uninterrupted coastline, its access is also constricted by thousands of offshore islands. The so-called First Island Chain runs from the Aleutian Islands, through Japan, Okinawa, Taiwan, and then down through the Philippines. In many ways Taiwan functions like Gibraltar, as a cork plugging access to and from the PRC's near seas. So long as Taiwan remains nominally independent, the three

PLAN fleets—the North Sea Fleet, East Sea Fleet, and South Sea Fleet—may have difficulty combining unopposed in wartime.

Due in part to these constricted seas, in both the First and Second Sino-Japanese wars, China made little use of its navy and proved susceptible to blockade.[11] The Nationalists later imposed a highly effective blockade against the PRC in the 1950s.[12] The twenty-one-year economic embargo by the United States and its allies from 1950 to 1971 forced the PRC to trade more and more with the USSR. Dependence created tensions, particularly given the Soviet Union's land power proclivities for control over immediate neighbors. During the 1960s, Mao Zedong concluded that the Soviet Union, not the United States, posed the greatest threat. This paved the way for Sino-American diplomatic normalization and cooperation to undermine the Soviet Union—then the common primary enemy of the PRC and the United States. This shows the overwhelming importance of alliances and coalitions to sea powers.

ALLIANCES AND COALITIONS

Whereas land powers have historically viewed the world in terms of sovereign territory and a zero-sum quest for control, sea powers have increasingly viewed it in terms of markets and commons for positive-sum economic growth and trade. Where land powers have seen land and seas to be taken, maritime powers have seen markets where money can be made. Where land powers have seen exclusive zones, sea powers have perceived vast commons in the oceans, air, and now cyberspace. According to Hugo Grotius (1583–1645), the founding father of international law, the Western view of seas as commons goes back to the Romans.[13]

The world order traditionally favored by land powers, based on exclusion zones and the domination of neighbors, is at best a zero-sum order: One side wins; the other side loses; the sum of the winnings and losses is zero. If the smaller power resists, territory becomes damaged in the fight, producing a negative sum. The post-Industrial Revolution maritime order has increasingly become a positive-sum international order: All participants win, with ever greater positive sums deriving from economic growth. The developing rules and institutions protect the weak and the strong alike, who all profit from a stable, rule-based system. The vision behind the League of Nations and the United Nations has been to have all nations ultimately join this order as constructive members and full participants. A comparison of the combined GNPs of all former Soviet allies and those of the United States illustrates the stark economic difference between a zero-sum continental and a positive-sum maritime world order.

Historically, land power alliances have been less effective than sea power coalitions. This is because of the negative-sum global order they prefer, the existential threat they pose to their closest foes, and the long-term threat posed by the dominant land power to its smaller allies. Since land borders can change over time and great land powers often believe what's mine is mine and what's yours is negotiable, neighboring land power allies often fear each other. This does not bode well for long-term alliance cohesion. Often they fear each other more than the distant sea power enemies, as became the case for Russia and China vis-à-vis the United States at the end of the Cold War. This situation allowed the United States to leverage the Sino-Soviet disagreements to help win the Cold War. The positive-sum maritime order does not suffer from these zero-sum land power alliance problems.

Theaters abutting land powers are inherently of greater value to them than to a distant sea power. Unlike the distant power separated by the seas, land powers do not necessarily intend to depart from occupied contiguous areas. They are often bent on territorial expansion and focus on geographic control. This boots-on-the-ground approach is expensive. Occupied countries do not tend to be as economically productive as free countries. Large standing armies in the capital tend to influence both politics and economics. Sea powers, by contrast, resent away-game wars, which interfere with economic growth at home. For them, the key is to win at acceptable costs.

Sea powers have the ability to open new theaters in inconvenient places for land powers and can supply them by sea, whereas land powers are limited to a finite set of contiguous fronts. These new theaters tend to be peripheral theaters and overall victory usually requires victory on the main front, bordering on the land power, or a contiguous land power ally. Land powers can benefit from their central position, providing internal lines of communication with their bordering allies. Sea powers find fighting land powers with neighboring allies particularly challenging—as was the case for the United States in the Korean and Vietnam wars—because contiguous friends can provide each other military and economic aid overland, and even sanctuary deep inland, where sea powers have the most difficulty sustaining forces, or where they may be reluctant to widen the war.

Sea powers tend to adopt layered strategies. Since for reasons of cost they are reluctant to go toe-to-toe against the land power on the main front, they often combine an array of military and non-military instruments of national power. Military strategies include blockade, commerce raiding, sea denial operations, expeditionary warfare on the enemy's periphery, and naval diplomacy, including sending ships into sensitive areas to act as a tripwire for full-scale retaliation. Sea powers also often combine non-military instruments such as economic embargoes, sanctions, and propaganda.

In the many wars between land and sea powers, the side with the largest naval component usually has the larger number of coalition partners and so has tended to win. Over the past two centuries, land powers have sustained more damage than have sea powers during attempts by either to close down the maritime commons. Favorable geography, naval dominance, and more numerous allies have better positioned sea powers than land powers to make use of the seas for military and civil traffic in wartime. Land powers by their constricted geography are more susceptible to blockade, while sea powers by their open geography and naval dominance are better positioned to conduct commerce raiding. Unimpeded access to oceanic trade better situates sea powers to endure protracted conflicts. While their economies continue to receive overseas resources and grow, those of their land enemies do not. This allows sea powers to increase their inventory of armaments, equipment, and merchant marine capacity despite wartime losses, while the constricted land power eventually falls behind.

Although dominance of the seas can set the conditions for a prevent-defeat strategy, since a land opponent cannot impose regime change, a deliver-victory strategy against a determined land power has usually also required military victory on the main front. During the Napoleonic Wars, it was France's failed attack on Russia that contributed to Napoleon's defeat. In World War I, Britain paid dearly when it broke with its sea power model to deploy its own armies to the main front in France. During World War II, Britain and the United States orchestrated a sea power strategy more efficiently when they allied with and supplied large land powers that did the bulk of the fighting, in this case Russia in the European theater and China in the Asian theater. The Cold War did not require a decisive battle. Some emphasize the military pressure from the surrounding maritime allies; others stress the implosion of the USSR's non-performing economy.

FINAL THOUGHTS

Layered positive-space strategies of blockade, commerce raiding, and expeditionary warfare were not strategically decisive alone, but worked together with such negative-space strategies as sea denial, embargo, and sanctions to become strategically effective. Sea powers were more financially able to conduct these strategies than their land adversaries were to endure them. Over time the cumulative effects changed the balance of forces in favor of the sea powers, by inducing the financial and military exhaustion of their land adversaries.

From the heyday of the British Empire to the present, sea powers have set the global order, and land powers have contested it. This dynamic is still with us, as the PRC seems to be readying its naval forces to pressure its neighbors. A zero-sum, big-power-take-all solution for territorial disputes is unlikely to garner the PRC many allies. In fact, its domineering approach to its foreign policy can be counted on to set the conditions for a vigorous opposing sea power coalition.

A strategically minded sea power could take advantage of the PRC's anachronistic land power strategy to help those Asian countries most threatened by its bullying to become more deeply integrated into the maritime system through greater participation in multinational organizations and through the careful setting of international legal precedents. This would strengthen the system and, in so doing, better position the growing list of those favoring the positive-sum maritime approach to wait out a change of heart in Beijing. It is unknown how long it will take for PRC leaders to conclude that their zero-sum approach benefits no one in the long run and their own trade-dependent country least of all.

NOTES

1. Alfred Thayer Mahan, *The Influence of Sea Power on History 1660–1783* (Boston, MA: Little, Brown & Co., 1890), chapter 1, 29–59. http://www.gutenberg .org/files/13529/13529-h/13529-h.htm

2. Michael Duffy, "Festering the Spanish ulcer: The Royal Navy and the Peninsular War, 1808–1814," in Bruce A. Elleman and S.C.M. Paine, eds. *Naval Power and Expeditionary Warfare: Peripheral Campaigns and New Theatres of Naval Warfare* (London: Routledge Press, 2011), 15–28.

3. Aleksei N. Kuropatkin, *The Russian Army and the Japanese War,* trans. A. B. Lindsay, vol. 1 (New York: E. P. Dutton, 1909), 36–37.

4. Andrew D. Lambert, "The Crimean War Blockade, 1854–56," in Bruce A. Elleman and S.C.M. Paine, eds., *Naval Blockades and Seapower: Strategies and Counter-Strategies, 1805–2005* (London: Routledge Press, 2006), 46–60; Andrew D. Lambert, "The Royal Navy's White Sea campaign of 1854," in Elleman and Paine, *Naval Power and Expeditionary Warfare,* 29–44; Andrew Lambert, "Arms Races and Cooperation: The Anglo-French Crimean War Coalition, 1854–1856," in Bruce A. Elleman and S.C.M. Paine, eds., *Naval Coalition Warfare: From the Napoleonic War to Operation Iraqi Freedom* (London: Routledge Press, 2008), 33–47.

5. Bruce A. Elleman, "Soviet Sea Denial and the KMT-CCP Civil War in Manchuria, 1945–1949," in Elleman and Paine, *Naval Coalition Warfare,* 119–29.

6. Donald Chisholm, "Amphibious Assault as Decisive Maneuver in Korea," in Elleman and Paine, *Naval Power and Expeditionary Warfare,* 113–128; Malcolm Muir, Jr., "A Failed Blockade? Air and Sea Power in Korea, 1950–53," in Elleman and Paine, *Naval Blockades,* 145–156.

7. Jeffrey G. Barlow, "The 1962 Cuban Missile Crisis," in Elleman and Paine, *Naval Blockades,* 157–68.

8. Spencer C. Tucker, "Naval Blockades During the Vietnam War," in Elleman and Paine, *Naval Blockades*, 169–80; Edward J. Marolda, "Changing Tides: Naval Coalitions and the Vietnam War," in Elleman and Paine, *Naval Coalition Warfare*, 130–45.

9. Bruce A. Elleman, "China's 1974 Naval Expedition to the Paracel Islands," in Elleman and Paine, *Naval Power and Expeditionary Warfare*, 141–51.

10. Gerhard L. Weinberg, "Germany and Assorted Allies in World War II," in Elleman and Paine, *Naval Coalition Warfare*, 110–18.

11. S.C.M. Paine, "Missed Opportunities in the First Sino-Japanese War, 1894–1895," in Elleman and Paine, *Commerce Raiding*, 105–20; Ken-ichi Arakawa, "Japanese Naval Blockade of China in the Second Sino-Japanese War, 1937–41," in Elleman and Paine, *Naval Blockades*, 105–16.

12. Bruce A. Elleman, "The Nationalists' Blockade of the PRC, 1949–58," in Elleman and Paine, *Naval Blockades*, 133–44.

13. Grotius, Hugo. *The Law of War and Peace* (*De Jure Belli ac Pacis*), trans. Louise R. Loomis (New York: Walter J. Black, 1949), 91–92; Hugo Grotius, *Freedom of the Seas*, trans Ralph van Demen Magoffin, ed. James Brown Scott, Carnegie Endowment for International Peace, Division of International Law (New York: Oxford University Press, 1916).

Compiled List of Naval Case Studies

1. The Battleship *Potemkin* and Its Discontents, 1905
   Robert Zebroski
2. The Revolt of the Lash, 1910
   Zachary R. Morgan
3. The Cattaro Mutiny, 1918
   Paul G. Halpern
4. "Red Sailors" and the Demise of the German Empire, 1918
   Michael Epkenhans
5. The French Naval Mutinies, 1919
   Philippe Masson
6. The HMAS *Australia* Mutiny, 1919
   David Stevens
7. Mutiny in the Chilean Navy, 1931
   William F. Sater
8. The Invergordon Mutiny, 1931
   Christopher M. Bell
9. The Port Chicago Mutiny, 1944
   Regina T. Akers
10. The Royal Indian Navy Mutiny, 1946
    Chris Madsen
11. The *Chongqing* Mutiny and the Chinese Civil War, 1949
    Bruce A. Elleman
12. The Post-war "Incidents" in the Royal Canadian Navy, 1949
    Richard H. Gimblett
13. Naval Blockade and International Law
    Wolf Heintschel von Heinegg

14. Napoleon's Continental Blockade: An Effective Substitute to Naval Weakness?
    Silvia Marzagalli
15. The Flawed British Blockade, 1812–1815
    Wade G. Dudley
16. The Crimean War Blockade, 1854–1856
    Andrew D. Lambert
17. The Union Navy's Blockade Reconsidered
    David G. Surdam
18. The First Sino-Japanese War: Japanese Destruction of the Beiyang Fleet, 1894–1895
    S. C. M. Paine
19. The Naval Blockade of Cuba during the Spanish-American War
    Mark L. Hayes
20. World War I: The Blockade
    Paul G. Halpern
21. Japanese Naval Blockade of China in the Second Sino-Japanese War, 1937–1941
    Ken-ichi Arakawa
22. Naval Blockade and Economic Warfare in the European War, 1939–1945
    Geoffrey Till
23. The Nationalists' Blockade of the PRC, 1949–1958
    Bruce A. Elleman
24. A Failed Blockade? Air and Sea Power in Korea, 1950–1953
    Malcolm Muir Jr.
25. The 1962 Cuban Missile Crisis
    Jeffrey G. Barlow
26. Naval Blockades during the Vietnam War
    Spencer C. Tucker
27. The Beira Patrol: Britain's Broken Blockade against Rhodesia
    Richard A. Mobley
28. SLOCs and Sidewinders: The 1982 Falklands War
    Charles W. Koburger, Jr.
29. Maritime Sanctions Enforcement Against Iraq, 1990–2003
    James Goldrick
30. Ballistic Missiles in China's Anti-Taiwan Blockade Strategy
    Chris Rahman
31. "To disrupt, deter and deny": Sealing Australia's Maritime Borders
    David M. Stevens
32. International Law and Coalition Operations
    Jane G. Dalton
33. Caging the Eagle: Napoleonic War Coalitions

Steve Ross

34. Arms Races and Cooperation: The Anglo-French Crimean War Coalition, 1854–1856
    Andrew Lambert
35. The Second Opium War Anglo-French Coalition
    Douglas Hurd
36. Seapower and Alliances in the Era of Bismarck and William II
    Lawrence Sondhaus
37. The Triple Intervention and the Termination of the First Sino-Japanese War
    S. C. M. Paine
38. "Dash to Peking": The International Naval Coalition during the Boxer Uprising in 1900
    T. G. Otte
39. The Naval Coalition against the Central Powers, 1914–1918
    Paul Halpern
40. Germany and Assorted Allies in World War II: Cooperation with the Soviet Union, Spain, Italy, and Japan
    Gerhard L. Weinberg
41. Soviet Sea Denial and the KMT-CCP Civil War in Manchuria, 1945–1949
    Bruce A. Elleman
42. Changing Tides: Naval Coalitions and the Vietnam War
    Edward J. Marolda
43. The Cold War as a Coalition Struggle
    Bradford A. Lee
44. The Maritime Element in the 1990–1991 Gulf Crisis: Drawing on the Dividends of Half a Century of Multinational Naval Operations
    James Goldrick
45. Western Intervention in Bosnia: Operation *Deliberate Force*
    Charles Ingrao
46. Coalition Warfare over Kosovo
    Andrew L. Stigler
47. Operation *Enduring Freedom*: Coalition Warfare from the Sea and on the Sea
    Robert J. Schneller, Jr.
48. The Formation of a Coalition of the Willing and Operation *Iraqi Freedom*
    David B. Crist
49. A Modern History of the International Legal Definition of Piracy
    Penny Campbell
50. Piracy on the South China Coast through Modern Times

Robert J. Antony

51. The Taiping Rebellion, Piracy, and the *Arrow* War
    Bruce A. Elleman
52. *Selamat Datang, Kapitan*: Post-World War II Piracy in the South China
    Sea
    Charles W. Koburger, Jr.
53. The Political Economy of Piracy in the South China Sea
    David Rosenberg
54. The Looting and Rape of Vietnamese Boat People
    Bruce A. Elleman
55. Piracy and Armed Robbery in the Malacca Strait: A Problem Solved?
    Catherine Zara Raymond
56. Piracy in Bangladesh: What Lies Beneath?
    Samuel Pyeatt Menefee
57. Confronting Maritime Crime in Southeast Asian Waters: Reexamining
    "Piracy" in the Twenty-First Century
    Sam Bateman
58. President Thomas Jefferson and the Barbary Pirates
    Robert F. Turner
59. The Limits of Naval Power: The Merchant Brig *Three Sisters*, Riff
    Pirates, and British Battleships
    Andrew Lambert
60. Guns, Oil, and "Cake"—Maritime Security in the Gulf of Guinea
    Arild Nodland
61. Fish, Family, and Profit: Piracy and the Horn of Africa
    Gary E. Weir
62. Legal issues in expeditionary campaigns
    Eric Talbot Jensen
63. Festering the Spanish ulcer: The Royal Navy and the Peninsular War,
    1808–1814
    Michael Duffy
64. The Royal Navy's White Sea campaign of 1854
    Andrew D. Lambert
65. Gallipoli as a combined and joint operation
    Robin Prior
66. The British Mesopotamia campaign: 1914–1918
    Paul G. Halpern
67. Pearl Harbor and beyond: Japan's peripheral strategy to defeat China
    S. C. M. Paine
68. A pivotal campaign in a peripheral theatre: Guadalcanal and World War
    II in the Pacific
    Bradford A. Lee

69. The New Guinea Campaign during World War II
   David Stevens
70. Amphibious assault as decisive maneuver in Korea
   Donald Chisholm
71. Naval operations in peripheral conflicts: The Malayan Emergency (1948–1960) and Confrontation (1962–1966)
   Jeffrey Grey
72. China's 1974 naval expedition to the Paracel Islands
   Bruce A. Elleman
73. "Always Expect the Unexpected": The Falklands/Malvinas war of 1982
   Eric Grove
74. The Maritime Campaign in Iraq
   Peter Jones
75. U.S. Naval Operations and Contemporary Geopolitics: The War on Terror and the New Great Game in the Early-Twenty-First Century
   John Reeve
76. The Breakdown of Borders: Commerce Raiding during the Seven Years' War, 1756–1763
   Thomas M. Truxes
77. *Guerre de Course* and the First American Naval Strategy
   Christopher P. Magra
78. French Privateering during the French Wars, 1793–1815
   Silvia Marzagalli
79. Waging Protracted Naval War: U.S. Navy Commerce Raiding during the War of 1812
   Kevin D. McCranie
80. CSS *Alabama* and Confederate Commerce Raiders during the U.S. Civil War
   Spencer C. Tucker
81. Two Sides of the Same Coin: German and French Maritime Strategies in the Late Nineteenth Century
   David H. Olivier
82. Missed Opportunities in the First Sino-Japanese War, 1894–1895
   S. C. M. Paine
83. Chinese Neutrality and Russian Commerce Raiding during the Russo-Japanese War, 1904–1905
   Bruce A. Elleman
84. *"Handelskrieg mit U-Booten"*: The German Submarine Offensive in World War I
   Paul G. Halpern
85. The Anglo-American Naval Checkmate of Germany's *Guerre de Course*, 1917–1918

Kenneth J. Hagan and Michael T. McMaster

86. Logistic Supply and Commerce War in the Spanish Civil War, 1936–1939
    Willard C. Frank, Jr.

87. The German U-boat Campaign in World War II
    Werner Rahn

88. The Shipping of Southeast Asian Resources Back to Japan: National Logistics and War Strategy
    Ken-ichi Arakawa

89. Unrestricted Submarine Victory: The U.S. Submarine Campaign against Japan
    Joel Holwitt

90. *Guerre de Course* in the Charter Era: The Tanker War, 1980–1988
    George K. Walker

91. Twenty-First-Century High-Seas Piracy off Somalia
    Martin N. Murphy

92. Sailors and Slaves: USS *Constellation* and the Transatlantic Slave Trade
    John Pentangelo

93. Overwhelming Force and the Venezuelan Crisis of 1902–1903
    Henry J. Hendrix

94. Starvation Blockade and Herbert Hoover's Commission for Relief in Belgium, 1914–1919
    Bruce A. Elleman

95. The Allied Embargo of Japan, 1939–1941: From Rollback to Deterrence to Boomerang
    S. C. M. Paine

96. After the Fall of South Vietnam: Humanitarian Assistance in the South China Sea
    Jan K. Herman

97. Continuing to Serve: Deploying Naval Vessels as Artificial Reefs
    Tom Williams

98. Naval Sonars, Strandings, and Responsible Stewardship of the Seas
    Darlene R. Ketten

99. U.S. Coast Guard Response to the *Deepwater Horizon* Oil Spill
    Rear Adm. Mary Landry

100. Deep Blue Diplomacy: Soft Power and China's Antipiracy Operations
    Andrew S. Erickson and Austin M. Strange

List of Strategic Terms

1. **active vs passive enemy:** adopting a set strategy and actions versus discounting strategy and taking no action.
2. **active defense:** a defensive posture that is conducted with activity so is actually offensive in nature, as versus a traditional passive defense that reacts to the enemy or includes no action; see also defense, offense, passive defense.
3. **adaptation:** change of behavior to suit new circumstances.
4. **Adaptive Planning and Execution (APEX) system:** as per DOD CJCS Guide 3130, "APEX integrates strategic and operational planning and execution activities of the Joint Planning and Execution Community (JPEC) to seamlessly transitions [*sic*] planning to execution."
5. **adversary:** a political or military opponent.
6. **airpower:** exerting military authority from the air.
7. **air-sea battle:** combination of air and naval assets working jointly.
8. **air-land campaign:** a joint campaign utilizing both air and land assets.
9. **air mobility:** capable of moving forces by means of airpower.
10. **air superiority:** more powerful than the enemy when exerting control of the air.
11. **air supremacy:** paramount power compared to the enemy when exerting control of the air.
12. **alliance:** as per *American Heritage*, "a formal pact of union or confederation between nations in a common cause."
13. **alternate land line of communication (LLOC):** to deliver goods along a new land line not being blockaded.
14. **alternate foreign port:** to deliver goods to a port not being blockaded that can then transship them over land to the blockaded country.

15. **amphibious assault:** a military attack against the land carried out from the sea.
16. **amphibious defense zone (ADZ):** area encompassing the amphibious objective area and the adjoining airspace required by accompanying naval forces for the purpose of air defense.
17. **amphibious landing:** the landing of troops and equipment from the sea.
18. **amphibious operations:** operations linking land and sea forces.
19. **anti-ship ballistic missile (ABM):** a missile fitted with an anti-ship seeker head capable of sinking a variety of ships including an aircraft carrier.
20. **antisubmarine warfare (ASW):** locating, deterring, and when possible destroying enemy submarines.
21. **appeasement:** as per *American Heritage*, the "policy of granting concessions to a potential enemies to maintain peace."
22. **assessment:** to evaluate a military situation and determine strengths and weaknesses; see also commander's intent.
23. **assumptions:** military issues one takes for granted, regardless whether true or false.
24. **asymmetrical warfare:** the attempt to sidestep enemy strengths by using other means.
25. **attrition warfare:** as per *American Heritage*, the "gradual diminution in number or strength due to constant stress," with the goal of wearing an enemy down over time.
26. **audiences—direct vs indirect:** direct audiences are those a military operation is knowingly trying to influence, while an indirect audience—either by intention or happenstance—is an audience that is also influenced by military operations.
27. **away game wars:** fighting on another country's territory.
28. **bait and bleed:** entice an enemy into a trap and then bleed it to death.
29. **balance of powers:** the comparative strength of various powers, with sea powers tending to get stronger over time vis-à-vis land powers.
30. **balance of power:** as per *American Heritage*, "a distribution of power between nations, often by means of alliance and counteralliance, whereby no one nation is able to dominate or conquer the others."
31. **balancing vs bandwagoning:** not allowing one nation to dominate versus shifting support to a nation whose fortunes appear to be rising.
32. **base raids:** to attack land bases of pirates and other military forces; for example, one of the best methods for stopping commerce raiding is to attack the base where they are sailing from.
33. **battlefield intelligence:** obtaining first-hand and rapid reports from the actual locations where fighting is taking place.

34. **beachhead:** as per *American Heritage*, a "position on an enemy shore-line captured by advance troops of an invading force."
35. **belligerent blockade:** a blockade that uses force.
36. **best case vs worst-case scenarios:** process of determining the best strategy to obtain a military objective.
37. **biological warfare:** as per *Webster's*, "warfare that makes use of bacteria, viruses, toxins, etc., to disable or destroy man, domestic animals, and food crops."
38. **blitzkrieg:** lightning warfare, or according to *American Heritage*, a "swift, sudden military offensive, usually by combined air and land forces."
39. **blockade:** the attempt to cut off enemy military or economic lines of communications or to prevent sortie of enemy forces.
40. **blockade distances:** close and distant vs near and far and also "open."
41. **blockade kinds:** different kinds include paper, pacific, belligerent, and commercial.
42. **blockade of ports:** either keeping a fleet trapped or drawing it out to battle.
43. **blockade porosity:** partial vs total stoppage of goods.
44. **blockade runners:** ships that try to escape capture when they enter or leave a blockaded port.
45. **blue vs green vs brown water navy:** deep seas versus continental waters versus coastal waters.
46. **boomerang effects:** an unintended effect that recoils against the perpetrator.
47. **bottleneck:** a constraining factor of some sort.
48. **bottleneck capability:** any capability that is in short supply and so the destruction of which will cause the enemy to lose; for example, at Guadalcanal so many Japanese pilots were shot down and killed that it became impossible for Japan to replace them.
49. **bottleneck substitution:** to replace a particular item that is not being allowed through a blockade or is being sanctioned.
50. **branches and sequels:** determining possible variations to a strategy early and midway through an operation as well as possible post-operation impacts.
51. **breakthrough:** according to *Webster's*, "a movement or advance all the way through and beyond an enemy's defensive system into the unorganized areas in the rear."
52. **buffer moat:** using a piece of water, such as a sea channel or river, to act as a buffer to keep an enemy out.

53. **buffer patrol:** sending ships on patrol through contested waters to intercede between two adversaries in such a fashion that any attack will spur third-party intervention; see also tripwire patrol.
54. **buffer state:** according to *Webster's*, "a small state lying between potentially hostile larger areas."
55. **buffer zone:** an area that cushions, shields, or protects another area.
56. **cannon-shot rule:** the distance offshore, usually 3 nautical miles, that a coastal state could traditionally claim as sovereign waters.
57. **capabilities-based planning:** working to integrate all DOD assets so as to decrease cost even while increasing overall capability.
58. **center of gravity (COG):** the source of an enemy's strength; either an operational or strategy weakness that, when exploited, can seriously weaken an enemy and result in their defeat; a good example was the vulnerability of the two British carriers in the Falklands.
59. **chain of command:** the vertical structure through which orders are passed from top to bottom, and information passed from bottom to top of a military command.
60. **Chairman of the Joint Chiefs of Staff (CJCS):** the head of the Pentagon-based military service leaders group which reports directly to the Secretary of Defense and also functions as the President's principal military advisor.
61. **choke point:** a bottleneck, especially in a sea line of communication (SLOC); see also gag point.
62. **citizen soldier:** a military drawn from the civilian population, for example the French Army under Napoleon.
63. **civil-military relations:** the interaction between civilians and their military counterparts.
64. **clandestine:** the use of secrecy and concealment for purposes of subversion or deception.
65. **clash of civilizations:** the view that different cultures and races are bound to fight.
66. **close blockade:** a blockade line close to the country being blockaded.
67. **closed sea:** any water that can be closed off to access, either by closing a strait or blockading a sea line of communication.
68. **cluttered sea:** any water that has numerous islands or other impediments to navigation.
69. **coalition:** a temporary combination of states, usually to defeat one specific enemy or accomplish one strategic objective.
70. **coalition membership stability:** successfully retaining allies within a coalition.
71. **coast watchers:** personnel who were stationed along critical waterways and reported on enemy ship movements, for example Australian coast watchers during World War II in the Pacific.

72. **coastal state:** the government of a state that is located next to a body of water, and over which it has legal authority to administer territorial waters up to 12 nautical miles from shore.
73. **coercion:** to compel by pressure or threat of violence.
74. **cohesion vs reach:** Corbett's view of concentration.
75. **combined operations:** the militaries of two or more countries working together closely, not to be confused with joint operations; see also joint operations.
76. **command and control (C2):** the process of planning and supervising the operations of military forces.
77. **command of the sea:** establishing one's forces in such a position that they can control the maritime communications of all parties concerned; see also sea command.
78. **commander's critical information requirement (CCIR):** identifies reconnaissance objectives and drives the commander's reconnaissance guidance.
79. **commander's intent:** a process whereby one's own and the enemy's forces are assessed in terms of times, space, and force, and then various courses of action (COA) are developed.
80. **commerce destruction vs commerce prevention:** the incremental difference between destroying a number of commercial ships versus exerting sea command (or sea control) that attempts to stop all enemy shipping.
81. **commerce raiding (guerre de course):** the legal taking or sinking of goods and ships under authorization from a national state.
82. **commission to privateer:** permission granted by a national state for a shipowner to conduct commerce raiding against an enemy of that state.
83. **common operating picture (COP):** the use of sensing devices to collate data into one comprehensive view of ship locations and movements.
84. **comparative economic growth rates:** how much each side in a conflict grows its economy during the course of the conflict.
85. **competing interests:** if two coalition partners disagree on a national goal, in particular if it has the potential of undermining the coalition cohesion.
86. **competitive advantage:** an advantage accruing to a country due to its geographic location, work force, or natural resources.
87. **compounding effects:** the additive impact of one or more strategies against an adversary's will to fight.
88. **concentration:** the unification or coordination of force in space, time, and effect to overwhelm the enemy.
89. **concentration of forces vs dispersal of forces:** putting all of one's forces together for maximum strength versus dividing them up for

maximum coverage; in the age of precision weapons, concentration could become a vulnerability.

90. **concentration vs opening new fronts:** a very important decision about force distribution, either by putting all forces in one place or dividing them among two or more fronts; see also peripheral campaigns.

91. **conquest:** the taking of the opponent's land or resources, up to and including the entire country, often permanently.

92. **consensual vs non-consensual invasion:** a situation where the national government is either asked in advance if it will allow foreign troops on its territory or if it is not asked.

93. **constrainment:** the strategy of using naval power to convince a Great Power adversary to continue to respect international norms and legalities.

94. **containment:** to hold a Great Power adversary within its current borders or area of influence.

95. **contiguous ally:** an ally on one's own border, thus making possible a secure land line of communication (LLOC); see also non-contiguous ally.

96. **contiguous zone:** the 12-nautical-mile zone beyond territorial waters according to UNCLOS in which customs law may be enforced.

97. **continental blockade:** Napoleon's failed attempt to cut the British Empire off from the European Continental System.

98. **continental shelf:** the part of a continent that is submerged in relatively shallow sea.

99. **continental power:** see land power.

100. **continental United States (CONUS):** all parts of the United States but Alaska, Guam, Hawaii, and Puerto Rico.

101. **conventional forces:** non-nuclear and non-irregular military forces.

102. **convoy:** a group of ships under the protection of an escort, particularly important for protecting shipping against commerce raiders.

103. **convoy escort:** an armed ship, usually a naval ship or Q-ship, that accompanies the convoy as a guard.

104. **cooperative adversary:** an enemy that does exactly what its opponent wants it to do, either through ignorance or lack of options.

105. **core territory:** the traditional land of a country, not counting colonies or other territories obtained during the conflict.

106. **counterattack:** to move the adversary from the offensive to the defensive.

107. **countermeasures:** actions adopted to offset an adversary's actions.

108. **course of action (COA):** a possible plan, often one of several, that can be used to obtain tactical, operational, or strategic objectives.

109. **covert operation:** a secret or concealed action.

110. **critical vulnerability:** a weakness in the overall strength of a nation or force, the neutralization of which would likely lead to defeat.

111. **culminating point of attack:** the point of an offensive in which the strength of the attacker no longer exceeds that of the defender; any attacker who proceeds beyond this point may be subject to successful counterattacks.
112. **culminating point of victory:** point of maximum military leverage to achieve the policy objective.
113. **cumulative strategy:** a strategy of aggregating effects, such as shipping losses to commerce raiders.
114. **cut logistical lines:** the act of cutting either sea lines of communication or land lines of communication in such a way that the adversary is not able to receive additional supplies, including more troops, ammunition, food, water.
115. **cyber terrorism:** using the internet to conduct a terrorist attack.
116. **cyber warfare:** using computers and the internet to organize and potentially carry out an attack either against a hard target or more likely against the adversary's computers and internet access.
117. **death ground:** to put an adversary in a position where death is the likely outcome, and fighting harder provides the only possible escape.
118. **decapitation:** to kill or disable either a civil or military leader or leaders.
119. **deception:** to use a ruse to confuse and confound the enemy.
120. **decisive point:** the point in time and/or space in which military success produces significant operational or strategic effects.
121. **decisiveness:** whether a naval operation, or type of operation, could alone end a conflict.
122. **decisive victory:** a wartime victory that obtains the national goals set at the beginning.
123. **deconfliction:** to decrease friction that might lead to disagreement, especially among allies or coalition partners.
124. **defection:** when the ship's crew, after a successful mutiny, decides to switch from one side to another, usually as a way of avoiding punishment; if a member of an alliance or coalition decides to pull out and join the other side.
125. **defense:** the use of force to oppose an attack.
126. **defense in depth:** trade space for time; while usually requiring fewer resources it can rarely bring victory; also see prevent defeat strategy.
127. **defilade:** protection or shielding from hostile ground observation or flat projecting fire.
128. **deliver victory strategy:** a strategy designed to obtain victory; the opposite is often a prevent defeat strategy, which if done correctly can undermine and checkmate a deliver victory strategy.
129. **detailed defeat:** to defeat enemy forces piecemeal.

130. **deterrence:** measures taken by a state or a group of allied states to prevent hostile action by an enemy state or states.
131. **diarchical hierarchy:** a system where dual officials, one representing the skilled bureaucracy or military and the other the ethnic or political group in charge, share decision making responsibility.
132. **diplomacy, information, military, and economics (DIME):** one method of assessing another country's military prowess.
133. **diplomatic leverage:** using diplomacy to put additional pressure on an adversary.
134. **diplomatically isolated:** the state of being bereft of allies.
135. **direct vs indirect effects:** immediate versus follow-on effects.
136. **disaster relief:** a humanitarian operation conducted after a natural disaster, such as a volcanic eruption, tsunami, earthquake, etc.
137. **discipline:** adherence to the chain of command and rules of military conduct; see also mutiny.
138. **disinformation:** giving out wrong or incomplete information to confuse the enemy.
139. **disposal force (not disposable force):** troops not critical for homeland defense deployed for a high risk, high reward, mission.
140. **disproportionate costs:** the goal of a strategy, in particular one based on protraction and/or attrition, that forces one's adversary to spend more than the protagonist, thereby obtaining cumulative advantages over time.
141. **distant blockade:** a blockade line distant from the country being blockaded, often to draw an opponent out to fight.
142. **diversion:** to create an event in one area to draw the adversary's attention away from another; also see feint.
143. **divide and conquer:** attempt to break up an adversary's alliances, or perhaps divide its military, so as to attack and destroy a smaller part of the whole.
144. **doctrine:** a set of guides for action both held and taught by a particular group.
145. **doctrinaire:** seeks to impose a doctrine in all situations regardless of circumstances.
146. **dogma:** a principle that is followed slavishly.
147. **dominant naval power:** the strongest sea power in a particular theater at a particular time.
148. **domino effect:** the fear of countries falling to Communism one by one; see also reverse domino effect.
149. **Donkey work:** a term used by Corbett to describe time-consuming actions that are part of exercising command of the sea.

150. **downsizing:** lessening the size of one's forces, often taken as a good opportunity by an adversary to attack; for example, Argentina attacked the Falklands right as the Royal Navy was undergoing downsizing.
151. **dream scenario:** when wartime conditions are such that the best possible outcome occurs for the winning side; see also nightmare scenario.
152. **dual-use equipment:** military equipment, such as navy ships, that can be used equally well for both humanitarian operations and military missions.
153. **duration:** the length of time an operation continues, often either shortened or lengthened depending on the capabilities of the opponent's military; see also war protraction.
154. **eccentric attack:** to take an object or place away from the enemy's main theater, often in the hopes that it divide its forces in an effort to get it back.
155. **economic sparkplug:** a strategy or operation that can boost economic revenues, such as sinking unused naval ships to create artificial reefs.
156. **economic strangulation:** to put strict limits on another country's imports and exports.
157. **effects:** can be direct vs indirect—both intended and unintended impact of a strategy.
158. **effort vs force:** Corbett's analytical terms for concentration.
159. **elasticity:** how to maximize concentration vs dispersal.
160. **embargo:** any restriction imposed upon commerce, usually of an enemy.
161. **embarkation:** the act of boarding a ship for a voyage.
162. **end state:** what a strategy's final objective should look like.
163. **enemy adaptation:** change of behavior by the enemy to suit new military circumstances.
164. **enemy is not a potted plant:** a saying in the Strategy and Policy Department at the U.S. Naval War College intended to remind the audience that the adversary also has a vote during any military encounter.
165. **enemy of my enemy is my friend:** a famous saying justifying alliances and coalitions with countries with similar enemies.
166. **envelopment:** the act of trying to surround an enemy partially or completely.
167. **environmental disaster response:** military operations intended to assist after an environmental problem, like a leaking oil pipeline or a stranded oil tanker.
168. **escalating costs:** putting more of a burden over time on an adversary and its coalition.
169. **escalation:** the tendency toward the use of maximum available strength or capability; in mutinies, the tendency to spread to more ships or add new demands, see horizontal escalation and vertical escalation.

170. **espionage:** use of spies by a government to obtain secret military, diplomatic, economic, or political information from another government, usually an enemy or ally of an enemy but sometimes one's own allies.
171. **exclusion zone:** an area of the ocean where one country has announced there will be military exercises as part of an operation, such as a blockade, usually a location where sea or air traffic is greatest.
172. **exclusive coalition:** a coalition that does not accept all willing members, but only those with similar and usually overlapping naval capabilities.
173. **exclusive economic zone (EEZ):** control of maritime resources out to 200 nautical miles from shore according to UNCLOS.
174. **execution:** carrying out a strategy or operation exactly as it was intended.
175. **exercises:** joint with other services participating or combined with other countries' militaries participating.
176. **exit strategy:** determining the end point of a strategy well in advance of its actual termination, in the hopes of being able to disengage with the least amount of friction.
177. **expeditionary warfare:** the act of using naval or air forces to land troops at a new location, often non-contiguous with the main front.
178. **expeditionary warfare type:** can include invasion, small-scale diversions, or eccentric attack.
179. **extension packages:** hard vs soft add-ons.
180. **Eyes in the Sky:** a combined patrol by Malaysia, Singapore, and Indonesia to patrol by air the Malacca Strait; often referred to by the acronym MALSINDO.
181. **Fabian strategy:** a cautious strategy avoiding direct confrontation, usually associated with a cumulative process of wearing down the enemy.
182. **face (losing vs gaining):** the fear of losing face by appearing to be weak as versus gaining face by putting on an appearance of strength; see also prestige.
183. **failed state:** a state that does not have an effective government and so is perceived by the international community to be a failure; also see pariah state.
184. **failsafe:** a mechanism built into a system to ensure safety should the system fail to operate properly.
185. **far blockade:** a blockade line far away from the country carrying out the blockade.
186. **fear:** the belief, whether founded or unfounded, that another person or country poses a threat; one of Thucydides' three fundamental motives: fear, honor, and interest.
187. **feasibility:** determining what is capable of being done.

188. **feigned withdrawal:** to pretend to withdraw in order to lure the enemy in deeper.
189. **feint:** a stratagem intended to mislead, such as a feigned attack designed to draw defensive action away from an intended target; also see diversion.
190. **first strike:** the first military attack, usually to take advantage of surprise.
191. **flag states:** a national government that agrees to let a ship function under its protection.
192. **flags of convenience:** as per *Webster's,* "the national flag of a nation with which merchant ships owned by persons of other nations are registered in order to effect a saving on taxes, wages, etc."
193. **flagship:** a ship bearing a flag officer or a commander of a fleet, squadron, or contingent, and displaying their flag.
194. **flanking maneuver:** to threaten or attack the right or left side of an enemy's military formation.
195. **fleet-in-being:** a naval fleet that poses a potential threat because it merely exists.
196. **fleet in port:** a fleet sitting in port that can become an easy target of attack, such as the Chinese fleet at Weihaiwei or the U.S. fleet at Pearl Harbor.
197. **fleet-on-fleet battle:** the classic battle of one Navy's fleet against the other.
198. **flexibility:** the capability of being able to adapt quickly to changing circumstances
199. **focal point:** where a convoy begins.
200. **fog of war:** the uncertainties involved in warfare stemming from lack of, inaccurate, or misleading information.
201. **force equation:** the determination of two opponents' military forces; see also war by algebra.
202. **force introduction:** simultaneous vs incremental vs sequential, plus strengthening vs intermittent vs weakening.
203. **force multiplier:** a weapon, technique, or technology that gives the owner a means of increasing their forces' impact, sometimes exponentially.
204. **fortress fleet:** a fleet tied to the area around the port it was tasked to defend, thereby ceding command of the sea to the adversary.
205. **forward operating base (FOB):** keeping personnel, weapons, and supplies close to the enemy position.
206. **forward presence:** keeping forces close to the adversary's geographic location.

207. **free strategical design:** a term Corbett used to argue that sea powers have a greater range of strategic options than land powers.
208. **free trade:** the long-held belief dating back to Grotius in the early 17th century that all countries have an inherent right to trade, and that using the seas for commerce should be common to all.
209. **freedom of navigation (FON):** unhindered ship movements anywhere on the high seas.
210. **freedom of navigation operations (FONOPS):** sending ships into disputed waters on purpose to challenge illegitimate territorial claims.
211. **freedom of the seas:** a concept established by the Dutch legal theorist Grotius in 1609 that all nations should have an equal right to use the seas.
212. **freight insurance:** insurance costs influenced by blockades, commerce raiding, sanctions, and embargoes.
213. **freight rates:** transportation costs influenced by blockades, commerce raiding, sanctions, and embargoes.
214. **friction:** a physics metaphor coined by Clausewitz to denote all the difficulties that impede military operations.
215. **friendly fire:** when one part of the military mistakenly fires on another part of its same military, often another service or an ally; see also joint operations and combined operations.
216. **friendly coalition fire:** when one coalition partner mistakenly attacks another's forces.
217. **gag point:** a bottleneck, especially in a land line of communication (LLOC); see also choke point.
218. **gap:** an empty area of water, usually between two regions that are patrolled by naval forces.
219. **genocide:** the deliberate and systematic extermination of a racial or national group; for example, the Turkish genocide of Armenians in 1914 began on the very day the British had originally planned to land forces at Gallipoli, later delayed by one day.
220. **geography:** open vs enclosed, maritime vs land-locked.
221. **ghost ship:** a ship taken by pirates and used to carry goods or conduct other piracies; see also phantom ship.
222. **global commons:** the concept that the oceans are free for all countries to use.
223. **global order:** the normal unimpeded workings of a maritime economy, based on a system of international institutions.
224. **global positioning system (GPS):** using satellite positioning to keep track of ships' locations.
225. **global war on terror (GWOT):** the anti-terrorist effort after 9-11 conducted by the United States with the assistance of allies and coalition partners.

226. **global warming vs climate change:** global warming is only temperature rise while climate change could include all climate changes.
227. **globalization:** the spread of a common legal system, economic system, plus communication systems across the entire world.
228. **glues and solvents:** those positive elements (glue) that can hold an alliance or coalition together versus those negative elements (solvent) that tears them asunder.
229. **graduated advance:** another term for an escalation of operations over time.
230. **grand strategy:** the highest level of strategy set by a national government, integrating all the elements of national power.
231. **great power:** a country that possesses military, economic, and diplomatic strength and whose national interests extend beyond its own borders.
232. **Great Wall:** the lengthy and large wall in China, but when applied to the sea suggests a line of ships conducting a blockade operation.
233. **guerre de course:** meaning "war of the chase," was considered to be the best method for countries with smaller navies to fight larger countries with bigger navies, see commerce raiding.
234. **guerrilla warfare:** as per *Webster's*, a type of warfare whose members belong to a "small independent band of soldiers that harasses the enemy by surprise raids, attacks on communication and supply lines, etc."
235. **gunboat diplomacy:** the classic use of navies to force another country to accept a diplomatic solution to a conflict.
236. **hammer and anvil:** having one force be a holding force (anvil) keeping the adversary from moving, while a second force (hammer) attacks.
237. **hard platforms vs soft platforms:** combatant ships versus ships designed or used for functions not involving kinetic warfare.
238. **hard power vs soft power:** military force as compared to humanitarian aid, disaster relief, plus a wide range of economic policies; hard-power assets tend to be equally useful delivering soft-power benefits, while soft-power assets can rarely exert hard-power benefits.
239. **hearts and minds:** the allegiance of the general population; convincing the adversary's citizens that their cause is hopeless, such as occurred in the United States during the Vietnam War, resulting in a withdrawal.
240. **hegemony:** as per *American Heritage*, "preponderant influence of one state over others."
241. **heterogeneous coalition:** navies with different capabilities working together in a coalition; also see homogeneous coalitions.
242. **high seas vs territorial waters:** the sea or ocean beyond 12 nautical miles (it used to be 3 nautical miles) from shore, whereas territorial waters are from the shore out to 12 nautical miles.

243. **holding (maintaining) command vs exercising command:** once secured, command of the sea is held by maintaining a sufficiently large navy to dissuade and deter challenges. Exercising command consists of deploying that navy.
244. **home front wars:** the civilian population of a country at war; also see away game wars.
245. **home guard:** a volunteer force formed to protect and defend a homeland while the regular army is fighting in the field.
246. **homeland security:** the security apparatus defending the country of one's allegiance.
247. **home turf:** land that is of greater value because it is considered traditionally part of a country.
248. **homogeneous coalition:** a coalition of similar states, usually with overlapping naval capabilities; also see heterogeneous coalition.
249. **honor:** adherence to what is thought to be a correct standard of conduct; part of Thucydides' three fundamental motives: fear, honor, and interest.
250. **hope is not a strategy:** fervent desires for an outcome cannot substitute for a strategy capable of achieving that outcome.
251. **horizontal escalation:** when a demonstration or mutiny spreads outward to include other ships, fleets, or the entire navy; see also vertical escalation.
252. **host country:** a country housing foreign troops, ships, etc.
253. **human trafficking:** the modern-day equivalent of slavery or endentured servitude, often carried out against unsuspecting or desperate refugees fleeing a humanitarian disaster seeking to find a better life in a new country.
254. **humanitarian assistance/disaster relief (HA/DR):** giving aid to a country after a disaster of some type.
255. **humanitarian disaster:** any type of disaster where people's lives are at risk.
256. **humanitarian relief:** operations to assist in any kind of human-related emergency.
257. **illegal immigration:** the unchecked movement of people across national borders, halted by the Australian government by adopting a reverse blockade.
258. **inclusive coalition:** adding in other powers with lesser capabilities to form larger coalitions.
259. **incremental dividends:** taking small gains and adding them together; for example, in World War II in the Pacific, Secretary of War Stimson called the U.S. strategy against Japan "pinprick" warfare, because it was based on adding together incremental dividends.

260. **infertile areas:** an area where there is little or no commerce so anti-pirate or anti-commerce raiding patrols are unnecessary.

261. **information superiority:** having greater intelligence assets than the adversary.

262. **instruments of national power:** the elements of a grand strategy, including economic, military, diplomatic, political, and information assets.

263. **insurance rate rise:** rising insurance rates, often a goal of a naval blockade, or threatened naval blockade, in order to put pressure on an adversary through increased insurance premiums.

264. **insurgency:** as per *Webster's*, "insurrection against an existing government by a group not recognized as having the status of a belligerent."

265. **insurrection:** as per *Webster's*, "any act or instance of revolt or open resistance to established authority."

266. **interception:** the stopping of goods during a blockade by finding and halting a ship or other transportation carrier.

267. **interdiction:** the stopping of goods during a blockade by any means.

268. **interest:** pertaining to obtaining one's goals and ambitions; one of Thucydides' three fundamental motives: fear, honor, and interest.

269. **interior lines:** continental countries enjoy the advantage of interior land lines of communication (LLOC).

270. **intermittent:** alternately beginning an action and then ceasing for a time before beginning again.

271. **international law:** the established set of laws determining legal and illegal use of the seas.

272. **international waters:** see high seas vs territorial waters.

273. **interoperability:** the ability of different ships, fleets, or navies to operate with each other.

274. **intervention:** a third country choosing to interject itself in the military affairs of two belligerent powers; see also third-party intervention.

275. **inverse rule:** the counter-intuitive view that a country with more shipping is actually less vulnerable to commerce raiding and blockade than a country with a lower level of shipping; for example, Great Britain had enormous shipping capability at the beginning of World War I.

276. **island:** land surrounded completely by water, the best place to conduct a blockade, since all sea lines of communication (SLOCs) are vulnerable to being cut.

277. **island-hopping:** a concept first proposed by Alfred Thayer Mahan in 1911 of skipping over certain Japanese-held islands, isolating them, and letting them "die on the vine" on the way to Japan.

278. **jackal state:** a lawless state, often a pariah state, that preys on international trade.

279. **Joint Chiefs of Staff (JCS):** Principal military advisory group reporting to the president of the United States, composed of the chiefs of the Army, Navy, and Air Force.
280. **joint operations:** two or more services working together, such as army with navy, or navy with air force; see also combined operations.
281. **kamikaze attacks:** Japanese air attacks in which the pilots intentionally flew their planes into enemy ships.
282. **key capabilities:** those capabilities that when degraded will lead to defeat.
283. **kill box:** an area where fire can be concentrated against an enemy.
284. **land line of communication (LLOC):** land access allowing for the delivery of necessary materials, including weapons, ammunition, fuel, and food.
285. **land operations:** conducting military actions against the territory of an adversary.
286. **land power:** a continental-based country with inadequate access to oceans and seas.
287. **law of armed conflict:** legal rules for warfare.
288. **law of the seas:** legal rules for oceans, updated in 1994 by UNCLOS.
289. **leap-frog:** jump over an opponent by adopting technology or tactics first.
290. **learn from mistakes of others:** a famous phrase by Bismarck.
291. **letter of marque:** an official letter allowing the holder to commerce raid a particular country for a particular time to obtain a certain amount of money in restitution.
292. **levels of warfare:** tactical, operational, strategic, and grand strategy.
293. **liminal space:** areas on the threshold of a change, such as from sea to shore, or from the sea to the air.
294. **liminal space tax:** the ability to charge money to expedite the transition of goods and persons from one side of a liminal space to another, such as embarking on a ship at a port or boarding a plane at an airport.
295. **liminal space eradication:** the longtime movement toward eliminating all liminal spaces, such as by digging tunnels under straits, or bridges over any body of water, so as to avoid paying liminal space taxes.
296. **limited objectives:** a goal less than regime change requiring a negotiated settlement between the two sides, possibly including a ship demonstration or mutiny.
297. **littoral:** the liminal water space close to the shores of a country.
298. **littoral state:** a state located adjacent to oceans and seas.
299. **local population allegiance:** local support necessary for a peripheral campaign on a new front to be successful.

300. **logistics:** support for armed forces, arguably the most critical element of modern warfare.
301. **loosening:** getting less stringent over time.
302. **lose all battles but the last one:** during a protracted war every battle can be lost so long as the final one is victorious.
303. **lose battles but win the war:** a war can still be won if operational battles are lost but the overall strategy is victorious; for example, pundits argue that the United States lost the Vietnam War, but not winning in Vietnam helped flip China to the U.S. side of the conflict, which ultimately led to victory in the Cold War.
304. **luck vs fate:** considered two important elements of Asian thinking, with luck able to delay one's fate or hasten it.
305. **Mandate of Heaven:** the belief in China that disasters—including defeat in war—can signal the end of a dynasty, a particular leader, or a national government.
306. **manifest destiny:** the view that God has given a country a guaranteed path.
307. **maritime crime:** illegal acts that occur within the sovereign territory of a coastal state.
308. **maritime domain awareness (MDA):** using sensing devices to collate data on ship movements to create a real time common operating picture.
309. **maritime surveillance:** the use of land, air, and space sensors to track ship locations and movements.
310. **maritime vs continental power (whale vs elephant):** the view that some countries are naturally sea powers and others are land powers; for example, America is often portrayed as a maritime power and Russia as a continental power.
311. **mass:** a type of concentration.
312. **mass communications:** all forms of media, including government propaganda, news organizations, and social media.
313. **media war:** the use of the press, network news, and more and more the internet to present one's own side of the conflict, and to undermine the propaganda of the adversary.
314. **midair refueling:** replenishing fuel in a moving aircraft, which is an absolutely critical capability if the goal is to assert air control.
315. **military operations other than war (MOOTWA):** a whole range of military operations that include humanitarian relief, disaster relief, plus antipiracy patrols.
316. **mine countermeasure (MCM):** using mine clearing ships to locate and defuse enemy sea mines.
317. **minor counterattacks:** a small effort to turn the adversary from the offensive to the defensive; see also counterattack.

318. **mirror-imaging:** assuming (usually mistakenly) that one's opponent thinks and behaves as one does.
319. **missile blockade:** the firing of missiles into a set exclusion zone, usually intended to interfere with either sea or air traffic or to increase insurance rates.
320. **mission creep:** when the original objectives of an operation are expanded, either on purpose or most often unconsciously, in such a way that it becomes impossible to obtain the original objective; for example, after the Inchon landing in Korea the U.S. forces pushed back the North Koreans so quickly that they were soon at the Yalu River, which precipitated a Chinese intervention, whereas if the movement north had stopped at Pyongyang as originally planned Chinese intervention might have been avoided.
321. **mobility:** the characteristic to be able to move when necessary.
322. **mother ship:** the use by pirates of a single ship, usually larger than their attack skiffs, to live on while waiting for a ship to pirate.
323. **mutiny:** when discipline breaks down on a ship between officers and crew, and an organized protest occurs, either opposing leadership decisions or, in the most extreme cases, attempting to take control of one ship, several ships, or an entire fleet or navy.
324. **narrow sea:** any water where access is through a narrow channel, such as a strait, that can be closed.
325. **national goals:** goals set by a national government body.
326. **national interests:** what nations consider to be necessary to their livelihood and continued growth.
327. **national prosperity:** how wealthy a state is and how much can it devote to conducting a war.
328. **national resilience:** how quickly a state can bounce back after a war.
329. **national security interests:** a government's main goal is to promote its security interests.
330. **naval coalition duration:** shrinking, shifting, stable, or asymmetric.
331. **naval coalition membership:** bilateral, regional, or global.
332. **naval coalition types:** homogeneous vs heterogeneous and inclusive vs exclusive.
333. **naval parity:** two navies of approximately equal size and quality.
334. **near blockade:** a blockade line close to the country conducting the blockade, usually directed at an opposing fleet.
335. **negative space:** a non-event, either something that was stopped from happening or an expected event that did not happen for some reason; see also positive space.
336. **negotiated settlement:** a settlement dependent on the agreement of both sides.

337. **negotiations:** the manner in which most limited wars are concluded.
338. **nested wars:** having two or more conflicts going simultaneously, such as a civil war within a country also fighting the Cold War.
339. **net assessment:** evaluation of strengths and weaknesses of all sides in the theater of conflict.
340. **network centric:** use of communication networks to centralize command and control.
341. **neutral powers:** non-aligned powers in adopting a blockade strategy, great effort should be made not to impact neutral powers who might then form alliances or coalitions with the adversary.
342. **neutrality:** policy or status of a country that is not part of a war between other nations.
343. **neutralization policy:** to make a contested area out of bounds for all aggressors, similar to when the Taiwan Patrol Force was created in 1950, and was then run until 1979, to make sure neither the ROC nor the PRC could attack across the strait; see also buffer patrol and tripwire patrol.
344. **niche capabilities:** special abilities that different navies bring to the table.
345. **nightmare scenario:** when wartime conditions are such that the worst possible outcome occurs; see also dream scenario.
346. **noncombatant evacuation operation (NEO):** naval forces assisting civilians to evacuate out of a dangerous situation.
347. **non-contiguous:** not adjacent to the main front.
348. **non-contiguous ally:** an ally not on one's own border, thus making secure land lines impossible and more likely that vulnerable sea lines of communication (SLOCs) will be necessary.
349. **objective:** something that one's efforts are intended to attain or accomplish.
350. **ocean enclosure movement:** the use of laws to claim ever greater national rights over neighboring waters.
351. **oceanic moat:** security protection offered by surrounding waterways, such as the English Channel or the Taiwan Strait.
352. **offense:** the attack.
353. **one-shot use:** a tactic, operation, or strategy that can only be used once.
354. **open registries:** the government of a state that allows any ship to register.
355. **operational goals:** goals set by a military authority to achieve operational objectives below the level of strategic goals.
356. **operational objectives:** specific endpoints to be achieved to further operational parameters.
357. **outcomes:** intended vs unintended.

358. **over-extension:** when the military's areas of responsibility exceed its capacity; one of the main goals of adopting a protracted and/or attrition strategy.
359. **over-the-horizon amphibious operation:** ships located out of sight well offshore sending in landing parties.
360. **overt vs covert operation:** regular military operation vs secret military operation.
361. **pacific blockade:** a blockade that does not use force.
362. **paper blockade:** a blockade that has been declared on paper but is not being enforced by the use of ships or any other patrol method.
363. **pariah state:** a national government that refuses to abide by international law; see also failed state.
364. **partial blockade:** a blockade that is not total, in which case either a percentage of goods or particular types of goods are allowed through.
365. **passive defense:** to oppose an attack by adopting only non-active measures; see also active defense.
366. **patrol:** one or more ships cruising through a set body of water; for example, one method of deterring pirates is to patrol waters prone to piracy.
367. **peninsulas:** land surrounded by water on three sides; a fairly good geographic location to conduct a naval blockade, in particular if the land lines can be cut, although inferior to island blockades where all sea lines of communication can be cut.
368. **peripheral campaign:** a campaign outside the main theater that might impact the main front by draining much-needed troops, supplies, or ordnance from the adversary.
369. **permanent conquest:** taking an opponent's land or resources in perpetuity.
370. **phantom ship:** a ship taken by pirates, reflagged, and used to transport goods; see also ghost ship.
371. **pincer movement:** having at least two independent military attacks converging on a central point.
372. **pinprick warfare:** the use of multiple peripheral campaigns to attack an enemy at many points; although criticized by Secretary of War Stimson, pinprick warfare against Japan during World War II created significant cumulative effects over time.
373. **piracy:** the opportunistic or professional taking of ships at sea, either to steal goods from them or to use the ship itself as a phantom or ghost ship, sell it, or demand ransom from the owners.
374. **policy-strategy match:** picking a strategy that will accomplish the policy objectives.

375. **political movements:** after a successful mutiny, an attempt by the muti-neers to put pressure on the politicians of a particular country.
376. **porous blockade:** a blockade that is not total, but is partial in that there are some goods that make it through.
377. **port of embarkation:** the location where goods are exported.
378. **port of arrival:** the location where goods are imported.
379. **port state:** the government of a state that has a commercial port, and over which it has legal authority to administer all activities within that port.
380. **positive objective vs negative objective:** making something happen vs stopping something from happening.
381. **positive space:** an event that occurs that is visible to all; see also negative space.
382. **positive-sum strategy:** a course of action generally leaving both sides better off.
383. **potted plant:** the image of an inert adversary used to illustrate the point that adversaries are not inert, but will react.
384. **power projection:** the ability to put forces or ordnance anywhere into a given space.
385. **prestige:** a government's or leader's concern that it will look weak if a strategy fails, or if it loses a war; in Asia, a loss of prestige can often be discussed in terms of "losing face."
386. **prestige value:** the public relations utility of a particular thing or action, often to make the public think the government is doing a better job than it really is.
387. **prevent-defeat strategy:** a strategy designed to deny victory to one's adversary; for example, the North Vietnamese adopted an effective prevent defeat strategy in the Vietnam War.
388. **primary vs secondary enemy:** the second most important adversary, perhaps a coalition partner of the main adversary, which if attacked can weaken the primary adversary's coalition.
389. **primary vs ulterior objective:** while defeating the enemy's navy is usually the primary objective, obtaining the ulterior objective is to capture whatever the war is being fought over.
390. **principle vs practice:** the constant tug-of-war between vague truisms about maritime power versus the actual utilization of maritime power.
391. **privateering:** the legal pirating of goods and ships by having a letter of *marque* from a national government giving the shipowner permission to act on behalf of that government.
392. **prize court:** a special court set up by a government granting letters of *marque* to privateers intended to insure a fair distribution of the proceeds.

393. **prize law:** the laws adopted to determine the fair distribution of the proceeds of commerce raiding.
394. **promotion of interests movement:** a demonstration or mutiny on a ship intended to promote the financial or working interests of the crew.
395. **protracted:** to prolong or lengthen the time of a particular operation or conflict, often with the goal of gradually weakening the enemy; see also attrition warfare.
396. **Q-ship:** an armed merchant ship, often disguised.
397. **Quad:** the naval coalition composed of the United States, Japan, Australia, and India.
398. **quarantine:** a naval blockade in all but name.
399. **rate of execution:** rapid vs slow and strengthening vs intermittent vs weakening.
400. **reflagging:** to change the flag on a ship, often during a conflict, so as to avoid capture.
401. **regime change:** by the end of a conflict, one government has been overthrown and replaced with another.
402. **relative costs:** the comparative price.
403. **relative value:** the comparative value of two objectives, for example retaining home turf versus obtaining foreign territory.
404. **reverse blockade:** rather than stopping the flow of goods, the reverse blockade attempts to halt the unwanted inflow of illegal immigrants.
405. **reverse domino effect:** to prop up a country economically so that it can become a symbol of Western capitalism; see also domino effect.
406. **risk averse:** opposition to taking chances; while normally a good behavior, strategic advantages can be lost if one is too hesitant to assume risks.
407. **rules of engagement (ROE):** rules dictated by higher authority, often the commander-in-chief, that all echelons of the military must follow during the course of a conflict, usually to insure that a limited war does not inadvertently become unlimited, adheres to international law, and protects non-combatants.
408. **sanction enforcement:** using all available assets to patrol sanction limits.
409. **sanctions:** actions by one or more states against another to force it to comply with legal obligations.
410. **sanctuary:** a geographic location that is difficult to attack; for example, while Al Qaida thought that land-locked Afghanistan offered them perfect sanctuary from which to make the 9-11 attacks, a combination of special forces on the ground, plus air support from mainly naval assets, denied them this sanctuary.
411. **script-writing:** laying out the enemy's optimal strategy from one's own point of view, and assuming enemy will follow it.

412. **sea-based airpower:** aircraft operating from the sea, such as jets from an aircraft carrier.
413. **sea command:** the goal of securing dominance of the sea while denying it to one's adversary, but normally command is contested and so an uncommanded sea is the norm.
414. **sea control:** the function of protecting shipping, a beachhead, port, or other position or maritime object.
415. **sea denial:** actions to prevent access to a particular area of water to the forces of one's adversary, usually for a limited amount of time, to stop it from obtaining command of the sea; see also command of the sea and/ or sea command.
416. **sea lift capacity:** the amount of equipment and materiel that can be brought to the battlefield by sea.
417. **sea line of communication (SLOC):** sea lanes allowing for the delivery of necessary materials, including weapons, ammunition, fuel, and food.
418. **sea mine:** standard method for exerting sea denial.
419. **sea power:** a country, often an island nation, that has a combination of naval and maritime commercial strength.
420. **secession movements:** after a successful mutiny, an attempt by the mutineers to lead a movement to secede from the government in charge.
421. **seizure of power movements:** after a successful mutiny, an attempt by the mutineers to seize governmental power.
422. **sequential strategy:** adding troops and new assets one after the other in progressive steps to the same theater or to a succession of theaters, often to wear down the adversary over time.
423. **shelling from the sea:** using naval platforms to shoot at an adversary from the sea.
424. **shock and awe:** using overwhelming force to convince an adversary to give up; see also blitzkrieg.
425. **simultaneous engagement:** to act at the same time.
426. **smuggling:** to import or export goods secretly in violation of the law.
427. **social media:** internet-based pundits and bloggers outside the organized media structure.
428. **sovereign waters:** waters under the total authority of a state.
429. **special relationship:** a long-term cooperative relationship between two countries, such as the Anglo-American alliance during both world wars, or the post–World War II alliance between Japan and the United States.
430. **spheres of influence:** a land power concept of exerting power over bordering countries.
431. **spoiler:** a third party that intervenes in order to "spoil" the strategy of one of two or more belligerents, often by opening an alternate Land Line of Communication (LLOC) that cannot be easily stopped.

432. **stability of a coalition:** the trustworthiness of the membership of a naval coalition.
433. **stakeholders:** all groups impacted by a strategy, to include not just the protagonist and its adversary, but a wide range of foreign and domestic audiences including allies and coalition partners on the one hand, and voters, the press, and social media on the other hand.
434. **standoff capability:** the characteristics of sea powers being able to remain far off shore and yet influence events on land.
435. **standoff weapons:** allowing ships or aircraft to strike from beyond the enemy's defensive envelope, often with a missile of some type.
436. **starvation blockade:** a naval blockade focused specifically on cutting food to the enemy, often with a parallel humanitarian operation to feed neutrals adversely impacted by the starvation blockade.
437. **strait:** narrow passage of water connecting two large bodies of water.
438. **strategic goals:** goals set by a political or military authority to achieve national objectives.
439. **strategic victory:** to achieve the strategic goals for which the war was fought.
440. **strategic vision:** a strong sense of how to obtain the policy objective.
441. **submarine:** a weapon used for blockade and commerce raiding; for example, the bulk of the Japanese ships sunk during World War II were due to U.S. submarines.
442. **substitute markets:** another market to export goods to that cannot be cut off by a blockade; see also bottleneck.
443. **substitute products:** an alternate source of products to import that cannot be cut off by a blockade.
444. **sunk costs:** the amount of money, and/or work, put into a strategy, which would be wasted if the strategy is ended without first achieving victory.
445. **surface patrols:** the use of surface ships to conduct patrol operations, such as of a naval blockade.
446. **surprise:** taking advantage of an opponent's lack of attention.
447. **surprise attack:** taking advantage of an opponent's lack of attention to engage in attack on an unlikely or undefended target; for example, the Japanese air and naval attack on Pearl Harbor took U.S. military forces by surprise.
448. **sustainability:** the ability to bring in supplies and ordnance to keep a conflict going.
449. **symbolic vs hard targets:** a symbolic target does not necessarily hold any real military value, while a hard target does; for example, the 9-11 attacks on the World Trade Centers were mainly symbolic, while the

attack on the Pentagon was a hard target but the plane hit a section of the building under construction, and so had relatively little impact.

450. **target audience:** the main group a strategy is created to appeal to.
451. **targets:** the focus of military or political force, directly vs indirectly, and often with primary vs secondary vs tertiary targets.
452. **terminal point:** where a convoy ends.
453. **territorial integrity:** respecting the borders of nations.
454. **territorial waters:** waters right offshore that are considered to be sovereign, originally 3 nautical miles from the coast but now generally accepted to be 12 nautical miles.
455. **terror sponge:** creating a situation that attracts terrorists to one spot; similar to a Venus flytrap but with terrorists.
456. **theater of operations:** any geographic location where military actions are taking place.
457. **third-party intervention:** a country not engaged in a conflict comes to the aid of one of the adversaries.
458. **threat of invasion:** to position one's troops to appear that they might invade the adversary's territory, whether in actual fact or to put pressure on the adversary to relocate troops from one theater to another.
459. **threshold:** how close a ship's crew is to sponsoring a demonstration or mutiny.
460. **Thucydides Trap:** the view that two great powers are destined to go to war; opposing arguments point out that democratic states, especially democratic sea powers, rarely go to war with each other.
461. **tight blockade:** a blockade that is as close to total as possible, or is not stopping all goods but is halting close to all of a certain necessary good, like food or oil.
462. **time, space, force:** the main assessment methods for determining one's own military advantages versus an adversary's.
463. **time:** implementation rate, duration, and type of timing.
464. **tipping point:** the point at which an action—such as a mutiny—becomes inevitable.
465. **torpedo:** a weapon originally designed to allow a weaker navy to attack a stronger navy; for example, torpedo boats could shoot and sink much larger ships.
466. **total blockade:** a blockade in which all goods are halted.
467. **trade embargo:** one or more countries prohibit a category of trade with an adversary; greater than trade restrictions or sanctions but less than a blockade.
468. **trade restrictions:** one or more countries adopting restrictions on trade with an adversary; lesser than trade embargo.

469. **trade up:** to break with one ally or coalition partner in order to obtain an even better one; for example, after Nixon visited China in 1972 the U.S. government traded up from South Vietnam and Taiwan to the PRC.

470. **transformative psychological effect:** an event that changes public opinion on whether or not to go to war; for example, both Pearl Harbor and 9-11 had transformative psychological effects on the American public.

471. **trigger:** when discipline on a ship is precarious and only needs a single event to spark a mutiny.

472. **tripwire patrol:** sending ships through contested waters between two adversaries such that any attack will spur third-party intervention; for example, the Taiwan Patrol Force was a tripwire patrol; see also buffer patrol.

473. **Trojan horse:** pretending something is harmless when it is in fact dangerous; Trojan rabbits, by contrast, are generally harmless.

474. **unconditional surrender:** to demand complete surrender without stipulations of an adversary as a prerequisite for ending military conflict.

475. **unconditional victory:** to win a conflict without any conditions.

476. **unconventional warfare:** any type of warfare that makes use of non-traditional tactics, operations, or strategy.

477. **unlimited objectives:** when the goals of a demonstration, mutiny, or conflict include the overthrow of the national government; see also limited objectives.

478. **unrestricted submarine warfare:** submarines may sink merchant ships without warning them or taking actions to save the crew, similar to Germany in World War I and the U.S. Navy in World War II in the Pacific.

479. **value of the object (VOO):** the real worth of wartime objectives.

480. **vernier vs on/off switch:** the difference between increasing or decreasing gradually versus abruptly.

481. **vertical escalation:** when the goals of a demonstration or mutiny increase to include greater demands from the navy or national government up to and including regime change; see also horizontal escalation.

482. **vulnerable landing period:** a time space when troops are landing on a beach, or when air assets are delivering them to an in-land location, during which an adversary would have a window of opportunity to attack and destroy them.

483. **war by algebra:** the numeric evaluation of opposing forces to determine the likely winner in a conflict; see also force equation.

484. **war limited by contingent:** a peripheral campaign that is used by a sea power to "wrest the initiative from the land Powers . . . by giving

the Continental war a new direction" (McCranie, 240, citing Corbett); the Iberian campaign during the Napoleonic Wars is often cited as an example of a successful campaign of this type.

485. **war protraction:** keeping a conflict going longer.
486. **war termination:** bringing a conflict to a close.
487. **wargaming:** simulation of conflict in which actual forces are not used and in which player decisions are used to determine battle outcomes.
488. **weakest member:** to break apart an adversary's coalition it is important to focus on the weakest member and split them away first.
489. **wealth accumulation:** the ability of a country, usually a sea power, to expand their economy even while fighting a conflict.
490. **weapons impact:** while new weapons can impact the practice of naval warfare, they rarely change the underlying principles.
491. **weapons of mass destruction (WMD):** any weapon that has the potential for producing large casualties and/or extensive destruction, usually in reference to nuclear weapons.
492. **whisper diplomacy:** secret diplomacy that is conducted behind closed doors and never becomes known to the media or to public opinion; most useful when working with European leaders concerned with "honor" or "prestige" or Asian leaders concerned with "face" since any decision to back down will never become known to the public.
493. **win without fighting:** the epitome of warfare according to Sunzi, author of *The Art of War*.
494. **windjammer:** Mahan's term for a useless talker.
495. **winning vs prevent-defeat strategy:** the first attempts to defeat the enemy while the second attempts to not let the enemy defeat them.
496. **win-win vs win-lose vs lose-lose scenarios:** seeking to find strategic solutions where all parties can win or where the protagonist wins and its adversaries lose; lose-lose scenarios, such as Japan attacking every Pacific Ocean neutral power during December 1941, should be avoided at all costs.
497. **withdrawal of forces:** during a peripheral campaign it is critical to be able to remove land forces back to the sea if the situation calls for it.
498. **working conditions:** the treatment or mistreatment of a ship's crew, often source of lapses in discipline up to and including mutiny.
499. **zero sum strategy:** at the end of the conflict the losses on one side exactly equal the gains on the other; see also positive sum strategy.
500. **zone of fire:** the area where munitions are falling.

Selected Bibliography

Acerra, Martine, Merino, José, and Meyer, Jean, eds. *Les Marines de Guerre européennes, XVII–XVIIIe siècles*. Paris: Presses Universitaires de la Sorbonne, 1985.

Acerra, Martine, and Meyer, Jean. *Historie de la Marine française des origines à nos jours*. Rennes: Ouest-France, 1994.

Acerra, Martine, and Meyer, Jean. *Marines et Révolution*. Paris: Editions Ouest-France, 1988.

Aizawa Kiyoshi. "Differences Regarding Togo's Surprise Attack on Port Arthur," in *The Russo-Japanese War in Global Perspective: World War Zero*, eds. John W. Steinberg, et al. Leiden: Brill, 2005.

Albion, Robert Greenhalgh. *Naval & Maritime History: An Annotated Bibliography*, 4th ed., Revised and Expanded. Mystic, CT: Munson Institute of American Maritime History, 1972.

Alden, John. *The Fleet Submarine in the U.S. Navy: A Design and Construction History*. Annapolis, MD: Naval Institute Press, 1979.

Albion, Robert Greenhalgh, and Pope, Jennie Barnes. *Sea Lanes In Wartime: The American Experience, 1775–1942*. New York: W.W. Norton and Company, Inc., 1942.

Aldrich-Moodie, Benjamin. *Negotiating Coalition: Winning Soviet Consent to Resolution 678 against Iraq*. Princeton, NJ: Woodrow Wilson School of Public and International Affairs, 1999.

Alexander, Martin S., ed. *Knowing Your Friends: Intelligence Inside Alliances and Coalitions from 1914 to the Cold War*. Portland: Cass, 1998.

Allen, Gardner W. *A Naval History of the American Revolution*, Vol. 1. Boston, MA: Houghton Mifflin Company, 1913.

Allen, Gardner W. *Our Navy and the Barbary Corsairs*. Hamden, CT: Archon Books, 1965.

American Colonization Society, *African Repository*, Vol. 37. Washington, DC: C. Alexander, 1861.

Anderson, Fred. *Crucible of War: The Seven Years' War and the Fate of Empire in British North America, 1754–1766*. New York: Alfred A. Knopf, 2000.

Anonymous. "Extracts from An Epitome of the Chino-Japanese War," in *Chino-Japanese War, 1894–95*, ed. N.W.H. Du Boulay. London: typescript, ca. 1903.

Applegate, Michael F. *Coalition Warfare versus France, 1792–1815*. Strategy Research Project. Carlisle Barracks: U.S. Army War College, 1 April 1996.

Asada, Sadao. *From Mahan to Pearl Harbor: The Imperial Japanese Navy and the United States*. Annapolis, MD: Naval Institute Press, 2006.

Au, W. *The Sonar of Dolphins*. New York: Springer, 1993.

Baer, George W. *One Hundred Years of Sea Power*. Stanford, CA: Stanford University Press, 1993.

Bahadur, Jay. *The Pirates of Somalia: Inside Their Hidden World*. New York: Pantheon Books, 2011.

Baker, John C. and Wiencek, David G. *A Cooperative Monitoring Regime for the South China Sea: Satellite Imagery, Confidence-building Measures, and the Spratly Islands Disputes*. Westport, CT: Praeger, 2002.

Ballard, George A. *The Influence of the Sea on the Political History of Japan*. New York: E. P. Dutton, 1921.

Bane, Suda L. and Ralph H. Lutz, eds. *The Blockade of Germany after the Armistice, 1918–1919: Selected Documents of the Supreme Economic Council, Superior Blockade Council, American Relief Administration, and Other Wartime Organizations*. New York: Howard Fertig, 1972.

Barker, Ralph. *The Blockade Busters*. London: Chatto & Windus, 1976.

Barlow, Jeffrey G. *From Hot War to Cold. The U.S. Navy and National Security Affairs, 1945–1955*. Stanford, CA: Stanford University Press, 2009.

Barnett, Roger W. "Blockade and Maritime Exclusion," in *International Military and Defense Encyclopedia*, ed. Trevor N. Dupuy, Vol. 1, 381–85. Washington, DC: Brassey's, 1993.

Barnhart, Michael A. *Japan Prepares for Total War*. Ithaca, NY: Cornell, 1987.

Barrett, David P., and Shyu, Larry N., eds. *Chinese Collaboration with Japan, 1932–1945*. Stanford, CA: Stanford University Press, 2001.

Barrett, Raymond D., Jr. *Coalition Dynamics*. Study Project. Carlisle Barracks: U.S. Army War College, 15 April 1992.

Bartlett, Ruhl J., ed. *The Record of American Diplomacy*. New York: Alfred A. Knopf, 1964.

Baugh, Daniel A. *British Naval Administration in the Age of Walpole*. Princeton, NJ: Princeton University Press, 1965.

Baugh, Daniel A. *The Global Seven Years' War, 1754–1763: Britain and France in a Great Power Contest*. Harrow, UK: Longman, 2011.

Baugh, Daniel A. "Why Did Britain Lose Command of the Sea During the War for America?" in *The British Navy and the Use of Naval Power in the Eighteenth Century*, eds. J. Black and P. Woodfine. Leicester: Leicester University Press, 1988.

Bayly, Admiral Sir Lewis. *Pull Together: The Memoirs*. London: G. G. Harrap & Co., Ltd, 1939.

Beach, Commander Edward L. *Submarine!*, Bluejacket Books. Annapolis, MD: Naval Institute Press, 1952.

Beach, Edward L. *Salt and Steel*. Annapolis, MD: Naval Institute Press, 1999.

Beale, Howard K. *Theodore Roosevelt and the Rise of America to World Power*. Baltimore, MD: John Hopkins University Press, 1956.

Beasley, W. G. *A Modern History of Japan*, 2nd ed. New York: Praeger, 1974.

Beatson, Robert. *Naval and Military Memoirs of Great Britain from 1727 to 1783*, 6 Vols. London: Longman, Hurst, Rees, and Orme, 1804.

Bechtol, Denise L. *Group Dynamics: The Coalition Warfare Commander's Nightmare*. Newport, RI: U.S. Naval War College, Joint Military Operations Department, 15 June 1995.

Beckman, Robert. "Combating Piracy and Armed Robbery against Ships in Southeast Asia: The Way Forward," *Ocean Development and International Law* 33, no. 3/4 (July–December 2002): 317–41.

Beesly, Patrick. *Very Special Intelligence: The Story of the Admiralty's Operational Intelligence Centre, 1939–1945*. London: Greenhill Books, 2000.

Bell, A.C. *A History of the Blockade of Germany and of the Countries Associated with Her in the Great War: Austria-Hungary, Bulgaria, and Turkey, 1914–1918*. London: Her Majesty's Stationery Office, 1937.

Bendert, Harald. *Das UC-Boote der Kaiserlichen Marine, 1914–1918*. Hamburg, Berlin, Bonn: E.S. Mittler, 2001.

Bennett, Frank M. *The Monitor and the Navy Under Steam*. Boston, MA: Houghton Mifflin, 1900.

Benoit, Charles. "Vietnam's 'Boat People'," in *The Third Indochina Conflict*, eds. David W. P. Elliott. Boulder, CO: Westview Press, 1981.

Benzon, Anne Cipriano, ed. *The United States in the First World War: An Encyclopedia*. Garland Press, 1995.

Bernath, Stuart L. *Squall across the Atlantic: American Civil War Prize Cases and Diplomacy*. Berkeley, CA: University of California Press, 1970.

Best, Antony, ed. *Imperial Japan and the World, 1931–1945: Critical Concepts in Asian Studies*. London: Routledge, 2011.

Biddle, Alexander, ed. *Old Family Letters*. Philadelphia, PA: J.B. Lippincott, 1892.

Biddulph, Colonel John. *The Pirates of Malabar*. London: Smith, Elder & Co., 1907.

Binaud, Daniel. *Les corsaires de Bordeaux et de l'estuaire. 120 ans de guerres sur mer*. Biarritz: Atlantica, 1999.

Bix, Herbert P. *Hirohito and the Making of Modern Japan*. New York: HarperCollins, 2000.

Blair, Clay. *Hitler's U-Boat War. The Hunters 1939–1942*. New York: Random House, 1996.

Blair, Clay, Jr. *Silent Victory: The U.S. Submarine War Against Japan*. Philadelphia, PA: J.B. Lippincott Company, 1975.

Blyth, Captain Ken, with Corris, Peter. *Petro Pirates: The Hijacking of the Petro Ranger*. St. Leonards, Australia: Allen & Unwin, 2000.

Bogdenko, V.L. "Stranitsy starykh bloknotov," in *Leningradtsy v Ispanii: Sbornik vospominami*, 3rd ed. Leningrad: Lenizdat, 1989.

Bogolepov, V. P. *Blockade and Counterblockade: Struggle on Ocean-Sea Lanes in World War II*. Arlington, VA: Joint Publications Research Service, 1971.

Bonnel, Ulane. *La France, les États Unis et la guerre de Course (1797–1815)*. Paris: Nouvelles Éditions Latines, 1961.

Bosscher, Ph. M. *De Koninklijke Marine in de Tweede Wereldoorlog*. Franeker: Wever, 1984.

Boulle, Pierre Henri. "The French Colonies and the Reform of their Administration during and following the Seven Years' War," Ph.D. dissertation, University of California at Berkley, 1968.

Bourgerie, Raymond and Lesouef, Pierre. *Palikao (1860), Le Sac du Palais d'Été et la prise de Pékin*. Paris: Economica, 1995.

Bove, A. A., ed. *Bove and Davis' Diving Medicine*. Elsevier-Saunders Publishers, 2004.

Bowen, Herbert W. *Recollections Diplomatic and Undiplomatic*. New York: Grafton Press, 1926.

Bowler, R. Arthur. *Logistics and the Failure of the British Army in America, 1775–1783*. Princeton, NJ: Princeton University Press, 1975.

Bowman, M.L. *Multinational Maritime Operations*. Norfolk: U.S. Department of the Navy, Naval Doctrine Command, September 1996. 1 Vol.

Boxer, Charles R. *The Dutch Seaborne Empire: 1600–1800*. New York: Alfred A. Knopf, 1965.

Bradlee, Francis B. *Blockade Running during the Civil War and the Effect of Land and Water Transportation on the Confederacy*. Philadelphia, PA: Porcupine, 1974.

Brice, Martin. *Axis Blockade Runners of World War II*. Annapolis, MD: Naval Institute Press, 1981.

Briggs, Herbert W. *The Doctrine of Continuous Voyage*. Baltimore, MD: Johns Hopkins Press, 1926.

Brodie, Bernard. *A Guide to Naval Strategy*. Princeton, NJ: Princeton University Press, 1944.

Brooke, James. "A Friendly Encounter with Illanun Pirates," in *Adventures and Encounters: Europeans in South-East Asia*, ed. Gullick, J.M. Kuala Lumpur. Malaysia: Oxford University Press, 1995.

Brooks, George E., Jr. *The Kru Mariner in the Nineteenth Century: An Historical Compendium*. Newark, DE: Liberian Studies Association in America, 1972.

Browning, Robert M., Jr. *From Cape Charles to Cape Fear: The North Atlantic Blockading Squadron during the Civil War*. Tuscaloosa, AL: University of Alabama Press, 1993.

Browning, Robert M., Jr. *Success Is All That Was Expected: The South Atlantic Blockading Squadron during the Civil War*. Washington, DC: Brassey's, 2002.

Bruyneel, Mark. *Comparison of 2002 Figures of the International Maritime Bureau*. International Maritime Bureau, Piracy Reporting Centre, 19 April 2003.

Buel, Richard, Jr. *In Irons: Britain's Naval Supremacy and the American Revolutionary Economy*. New Haven, CT: Yale University Press, 1998.

Bulloch, James D. *The Secret Service of the Confederate States in Europe, or How the Confederate Cruisers were Equipped*. New York: Modern Library, 2001.

Burkman, Thomas W. *Japan and the League of Nations: Empire and World Order, 1914–1938.* Honolulu, HI: University of Hawai'i Press, 2008.

Burrell, William. *Reports of Cases Determined by the High Court of Admiralty and Upon Appeal Therefrom, . . . Together with Extracts from the Books and Records of the High Court of Admiralty and the Court of the Judges Delegates, 1584–1839,* ed. Reginald G. Marsden. London: William Clowes and Sons, Limited, 1885.

Butel, Paul. *The Atlantic.* London: Routledge, 1999.

Cababé, Michael. *The Freedom of the Seas: The History of a German Trap.* London: John Murray, 1918.

Canney, Donald L. *Africa Squadron: The U.S. Navy and the Slave Trade, 1842–1861.* Washington, DC: Potomac Books, Inc., 2006.

Canny, Nicholas, ed. *The Origins of Empire: British Overseas Enterprise to the Close of the Seventeenth Century,* Vol. 1 of *The Oxford History of the British Empire,* ed. Wm. Roger Louis. Oxford: Oxford University Press, 1998.

Capp, Bernard. *Cromwell's Navy: The Fleet and the English Revolution, 1648–1660.* Oxford: Clarendon Press, 1989.

Carse, Robert. *The Age of Piracy.* London: Robert Hale Ltd., 1957.

Carse, Robert. *Blockade: The Civil War at Sea.* New York: Rinehart, 1958.

Carter, Alice Clare. *The Dutch Republic in Europe in the Seven Years' War.* London: Macmillan, 1971.

Casse, Michel. "Un armateur en course bordelaise sous la Révolution et l'Empire: Jacques Conte, 1753–1836," in *Bordeaux, porte océane, carrefour européen,* Actes du 50ᵉ congrès de la Fédération Historique du Sud-Ouest. Bordeaux: FHSO, 1999.

Cassells' History of the Russo-Japanese War, Vol. II. New York: Cassell and Company Ltd, 1905.

Chaitin, Peter. *The Coastal War: Chesapeake Bay to Río Grande.* Alexandria, VA: Time Life, 1984.

Chalk, Peter. "Grey-Area Phenomena in Southeast Asia: Piracy, Drug Trafficking and Political Terrorism," *Canberra Papers on Strategy and Defence,* no. 123 (1997).

Chalk, Peter. *Non-Military Security and Global Order: The Impact of Extremism, Violence and Chaos on National and International Security.* London: Macmillan, 2002.

Chapelle, Howard I. *The History of The American Sailing Navy: The Ships and Their Development.* Reprint of Edition from New York: Norton, 1949.

Charbonnel, Nicole. *Commerce et course sous la Révolution et le Consulat à La Rochelle: autour de deux armateurs: les frères Thomas et Pierre-Antoine Chegaray.* Paris: PUF, 1977.

Chatterton, E. Keble. *The Big Blockade.* London: Hurst & Blackett, 1932.

Chatterton, E. Keble. *Danger Zone: The Story of the Queenstown Command.* Boston, MA: Little, Brown, 1934.

Chayes, Abram. *The Cuban Missile Crisis.* New York: Oxford University Press, 1974.

Chesneaux, Jean, ed. *Popular Movements and Secret Societies in China, 1840–1950.* Stanford, CA: Stanford University Press, 1972.

Choudhry, H. Mashhud. *Coalition Warfare: Can the Gulf War-91 Be the Model for Future?* Study Project. Carlisle Barracks: U.S. Army War College, 21 February 1992.

Chow, Jen Hwa. *China and Japan: The History of Chinese Diplomatic Missions in Japan 1877–1911.* Singapore: Chopmen Enterprises, 1975.

Ciano, Galeazzo. *Diary, 1937–1943.* New York: Enigma, 2002.

Civil War Naval Chronology, 1861–1865. Vol. 1. Washington, DC: Naval History Division, Navy Department, 1972.

Clarke, Frank G. *The History of Australia.* London: Greenwood Press, 2002.

Clark, John G. *La Rochelle and the Atlantic Economy during the Eighteenth Century.* Baltimore, MD: The Johns Hopkins University Press, 1981.

Clark, William Bell. *Ben Franklin's Privateers: A naval epic of the American Revolution.* Baton Rouge, LA: Louisiana State University Press, 1956.

Clark, William Bell. *George Washington's Navy: Being an Account of His Excellency's Fleet in New England Waters.* Baton Rouge, LA: Louisiana State University, 1960.

Clauder, Anne. *American Commerce as Affected by the Wars of the French Revolution and Napoleon, 1793–1812.* Philadelphia, PA: University of Pennsylvania, 1932 [reprint. 1972].

Clowes, William Laird. *The Royal Navy: A History from the Earliest Times to the Present,* 7 Vols. London: Sampson Low, Marston and Company, 1897–1903.

Clune, Frank and Stephensen, P.R. *The Pirates of the Brig Cyprus.* London: Rupert Hart-Davis, 1962.

Cochran, Hamilton. *Blockade Runners of the Confederacy.* Indianapolis, IN: Bobbs-Merrill, 1958.

Cohen, William S. "Allied and Coalition Efforts." in *Annual Report to the President and the Congress,* 145–46. Posture Statement presented to the 106th Cong., 1st sess. Washington, DC: U.S. Department of Defense, 1999.

Cohn, Elizabeth. "President Kennedy's Decision to Impose a Blockade in the Cuban Missile Crisis: Building Consensus in the ExComm after the Decision," in *The Cuban Missile Crisis Revisited,* ed. James A. Nathan, chap. 7, 219–35. New York: St. Martin's, 1992.

Collin, Richard H. *Theodore Roosevelt, Culture, Diplomacy, and Expansion: A New View of American Imperialism.* Baton Rouge, LA: Louisiana State University Press, 1985.

Collin, Richard H. *Theodore Roosevelt's Caribbean.* Baton Rouge, LA: Louisiana State University Press, 1990.

Collinge, Robert A., and Ayers, Ronald M. *Economics by Design: Principles and Issues.* Upper Saddle River, NJ: Prentice-Hall, 2000.

Colombos, C. John. *The International Law of the Sea,* 6th revised ed. London: Longman Group, 1967.

Coltman, Robert, Jr. *The Chinese, Their Present and Future: Medical, Political, and Social.* Philadelphia, PA: F. A. Davis, Publisher, 1891.

Commonwealth of Australia. *Select Committee on A Certain Maritime Incident: Report.* Canberra: Senate Printing Unit, 2002.

Condit, Howard. *General George C. Marshall, Strategic Leadership and Coalition Warfare*. Strategy Research Project. Carlisle Barracks: U.S. Army War College, 15 April 1996.

Conroy, Hilary, and Wray, Harry, eds. *Pearl Harbor Reexamined: Prologue to the Pacific War*. Honolulu, HI: University of Hawaii Press, 1990.

Consett, M.W.W.P. and Daniel, O. H. *The Triumph of Unarmed Forces (1914–1918): An Account of the Transactions by which Germany during the Great War Was Able To Obtain Supplies prior to Her Collapse under the Pressure of Economic Forces*. London: Williams and Norgate, 1928.

Conway, Stephen. *War, State, and Society in Mid-Eighteenth-Century Britain and Ireland*. Oxford: Oxford University Press, 2006.

Cooling, Benjamin Franklin. *Gray Steel and Blue Water Navy: The Formative Years of America's Military-Industrial Complex 1881–1917*. Hamden, CT: Archon Books, 1979.

Corbett, Julian S. *England in the Seven Years' War: A Study in Combined Strategy*, 2 Vols. London: Longmans, Green, and Co., 1907 [1918].

Corbett, Julian S. *Maritime Operations in the Russo-Japanese War: 1904–1905*, Vol. 2. Annapolis, MD: Naval Institute Press, 1994.

Corbett, Julian S. *Some Principles of Maritime Strategy with an Introduction and Notes by Eric J. Grove*. Classics of Sea Power Series. Annapolis, MD: Naval Institute Press, 1988.

Costello, John, and Tsarev, Oleg. *Deadly Illusions*. New York: Crown, 1993.

Cotran, R. S., Kumar, V., and Collins, T. *Robbins Pathologic Basis of Disease*, 6th ed. Philadelphia, PA: W.B. Saunders Publishers, 1999.

Coughlin, William J., and Theodore C. Mataxis. "Coalition Warfare," in *Encyclopedia of the American Military*, eds. John E. Jessup and Louise B. Ketz, Vol. 3, pp. 1709–36. New York: Scribner's, 1994.

Couteau-Bégarie, Hervé. *L'histoire maritime en France*. Paris: Economica, 1995.

Coverdale, John F. *Italian Intervention in the Spanish Civil War*. Princeton, NJ: Princeton University Press, 1975.

Cowman, Ian. *Dominion or Decline: Anglo-American Relations in the Pacific, 1937–1941*. Oxford: BERG, 1996.

Craig, Gordon A. "Problems of Coalition Warfare: The Military Alliance against Napoleon, 1813–1814," in *The Harmon Memorial Lectures in Military History, 1959–1987*, ed. Harry R. Borowski, 325–46. Washington, DC: U.S. Air Force, Office of Air Force History, 1988.

Croston, Glenn. *The Real Story of Risk: Adventures in a Hazardous World*. Amherst, NY: Prometheus Books, 2012.

Crouzet, François. *L'économie britannique et le blocus continental, 1806–1813*, 2nd ed. Paris: Economica, 1987.

Crow, Hugh. *The Memoirs of Captain Hugh Crow: The Life and Times of a Slave Trade Captain*. Oxford: Bodleian Library, 2007.

Crowhurst, Patrick. *The Defence of British Trade, 1689–1815*. Folkestone, Kent: Wm Dawson & Sons Ltd, 1975.

Crowhurst, Patrick. *The French War on Trade: privateering, 1793–1815.* London: Scolar Press, 1989.

Curwen, C. A. *Taiping Rebel, The Deposition of Li Hsiu-ch'eng.* London: Cambridge University Press, 1977.

Cushman, John H., Sr. *Command and Control of Theater Forces: Issues in Mideast Coalition Command.* Cambridge: Harvard University, Center for Information Policy Research, Program on Information Resources Policy, February 1991.

Cutler, Carl C. *Greyhounds of the Sea.* Annapolis, MD: Naval Institute Press, 1984.

Dalzell, George W. *The Flight from the Flag: The Continuing Effect of the Civil War Upon the American Carrying Trade.* Chapel Hill, NC: University of North Carolina Press, 1940.

Daniels, Josephus. *Our Navy at War.* New York: G. H. Doran, 1922.

Danzik, Wayne. *Participation of Coalition Forces in the Korean War.* Newport, RI: U.S. Naval War College, 17 June 1994.

David, Gregory S. *Piracy in Southeast Asia: A Growing Threat to the United States' Vital Strategic and Commercial Interests.* Quantico, VA: Marine Corps Command and Staff College, 2002.

Davis, Peter E. *United States Army Special Forces Coalition Support Operations: Mission or Collateral Activity.* M.A. Thesis. Fort Leavenworth: U.S. Army Command and General Staff College, 2 June 1995.

Davis, Sir John Francis. *China, During the War and Since the Peace.* Wilmington, Delaware: Scholarly Resources Inc., 1972.

de Guttry, Andrea, and Ronzitti, Natalino, eds. *The Iran-Iraq War* (1980–1988) *and the Law of Naval Warfare.* Cambridge: Grotius, 1993.

de Vattel, Emer. *The Law of Nations; or, Principles of the Law of Nature: Applied to the Conduct and Affairs of Nations and Sovereigns.* London: G. G. J. and J. Robinson, 1793.

Deane, Henry B. *The Law of Blockade: Its History, Present Condition, and Probable Future: An International Law Essay, 1870.* London: Longmans, Green, Reader, and Dyer, 1870.

Deane, James P. *The Law of Blockade as Contained in the Report of Eight Cases Argued and Determined in the High Court of Admiralty on the Blockade of the Coast of Courland, 1854.* London: Butterworths, 1855.

Defoe, Daniel. *A General History of the Robberies and Murders of the Most Notorious Pyrates.* New York: Garland Publishing, Inc., 1972.

Delaney, Norman C. *John McIntosh Kell of the Raider Alabama.* Tuscaloosa, AL: The University of Alabama Press, 1973.

DeLany, Walter S. *Bayly's Navy.* Washington, DC: Naval Historical Foundation, 1980.

Dennis, Alfred P. *Adventures in American Diplomacy, 1896–1906.* New York: E. P. Dutton, 1928.

Departement van Defensie. *Jaarboek van de Koninklijke Marine, 1936–37.* The Hague: Algemeene Landsdrukkerij, 1938.

Despain, Jeffrey W. *Operations of the Western Gulf Blockading Squadron and the Department of the Gulf in the Gulf of Mexico, 1862–1864.* Fort Leavenworth, KS: U.S. Army Command and General Staff College, 1996.

Dewey, George. *Autobiography of George Dewey.* Annapolis, MD: Naval Institute Press, 1987.

Diène, Doudou, ed. *From Chains to Bonds: The Slave Trade Revisited.* New York: Berghahn Books, 2001.

Dillon, Dana R. *Piracy in Asia: a Growing Barrier to Maritime Trade.* The Heritage Foundation. Policy Research & Analysis, 22 June 2000.

Do, Kiem and Kane, Julie. *Counterpart: A South Vietnamese Naval Officer's War.* Annapolis, MD: Naval Institute Press, 1998.

Dobson, [John]. *Chronological Annals of the War, from its Beginning to the Present Time.* Oxford: At the Clarendon Press, 1763.

Documents on British Foreign Policy, 1919–1939. 2nd Series, Vol. 18. London: HMSO, 1980.

Documents on German Foreign Policy, 1918–1945. Series D, Vol. 3: "Germany and the Spanish Civil War." Washington, DC: United States Government Printing Office, 1950.

Dodington, George Bubb. *The Diary of the Late George Bubb Dodington.* Salisbury: E. Easton, 1784.

Dönitz, Karl. *Memoirs. Ten Years and Twenty Days,* [with an Introduction and Afterword by Jürgen Rohwer]. Annapolis, MD: Naval Institute Press, 1990.

Dorn, Walter L. *Competition for Empire, 1740–1763.* New York: Harper & Row, Publishers, 1963.

Dow, George Francis. *Slave Ships and Slaving.* Salem, MA: Marine Research Society, 1927.

Dower, John W. *Embracing Defeat: Japan in the Wake of World War II.* New York: W.W. Norton & Company/The New Press, 1999.

Drake, Richard. *Revelations of a Slave Smuggler: Being the Autobiography of Capt. Rich'd Drake, An African Trader For Fifty Years—From 1807 to 1857; During Which Period He Was Concerned In The Transportation Of Half A Million Blacks From African Coasts to America.* New York: Robert M. DeWitt Publisher, 1860; Repub. Northbrook, Ill.: Metro Books, 1972.

Drea, Edward J. *Japan's Imperial Army: Its Rise and Fall, 1853–1945.* Lawrence, KS: University of Kansas Press, 2009.

Dreifort, John E. *Yvon Delbos at the Quai d'Orsay: French Foreign Policy during the Popular Front, 1936–1938.* Lawrence, KS: University Press of Kansas, 1973.

Du Pont, Samuel F. "The Blockade: 1862–1863," in *Samuel Francis Du Pont: Selection from His Civil War Letters,* Vol. 2, 3 Vols. Ithaca, NY: Cornell University Press for the Eleutherian Mills Historical Library, 1969.

Ducéré, Édouard. *Les corsaires basques et bayonnais sous la République et l'Empire.* Bayonne: A. Lamaignère, 1898.

Dudley, Wade G. *Splintering the Wooden Wall: The British Blockade of the United States, 1812–1815.* Annapolis, MD: Naval Institute Press, 2003.

Dudley, William S., and Crawford, Michael J., eds. *The Naval War of 1812: A Documentary History.* Washington, DC: Naval Historical Center, 1992.

Dull, Jonathan R. *The French Navy and the Seven Years' War.* Lincoln, NB: University of Nebraska Press, 2005.

Dunnigan, James F., and Austin Bay. *From Shield to Storm: High-Tech Weapons, Military Strategy, and Coalition Warfare in the Persian Gulf.* New York: Morrow, 1992.

Durkin, Michael F. *Naval Quarantine: A New Addition to the Role of Sea Power.* Maxwell Air Force Base, AL: Air University: Air War College, 1964.

Eargle, Lisa A., and Esmail, Ashraf, eds. *Black Beaches and Bayous: The BP Deepwater Horizon Oil Spill Disaster.* New York: University Press of America, 2012.

Earle, Peter. *The Pirate Wars.* New York: St. Martin's Press, 2003.

Easter, Cornelius. *Organizational Climate Building and Culture Integration in Coalition Warfare.* Strategy Research Project. Carlisle Barracks: U.S. Army War College, 15 April 1996.

Eastlake, Warrington, and Yamada Yoshi-aki. *Heroic Japan: A History of the War between China & Japan.* 1897; reprint, Washington, DC: University Publications of America, 1979.

Eckert, Edward K. *Navy Department in the War of 1812.* Gainesville, FL: University of Florida Press, 1973.

Edmonds, C., Lowry, C., Pennefather, J., and Walker, R. *Diving and Subaquatic Medicine,* 4th ed. London: Arnold Publishers, 2002.

Eklof, Stefan. *Pirates in Paradise: A Modern History of Southeast Asia's Maritime Marauders.* Copenhagen, Denmark: Nordic Institute of Asian Studies, 2006.

Elleman, Bruce A. *High Seas Buffer: The Taiwan Patrol Force, 1950–1979.* Newport, RI: NWC Press, 2012.

Elleman, Bruce A. *Modern Chinese Warfare, 1795–1989.* London: Routledge, 2001.

Elleman, Bruce A. *Seaborne Perils: Piracy, Maritime Crime, and Naval Terrorism in Africa, South Asia, and Southeast Asia.* Lanham, MD: Rowman & Littlefield, 2018.

Elleman, Bruce A. *Taiwan's Offshore Islands: Pathway or Barrier?* Newport, RI: NWC Press, 2019.

Elleman, Bruce A. *Waves of Hope: The U.S. Navy's Response to the Tsunami in Northern Indonesia.* Newport, RI: NWC Press, 2007.

Elleman, Bruce A. and Bell, Christopher M., eds. *Naval Mutinies of the Twentieth Century: An International Perspective.* London: Frank Cass, 2003.

Elleman, Bruce A., and Bussert, James C. *People's Liberation Army Navy: Combat Systems Technology, 1949–2010.* Annapolis, MD. Naval Institute Press, 2011.

Elleman, Bruce A., Forbes, Andrew, and Rosenberg, David, eds. *Piracy and Maritime Crime: Historical and Modern Case Studies.* Newport, RI: NWC Press, 2010.

Elleman, Bruce A., and Paine, S.C.M., eds. *Commerce Raiding: Historical Case Studies, 1755–2009.* Newport, RI: NWC Press, 2013.

Elleman, Bruce A., and Paine, S.C.M. *Modern China: Continuity and Change 1644 to the Present.* Boston, MA: Prentice Hall, 2010.

Elleman, Bruce A., and Paine, S.C.M., eds. *Naval Blockades and Seapower: Strategies and Counter-strategies, 1805–2005.* London: Routledge, 2006.

Elleman, Bruce A., and Paine, S.C.M., eds. *Naval Coalition Warfare: From the Napoleonic War to Operation Iraqi Freedom.* London: Routledge Press, 2008.

Elleman, Bruce A., and Paine, S.C.M., eds. *Naval Power and Expeditionary Warfare: Peripheral campaigns and new theatres of naval warfare.* London: Routledge Press, 2011.

Elleman, Bruce A., and Paine, S.C.M., eds. *Navies and Soft Power: Historical Case Studies of Naval Power and the Nonuse of Military Force.* Newport, RI: NWC Press, 2015.

Ellen, Eric. "Piracy Worldwide," in *Asia's Security Challenges*, ed. Wilfried A. Herrmann. Commack, NY: Nova Science Publishers, 1998.

Ellen, Eric, ed. *Shipping at Risk: "The Rising Tide of Organized Crime."* Paris: ICC Publishing SA, 1997.

Ellis, Eric. "Singapore's New Straits; Piracy on the High Seas Is on the Rise in Southeast Asia." *Fortune International* (29 September 2003): 24.

Ellis, John. *Brute Force: Allied Strategy and Tactics in the Second World War.* New York: Viking Books, 1990.

Epkenhans, Michael. "Technology, Shipbuilding and Future Combat in Germany, 1880–1914," in *Technology and Naval Combat in the Twentieth Century and Beyond*, ed. Phillips Payson O'Brien. London: Frank Cass, 2001.

Epkenhans, Michael. *Tirpitz: Architect of the German High Seas Fleet.* Washington, DC: Potomac Books, 2008.

Esthus, Raymond A. *Theodore Roosevelt and Japan.* Seattle, WA: University of Washington Press, 1967.

Evans, David C., and Peattie, Mark R. *Kaigun: Strategy, Tactics, and Technology of the Imperial Japanese Navy 1887–1941.* Annapolis, MD: Naval Institute Press, 1997.

Ewell, Judith. *Venezuela: A Century of Change.* Stanford, CA: Stanford University Press, 1984.

Falconer, William. *A New Universal Dictionary of the Marine.* London: T. Cadell and W. Davies, 1769 [1815].

Farrar, Marjorie M. *Conflict and Compromise: The Strategy, Politics and Diplomacy of the French Blockade, 1914–1918.* The Hague: Martinus Nijhoff, 1974.

Fauchille, Paul. *Du blocus maritime: étude de droit international et de droit comparé.* Paris: Librairie nouvelle de droit et de jurisprudence, 1882.

Fayle, C. Ernest. *Seaborne Trade.* 3 Vols. London: John Murray, 1920–1924, Vol. II.

Fernow, Berthold, ed. *New York (Colony) Council. Calendar of Council Minutes, 1668–1783.* Harrison, NY: Harbor Hill Books, 1987.

Fowler, William M., Jr. *Rebels Under Sail: The American Navy During the Revolution.* New York: Charles Scribner's Sons, 1976.

Francis, E.V. *The Battle for Supplies.* London: Jonathan Cape, 1942.

Franco, Lucas Molina, and Manrique, José María. *Legion Condor: La historia olvidada.* Valladolid: Quirón, 2000.

Frank, Willard. "The Atlantic in the Strategic Perspective of Hitler and Roosevelt, 1940–1941," in *To Die Gallantly. The Battle of the Atlantic*, eds. Timothy J. Runyan and Jan M. Copes. San Francisco: Westview Press 1994.

Frank, Willard. "The Campaign: The German Perspective," in *The Battle of the Atlantic 1939 1945. The 50th Anniversary International Conference*, eds. Stephen Howarth and Derk Law. London: Greenhill Books, 1994.

Frank, Willard. "Die deutsche Seekriegführung 1943 bis 1943 [German Naval Warfare 1943–1945]," in *Das Deutsche Reich und der Zweite Weltkrieg*, Vol. 10: *Der Zusammenbruch des Deutschen Reiches 1945, Part I: Die militärische Niederwerfung der Wehrmacht*. Munich: Deutsche Verlags-Anstalt, 2008.

Frank, Willard. "The War at Sea in the Atlantic and in the Arctic Ocean," in *Germany and the Second World War*, Vol. 6: *The Global War. Widening of the Conflict into a World War and the Shift of the Initiative 1941–1943*, eds. Horst Boog, Werner Rahn, Reinhard Stumpf, Bernd Wegner. Oxford: Clarendon Press, 2001.

Frank, Willard C., Jr. "German Clandestine Submarine Warfare in the Spanish Civil War, 1936," in *New Interpretations in Naval History: Selected Papers from the Ninth Naval History Symposium Held at the United States Naval Academy, 18–20 October 1989*, eds. William R. Roberts and Jack Sweetman. Annapolis, MD: Naval Institute Press, 1991.

Frank, Willard C., Jr. "The Nyon Arrangement 1937: Mediterranean Security and the Coming of the Second World War," in *Regions, Regional Organizations and Military Power: XXXIII International Congress of Military History, 2007*, ed. Thean Potgieter. Stellenbosch: South African Military History Commission/ African Sun Media, 2008.

Friends, Society of, Philadelphia, Yearly Meeting. *An Exposition of the African Slave Trade, From the Year 1840, to 1850, Inclusive, Prepared from Official Documents, and Published by Direction of the Representatives of the Religions Society of Friends, in Pennsylvania, New Jersey, and Delaware*. Philadelphia, PA: J. Rakestraw, 1851; repub. Detroit, Michigan: Negro History Press, 1969.

Fromm, D. M. and McEachern, J. F. *Acoustic Modelling of the New Providence Channel*. Washington, DC: U.S. Office of Naval Research, 2000.

Fuehrer Conferences in Matters dealing with the German Navy. 7 Vols. Washington, DC: Secretary of the Navy, 1947.

Fuehrer Conferences on Naval Affairs 1939–1945. Annapolis, MD: Naval Institute Press, 1990.

Fuehrer Directives and Other Top-Level Directives of the German Armed Forces 1939–1941. Naval War College, Henry E. Eccles Library. Typescript Translation [Office of Naval Intelligence] Washington, DC, 1948.

Fuller, William C., Jr. *Strategy and Power in Russia, 1600–1914*. New York: The Free Press, 1992.

Furlong, Ronald L. *Future Coalitions: Learning from the Past, Look to the Future and Listening to Our Allies*. Newport, RI: U.S. Naval War College, Department of Operations, 18 May 1998.

Gallois, Napoléon. *Les corsaires français sous la république et l'Empire*. 2 Vols. Le Mans: Julien, Lanier et Cie, 1854.

Gannon, Tina. "International Law of the Sea: Reconciling the Law of Piracy and Terrorism in the Wake of September 11th," *Tulane Maritime Law Journal* 27, no. 1(Winter 2002): 257–75.

Gantenbein, James W. *The Doctrine of Continuous Voyage, Particularly as Applied to Contraband and Blockade*. Portland, OR: Keystone, 1929.

Gardiner, Robert, ed. *The Naval War of 1812*. London: Caxton in association with the National Maritime Museum, 1998 [2001].

Gardiner, Robert, ed. *Navies and the American Revolution, 1775–1783*. London: Chatham Publishing, in association with the National Maritime Museum, 1996.

Gehrki, Frank J. *Coalition Warfare under the Duke of Marlborough during the War of Spanish Succession*. Study Project. Carlisle Barracks: U.S. Army War College, 15 April 1992.

Gemzell, Carl-Axel. *Organisation, Conflict and Innovation: A Study of German Naaval Strategic Planning, 1888–1940*. Lund: Esselte Studium, 1973.

Gerace, Michael P. *Military Power, Conflict and Trade*. London: Frank Cass, 2004.

Giangreco, D. M. *Hell to Pay: Operation DOWNFALL and the Invasion of Japan, 1945–1947*. Annapolis, MD: Naval Institute Press, 2009.

Gibson, R.H., and Prendergast, Maurice. *The German Submarine War, 1914–1918*. London: Constable, 1931.

Gill, Martin. "Security at Sea: Fraud, Piracy and the Failure of Police Cooperation Internationally," *International Relations* 13, no. 3 (December 1996): 43–58.

Gilliland, C. Herbert. *USS Constellation on the Dismal Coast: Willie Leonard's Journal, 1859–1861*. Columbia, SC: University of South Carolina Press, 2013.

Gilliland, C. Herbert. *Voyage to the Thousand Cares: Master's Mate Lawrence with the African Squadron, 1844–1846*. Annapolis, MD: Naval Institute Press, 2004.

Gipson, Lawrence Henry. *The British Empire Before the American Revolution*, 15 Vols. New York: Alfred A. Knopf, 1939–70.

Gleaves, Albert. *The Admiral*. Pasadena, CA: Hope Publishing, 1985.

Glete, Jan. *Navies and Nations: Warships, Navies and State Building in Europe and America, 1500–1860*. Vol. 2. Stockholm: Almqvist and Wiksell International, 1993.

Gol'dberg, David Isaakovich. *Внешняя политика Японии (сентябрь 1939 г.-декабрь 1941 г.)* (*The Foreign Policy of Japan [September 1939–December 1941]*). Moscow: Издательство восточной литературы, 1959.

Goldman, Emily O. *Sunken Treaties: Naval Arms Control Between the Wars*. University Park, PA: The Pennsylvania State University Press, 1994.

Görlitz, Walter, ed. *The Kaiser and His Court: The Diaries, Notebooks and Letters of Admiral George Alexander von Müller Chief of the Naval Cabinet, 1914–1918*. English translation. London: Macdonald, 1961.

Gottschalk, Jack A., and Flanagan, Brian P., with Kahn, Lawrence J., and LaRochelle, Dennis M. *Jolly Roger with an Uzi: the Rise and Threat of Modern Piracy*. Annapolis, MD: Naval Institute Press, 2000.

Gottschall, Terrell D. *By Order of the Kaiser*. Annapolis, MD: Naval Institute Press, 2003.

Graham, Gerald S. *The China Station: War and Diplomacy 1830–1860*. Oxford: Clarendon Press, 1978.

Grainger, John D. *The Maritime Blockade of Germany in the Great War: The Northern Patrol, 1914–1918*. Aldershot, Hants, UK: Ashgate for the Navy Records Society, 2003.

Grant, Bruce. *The Boat People: An 'Age' Investigation*. New York: Penguin Books, 1979.

Gregory, William A. *Opening Pandora's Box: The U.S. Army in Combined Contingency Operations*. Fort Leavenworth: U.S. Army Command and General Staff College, School of Advanced Military Studies, 1991.

Grissim, John. "Piracy Returns." *Coast Guard*, 6 (September 1997): 18–20.

Grivel, Richild. *De la guerre maritime avant et depuis les nouvelles inventions*. Paris: Arthus Bertrand, 1869.

Groth, Carl H. *Standardization and Interoperability in Future Army Operations*. Bethesda, MD: Logistics Management Institute, May 1992.

Guffey, Howard R. *Historical Review and Evaluation of Combined Army Operations for Deputy Chief of Staff for Doctrine, Training and Doctrine Command*. Alexandria: Military Professional Resources, 1990.

Guichard, Louis. *The Naval Blockade, 1914–1918*. New York: D. Appleton, 1930.

Guilliatt, Richard, and Hohnen, Peter. *The Wolf*. New York: Free Press, 2010.

Gustaitis, Peter J., II. *Coalition Special Operations: An Operational-Level View*. Strategy Research Project. Carlisle Barracks: U.S. Army War College, 1 June 1998.

Güth, Rolf. *Von Revolution zu Revolution: Entwicklungen und Führungsprobleme der deutschen Marine 1848–1918*. Herford: E.S. Mittler, 1978.

Hackworth, Green H. "Blockade," in *Digest of International Law*, Vol. 7, chapter XXII, parts 623–626, 114–134. Washington, DC: U.S. Gov't. Print. Off., 1943.

Hagan, Kenneth J. "The Birth of American Naval Strategy," in *Strategy in the American War of Independence*, eds. Donald Stoker, Kenneth J. Hagan, and Michael T. McMaster. New York: Routledge, 2010.

Hagan, Kenneth J. *This People's Navy: The Making of American Sea Power*. New York: The Free Press, 1991.

Halberstam, David. "Terrorism on the High Seas: The Achille Lauro—Piracy and the IMO Convention on Marine Safety," *American Journal of International Law* 82 (1988): 269–310.

Hall, John W., Jansen, Marius B., Kanai, Madoka, and Twitchett, Denis, eds. *The Cambridge History of Japan The Twentieth Century*, Vol. 6. Cambridge: Cambridge University Press, 1988.

Halpern, Paul G. *A Naval History of World War I*. Annapolis, MD: Naval Institute Press, 1994.

Halpern, Paul G. *The Naval War in the Mediterranean, 1914–1918*. London and Annapolis, MD: Allen & Unwin/Naval Institute Press, 1987.

Halusky, J. G., ed. *Artificial Reef Research Diver's Handbook*. University of Florida, Gainesville, FL: Florida Sea Grant College Program, 1991.

Hamilton, Keith, and Salmon, Patrick, eds. *Slavery, Diplomacy and Empire: Britain and the Suppression of the Slave Trade, 1807–1975*. Portland, Oregon: Sussex Academic Press, 2009.

Hampshire, A. Cecil. *The Blockaders*. London: William Kimber, 1980.

Hansard, T.C., ed. *Parliamentary Debates. From the Year 1803 to the Present Time*. 41 Vols. London: H.M.S.O., 1803–1820.

Hansen, Stig Jarle. *Piracy in the greater Gulf of Aden: Myths, Misconceptions and Remedies*. Oslo: Norwegian Institute for Urban Regional Research [NIBR], 2009.

Harman, Joyce Elizabeth. *Trade and Privateering in Spanish Florida, 1732–1763.* Tuscaloosa, AL: University of Alabama Press, 2004.

Harries, Meirion and Harries, Susie. *Soldiers of the Sun: The Rise and the Fall of the Imperial Japanese Army.* New York: Random House, 1991.

Hartwig, Dieter. *Großadmiral Karl Dönitz. Legende und Wirklichkeit.* Munich: Paderborn, 2010.

Hattendorf, John B. and Elleman, Bruce A., eds. *Nineteen-Gun Salute: Case Studies of Operational, Strategic, and Diplomatic Naval Leadership during the 20th and Early 21st Centuries.* Newport, RI: Naval War College Press/U.S. Government Printing Office, 2010.

Hawkins, Nigel. *The Starvation Blockades.* Barnsley, South Yorkshire, UK: Leo Cooper, 2002.

Hendrix, Henry J. *Theodore Roosevelt's Naval Diplomacy: the U.S. Navy and the Birth of the American Century.* Annapolis, MD: United States Naval Institute Press, 2009.

Herman, Donald L. "Democratic and Authoritarian Traditions," in *Democracy in Latin America: Colombia and Venezuela.* New York: Praeger, 1988.

Herman, Donald L. *Navy Medicine in Vietnam: Oral Histories from Dien Bien Phu to the Fall of Saigon.* Jefferson, NC: McFarland & Company, Inc., 2009.

Herman, Donald L. *Navy Medicine in Vietnam: Passage to Freedom to the Fall of Saigon.* Washington, DC: Naval History and Heritage Command, 2010.

Herrmann, Wilfried A. *Asia's Security Challenges.* Commack, NY: Nova Science Publishers, 1998.

Hervey, Frederick. *The Naval, Commercial, and General History of Great Britain,* 5 Vols. London: J. Bew, 1786.

Herwig, Holger H. *Germany's Version of Empire in Venezuela.* Princeton, NJ: Princeton University Press, 1986.

Herwig, Holger H. *'Luxury Fleet': The Imperial German Navy, 1888–1918.* London: Allen & Unwin, 1980.

Herwig, Holger H. *Politics of Frustration: The United States in German Naval Planning, 1889–1941.* Boston, MA: Little, Brown, 1976.

Herwig, Holger H. "Total Rhetoric, Limited War: Germany's U-Boat Campaign, 1917–1918" in *Great War, Total War: Combat and Mobilization on the Western Front, 1914–1918,* eds. Roger Chickering and Stig Förster. Washington, DC: German Historical Institute; New York: Cambridge University Press, 2000.

Herzog, James H. *Closing the Open Door: American-Japanese Diplomatic Negotiations, 1936–1941.* Annapolis, MD: Naval Institute Press, 1973.

Hezlet, Vice Admiral Sir Arthur. *The Submarine and Sea Power.* London: Peter Davies, 1967.

Hickey, Donald R. *The War of 1812: A Forgotten Conflict.* Urbana: University of Illinois Press, 1990.

Higginbotham, Don. *The War of American Independence: Military Attitudes, Policies, and Practice, 1763–1789.* Boston, MA: Northeastern University Press, 1971 [1983].

Hill, Howard C. *Roosevelt and the Caribbean.* Chicago: University of Chicago Press, 1927.

Hill, Howard C. "The Venezuelan Crisis," in *Roosevelt and the Caribbean*, chap. 5, 106–47. Chicago, IL: University of Chicago Press, 1927.

Hinsley, F. H. *British Intelligence in the Second World War. Its Influence on Strategy and Operations.* 5 Vols. Cambridge: Cambridge University Press, 1979–90.

Hobart-Hampden, C. Augustus. *Never Caught: Personal Adventures Connected with Twelve Successful Trips in Blockade-Running during the American Civil War, 1863–1864.* Carolina Beach, NC: Blockade Runner Museum, 1967.

Hobson, Rolf. *Imperialism at Sea: Naval Strategic Thought, the Ideology of Sea Power, and the Tirpitz Plan, 1875–1914.* Boston, MA: Brill, 2002.

Hogan, Albert E. *Pacific Blockade.* Oxford, UK: Clarendon, 1908.

Holmes, James R. *Theodore Roosevelt and the World Order.* Washington, DC: Potomac Books, 2007.

Hood, Miriam. *Gunboat Diplomacy, 1895–1905: Great Power Pressure in Venezuela.* South Brunswick, NJ: A. S. Barnes, 1977.

Hoogenboom, Ari. *Gustavus Vasa Fox of the Union Navy: A Biography.* Baltimore, MD: The Johns Hopkins University Press, 2008.

Horner, Dave. *The Blockade-Runners: True Tales of Running the Yankee Blockade of the Confederate Coast.* New York: Dodd, Mead, 1968.

Howard, Warren. *American Slavers and the Federal Law, 1837–1862.* Berkeley, CA: University of California Press, 1963.

Hsu, Immanuel C. Y. *China's Entrance into the Family of Nations: The Diplomatic Phase, 1858–1880.* Cambridge, MA: Harvard University Press, 1960.

Hubatsch, Walther, ed. *Hitlers Weisungen für die Kriegführung, 1939–1945.* Erlangen: K. Muller, 1962 [1983].

Hudson, H. *Northern Approaches.* Canberra: Australian Government Publishing Service, 1988.

Hugill, Paul D. *The Continuing Utility of Naval Blockades in the Twenty-first Century.* Fort Leavenworth, KS: U.S. Army Command and General Staff College, 1998.

Hull, Isabel V. *Absolute Destruction: Military Culture and the Practices of War in Imperial Germany.* Ithaca, NY: Cornell University Press, 2005.

Hunt, Peter C. *Coalition Warfare: Considerations for the Air Component Commander.* M.M.A.S. Thesis. Maxwell Air Force Base: U.S. Air University, Air Command and Staff College, School of Advanced Airpower Studies, March 1998.

Hunter, Janet E., comp. *Concise Dictionary of Modern Japanese History.* Berkeley, CA: University of California Press, 1984.

Hympendahl, Klaus. *Pirates Aboard! Forty Cases of Piracy Today and What Bluewater Cruisers Can Do About It.* New York: Sheridan House, 2003.

Ike, Nobutaka, trans. and ed. *Japan's Decision for War: Records of the 1941 Policy Conferences.* Stanford, CA: Stanford University Press, 1967.

International Maritime Bureau (IMB). *Piracy and Armed Robbery Against Ships Annual Report*, ICC International Maritime Bureau (2005).

International Maritime Bureau (IMB). *Piracy and Armed Robbery Against Ships, Annual Report, 1 January–31 December 2006.* ICC International Maritime Bureau, London, 2007.

International Military Tribunal for the Far East. *The Tokyo War Crimes Trial.* 17 Vols. Compiled by R. John Prichard and Sonia Magbanua Zaide. Project Director Donald Cameron Watt. New York: Garland Publishing, 1981.

Iriye, Akira. *The Cambridge History of American Foreign Relations,* Vol. 3, *The Globalizing of America, 1913–1945.* Cambridge: Cambridge University Press, 1993.

Ito, Masanori. *The End of the Imperial Japanese Navy.* New York: Jove Books, 1956.

Iwatake, Teruhiko. *Nanpo Gunseika no Keizai-Shisaku* (Economic Policies under the Southern Army's Administration), Vol. 1. Tokyo: Ryukei Shosha, 1995.

Jackson, Melvin H. *Privateers in Charleston, 1793–1796. An Account of a French Palatinate in South Carolina.* Washington, DC: Smithsonian Institution Press, 1969.

James, William. *Naval Occurrences of the War of 1812.* Reprint, London: Conway Maritime, 2004.

Japan, Army General Staff, ed. *Sugiyama Memo,* Vol. 1. Tokyo: Hara Shobo, 1967.

Japan, Imperial General Staff. *A History of the War between Japan and China.* Vol. 1, trans. Major Jikemura and Arthur Lloyd. Tokyo: Kinkodo Publishing, 1904.

Jen, Yu-wen. *The Taiping Revolutionary Movement.* New Haven, CT and London: Yale University Press, 1973.

Jennings, Francis. *Empire of Fortune: Crowns, Colonies & Tribes in the Seven Years War in America.* New York: W. W. Norton & Company, 1988.

Ji, Guoxing. *SLOC Security in the Asia Pacific.* Honolulu, HI: Asia-Pacific Center for Security Studies. Center Occasional Paper, 2000.

Johnson, Captain Charles. *Lives of the Most Notorious Pirates.* London: The Folio Society, 1962. Edited with an Introduction by Christopher Lloyd.

Johnson, Derek, and Valencia, Mark, eds. *Piracy in Southeast Asia: Status, Issues, and Responses.* Singapore: Institute of Southeast Asian Studies, 2005.

Jones, F. C. *Japan's New Order in East Asia: Its Rise and Fall 1937–1945.* London: Oxford University Press, 1954.

Jones, Jerry W. *U.S. Battleship Operations in World War I.* Annapolis, MD: Naval Institute Press, 1998.

Jones, Virgil C. "The Blockaders, January 1861–March 1862," in *The Civil War at Sea,* Vol. 1, 3 Vols. New York: Holt, Rinehart, Winston, 1960.

Kaeppelin, Jeanne, ed. *Surcouf dans l'océan Indien: journal de bord de la "Confiance".* Saint-Malo: Cristel, 2007.

Kahn, David. "Codebreaking in World War I and II: The Major Successes and Failures," in *The Missing Dimension: Governments and Intelligence Communities in the Twentieth Century,* eds. Christopher Andrews and David Dilks. London: Macmillan, 1984.

Kahn, David. *Seizing the Enigma. The Race to Break the German U-Boat Codes, 1939–1943.* Boston, MA: Houghton Mifflin Co., 1991.

Kamphausen, Roy, Lai, David, and Tanner, Travis, eds. *Learning by Doing: The PLA Trains at Home and Abroad.* Carlisle, PA: Army War College Press, 2012.

Karau, Mark D. *'Wielding the Dagger': The MarineKorps Flandern and the German War Effort, 1914–1918.* Westport, CT: Praeger, 2003.

Karnow, Stanley. *Vietnam: A History*. New York: Viking, 1983.

Karraker, Cyrus H. *Piracy was a Business*. Rindge, NH: Richard R. Smith Publishers, Inc., 1953.

Kell, John M. *Recollections of a Naval Life*. Washington, DC: Neale, 1900.

Kelly, Patrick J. *Tirpitz and the Imperial German Navy*. Bloomington, IN: Indiana University Press, 2011.

Kennedy, Paul M. *The Rise and Fall of British Naval Mastery*. New York: Scribner, 1976.

Kimball, Gertrude Selwyn, ed. *Correspondence of William Pitt*. 2 Vols. New York: The Macmillan Company, 1906.

Klachko, Mary, and Trask, David F. *Admiral William Shepherd Benson: First Chief of Naval Operations*. Annapolis, MD: Naval Institute Press, 1987.

Klooster, Wim. *Illicit Riches: Dutch Trade in the Caribbean, 1648–1795*. Leiden: KITLV Press, 1998.

Kneer, Warren G. *Great Britain and the Caribbean*. East Lansing: Michigan State University Press, 1975.

Knox, Dudley W. *The Naval Genius of George Washington*. Boston, MA: Riverside Press, 1932.

Knox, Dudley W. *A History of the United States Navy*. New York: G. P. Putnam's Sons, 1936.

Kryter, K. D. *Handbook of Hearing and the Effects of Noise*. New York: Academic Press, 1996.

Kubiak, Krzysztof. "Terrorism Is the New Enemy at Sea," *U.S. Naval Institute Proceedings* 129, no. 12 (December 2003): 68–71.

Kuehn, John T. *Coalition Tactics on the Napoleonic Battlefield and Their Influence on Unity of Effort*. Fort Leavenworth: U.S. Army Command and General Staff College, School of Advanced Military Studies, 13 November 1997.

Kuehn, John T. *The Reasons for the Success of the Sixth Coalition against Napoleon in 1813*. M.A. Thesis. Fort Leavenworth: U.S. Army Command and General Staff College, 7 June 1997.

Kuo, Ting-yee. *Sino-Japanese Relations, 1862–1927*. New York: Columbia University Press, 1965.

Labaree, Benjamin W. *A Supplement (1971–1986) to Robert G. Albion's Naval & Maritime History, An Annotated Bibliography, Fourth Edition*. Mystic, CT: Munson Institute of American Maritime Studies, 1988.

LaFeber, Walter. *The Cambridge History of American Foreign Policy*. Cambridge, MA: Cambridge University Press, 1993.

Lambi, Ivo Nikolai. *The Navy and German Power Politics, 1862–1914*. Boston, MA: Allen & Unwin, 1984.

Landers, Howard L. *The Virginia Campaign and the Blockade and Siege of Yorktown, 1781: Including a Brief Narrative of the French Participation in the Revolution Prior to the Southern Campaign*. Washington, DC: U.S. Gov't Print. Off., 1931.

Lasater, Martin L., ed. *Beijing's Blockade Threat to Taiwan: A Heritage Roundtable*. Washington, DC: Heritage Foundation, 1986.

Lavery, Brian. *Nelson's Navy: The Ships, Men and Organization, 1793–1815*. Reprint, Annapolis, MD: Naval Institute Press, 1997.

Le Guellaff, Florence. *Armements en course et Droit de prises maritimes (1792–1856)*. Nancy: Presses Universitaires de Nancy, 1999.

Leadam, I. S. *The History of England from the accession of Anne to the death of George II*. London: Longmans, Green and Company, 1909.

Leavelle, Clyde M. *An Analysis in Coalition Warfare: Napoleon's Defeat at the Battle of Nations—Leipzig, 1813*. Strategy Research Project. Carlisle Barracks: U.S. Army War College, 6 April 1998.

Lecky, William Edward Hartpole. *A History of England in the Eighteenth Century*, 8 Vols. New York: D. Appleton and Company, 1888.

Lee, Bradford A. *Britain and the Sino-Japanese War 1937–1939*. Stanford, CA: Stanford University Press, 1973.

Lee, Robert H. G. *The Manchurian Frontier in Ch'ing History*. Cambridge: Harvard University Press, 1970.

Legohérel, Henri. *Histoire de la Marine française*. Paris: PUF, 1999.

Lehr, Peter. *Violence at Sea: Piracy in the Age of Global Terrorism*. London: Routledge, 2006.

Lehr, Peter, and Lehmann, Hendrick. "Somalia – Pirates' New Paradise," in *Violence at Sea: Piracy in the Age of Global Terrorism*. ed. Peter Lehr. London: Routledge, 2006.

Leide, Jack. "Intelligence in Coalition Warfare: Desert Shield/Desert Storm," in *Intelligence in Partnership: Conference Proceedings, June 26–27, 1997*, 63–69. Washington, DC: Joint Military Intelligence College, 1997.

Leighton, John Langdon. *SIMSADUS London: The American Navy in Europe*. New York: H. Holt and Company, 1920.

Lewis, Ioan. *A Pastoral Democracy*. Oxford Press: James Currey for the International African Institute, 1999.

Lewis, Ioan. *Understanding Somalia and Somaliland*. London: Hurst, 2008.

Leyland, John, ed. *Dispatches and Letters Relating to the Blockade of Brest, 1803–1805*. 2 Vols. London. Printed for the Navy Records Society, 1899–1902.

Lindley, Augustus. *Ti-Ping Tien-kwoh, The History of the Ti-Ping Revolution*. New York: Praeger Publishers, 1970.

Lintner, Bertil. "The Perils of Rising Piracy (Posing a Challenge to Asian Navies)," *Jane's Defence Weekly* 34, no. 20 (15 November 2000): 18–19.

Liss, Sheldon B. *Diplomacy and Dependency: Venezuela, the United States, and the Americas*. Salisbury, NC: Documentary Publications, 1978.

Little, Benerson. *The Sea Rover's Practice: Pirate Tactics and Techniques, 1630–1730*. Washington, DC: Potomac Books, Inc., 2005.

Lloyd, Christopher. *The Navy and the Slave Trade: The Suppression of the Afriican Slave Trade in the Nineteenth Century*. London: Frank Cass & Co. Ltd., 1968.

Lloyd, Christopher. *William Dampier*. London: Faber and Faber, 1966.

Lockwood, Vice Admiral Charles A. *Sink 'Em All: Submarine Warfare in the Pacific*. New York: E.P. Dutton & Co., Inc., 1951.

Lone, Stewart. *Japan's First Modern War: Army and Society in the Conflict with China, 1894–95*. London: St. Martin's Press, 1994.

Loreburn, Earl. "Blockade," in *Capture at Sea*, chap. 4, 77–102. London: Methuen, 1913.

Lu, David J. *Japan a Documentary History: The Late Tokugawa Period to the Present*, Vol. 2. Armonk, NY: M.E. Sharpe, 1997.

Lucie-Smith, Edward. *Outcasts of the Sea*. New York: Paddington Press, 1978.

Lundgren, C. and Miller, J., eds. *The Lung at Depth*. New York: Marcel Dekker, 1999.

Luntinen, Pertii, and Menning, Bruce W. "The Russian Navy at War, 1904–05," in *The Russo-Japanese War in Global Perspective: World War Zero*, ed. John W. Steinberg, et al. Leiden: Brill, 2005.

Lustgarten, Abrahm. *Run to Failure: BP and the Making of the Deepwater Horizon Disaster*. New York: W.W. Norton & Company, 2012.

Lydon, James G. *Pirates, Privateers, and Profits*. Upper Saddle River, NJ: The Greg Press, Inc., 1970.

Lynn, John A. *Giant of the Grand Siècle. The French Army, 1610–1715*. Cambridge: Cambridge University Press, 1997.

Macpherson, David. *Annals of Commerce, Manufactures, Fisheries, and Navigation*, 4 Vols. London: Nichols and Son et al., 1805.

Magens, Nicolas. *An Essay on Insurances*, 2 Vols. London: J. Haberkorn, 1755.

Magner, Mike. *Poisoned Legacy: The Human Cost of BP's Rise to Power*. New York: St. Martin's Press, 2011.

Mahan, Alfred T. *The Influence of Sea Power upon History 1660–1783*. London: Sampson Low & Co., 1893, and New York: Dover Publications, Inc., 1987.

Mahan, Alfred T. *The Major Operations of the Navies in the War of American Independence*. London: S. Low, Marston, 1913.

Mahon, John K. *The War of 1812*. Gainesville, FL: University of Florida Press, 1972.

Malkin, H. W. "Blockade in Modern Conditions," in *British Year Book of International Law*, Vol. 3, 87–98. London: Henry Frowde and Hodder & Stoughton, 1922–1923.

Malo, Henry. *Les derniers corsaires. Dunquerque 1715–1815*. Paris: Emile-Paul Frères, 1925.

Mann, Michael. *China, 1860*. London: Michael Russell, 1989.

Marchand, John B. *Charleston Blockade: The Journals of John B. Marchand, U.S. Navy, 1861–1862*. Newport, RI: Naval War College Press, 1976.

Marder, Arthur J. *From the Dreadnought to Scapa Flow*. Vol. 4, *1917: Year of Crisis*. London: Oxford University Press, 1969.

Marks, Frederick W. *Velvet on Iron*. Lincoln, NB: University of Nebraska Press, 1979.

Marolda, Edward J. *By Sea, Air, and Land: An Illustrated History of the U.S. Navy and the War in Southeast Asia*. Washington, DC: Naval Historical Center, 1992.

Marr, D. and Wilkinson, M. *Dark Victory*. Sydney, Australia: Allen & Unwin, 2003.

Marriot, James. *The Case of the Dutch Ships Considered*. London: R and J. Dodsley, 1759.

Marshall P. J., ed. *The Eighteenth Century*, Vol. 2 of *The Oxford History of the British Empire*, ed. Wm. Roger Louis. Oxford: Oxford University Press, 1998.

Marvel, William. *The Alabama & the Kearsarge: The Sailor's Civil War*. Chapel Hill, NC: The University of North Carolina Press, 1996.

Marzagalli, Silvia, ed. *Bordeaux et la Marine de Guerre*. Bordeaux: Presses Universitaires de Bordeaux, 2002.

Marzagalli, Silvia. *Les boulevards de la fraude: le négoce de Bordeaux, Hambourg et Livourne au temps du Blocus continental, 1806–1813*. Villeneuve d'Ascq: Presses Universitaires du Septentrion, 1999.

Massie, Robert K. *Castles of Steel: Britain, German, and the Winning of the Great War at Sea*. New York: Ballantine Books, 2004.

Matloff, Maurice, and Snell, Edwin M. *Strategic Planning for Coalition Warfare*. United States Army in World War II: The War Department, 2 Vols. Washington, DC: U.S. Department of the Army, Office of the Chief of Military History, 1953–59.

Maurer, Martha E. *Coalition Command and Control: Key Considerations*. Washington, DC: National Defense University, Institute for National Strategic Studies, Center for Advanced Command Concepts and Technology, 1994.

May, Ernest R. *The World War and American Isolation*. Chicago: Quadrangle Books, 1966.

McBeth, Brian S. *Gunboats, Corruption, and Claims: Foreign Investment in Venezuela, 1899–1908*. Westport, CT: Greenwood Press, 2001.

McCusker, John J. *Money and Exchange in Europe and America, 1600–1775*. Chapel Hill, NC: University of North Carolina Press, 1978.

McGiffin, Lee. *Yankee of the Yalu: Philo Norton McGiffin, American Captain in the Chinese Navy (1885–1895)*. New York: E. P. Dutton, 1968.

McJoynt, Albert D. "Coalition Warfare," in *International Military and Defense Encyclopedia*, ed. Trevor N. Dupuy, Vol. 2, 533–37. Washington, DC: Brassey's, 1993.

McKee, Christopher. *A Gentlemanly and Honorable Profession: The Creation of the U.S. Naval Officer Corps, 1794–1815*. Annapolis, MD: Naval Institute Press, 1991.

McMillan, Lance. *The British Middle East Force, 1939–1942: Multi-Front Warfare with Coalition Forces*. Newport, RI: U.S. Naval War College, Department of Operations, 5 February 1994.

Medve, John P. *Integration, Interoperability and Coalition Warfare in the New World Order: A Monograph*. Fort Leavenworth: U.S. Army Command and General Staff College, School of Advanced Military Studies, 1993.

Mellor, Justin S. C. "Missing the Boat: the Legal and Practical Problems of the Prevention of Maritime Terrorism," *American University International Law Review* 18, no. 2 (2002): 341–97.

Melvin, Frank Edgar. *Napoleon's Navigation System. A Study of Trade Control During the Continental Blockade*. New York: Appleton, 1919 [1970].

Menkhaus, Ken. "Local Security Systems in Somali East Africa," in *Fragile States and Insecure People? Violence, Security and Statehood in the Twenty-first*

Century, eds. Louise Andersen, Bjom Moller, and Finn Sepputtat. New York: Palgrave Macmillan, 2007.

Merli, Frank J., and Ferrell, Robert H. "Blockades," in *Encyclopedia of American Foreign Policy*, 2nd ed., Vol. 1, 171–184. New York: Charles Scribner's, 2002.

Mevers, Frank C. "Naval Policy of the Continental Congress," in *Maritime Dimensions of the American Revolution*. Washington, DC: Naval History Division, Department of the Navy, 1977.

Meyer, Jean, and Bromley, John. "La seconde guerre de Cent Ans (1689–1815)," in *Dix siècles d'histoire franco-britannique. De Guillaume le conquérant au marché commun*, eds. Douglas Johnson, François Bédarida, François Crouzet. Paris: Albin Michel, 1979.

Michie, Alexander. *The Englishman in China during the Victorian Era*. Vol. 2. Edinburgh: William Blackwood and Sons, 1900.

Miller, Edward S. *War Plan Orange: The U.S. Strategy to Defeat Japan, 1897–1945*. Annapolis, MD: Naval Institute Press, 1991.

Miller, Harry. *Pirates of the Far East*. London: Robert Hale & Company, 1970.

Miller, Nathan. *Sea of Glory: A Naval History of the American Revolution*. Charleston, SC: The Nautical & Aviation Publishing Company of America, 1974.

Milner, Marc. *Battle of the Atlantic*. St. Catharines, ON: Vanwell, 2003.

Mitchell, Donald W. *A History of Russian and Soviet Sea Power*. New York: Macmillan, 1974.

Mo, John. "Options to Combat Piracy in Southeast Asia," *Ocean Development and International Law* 33, no. 3/4 (July/December 2002): 343–58.

Mokhtari, Fariborz L., ed. *Peacemaking, Peacekeeping and Coalition Warfare: The Future Role of the United Nations*. Washington, DC: National Defense University, 1994.

Moore, John B. "Blockade," in *A Digest of International Law as Embodied in Diplomatic Discussions, Treaties and Other International Agreements, International Awards, the Decisions of Municipal Courts, and the Writings of Jurists and Especially in Documents, Published and Unpublished, Issued by Presidents and Secretaries of State of the United States, the Opinions of the Attorneys-General, and the Decisions of Courts, Federal and State*, Vol. 7, chapter XXVII, parts 1266–1286, 780–858. Washington, DC: U.S. Gov't. Print. Off., 1906.

Morelock, Jerry D. "Blueprint for Victory: Leadership Strategy for Coalition Warfare," in *Essays on Strategy IX*, ed. Thomas C. Gill, 81–119. Washington, DC: National Defense University Press, 1993.

Mori, Kenkichi. *The Submarine in War: A Study of Relevant Rules and Problems*. Tokyo: Maruzen, 1931.

Morison, Elting E. *Admiral Sims and the Modern American Navy*. Boston, MA: Houghton Mifflin, 1942.

Morison, Samuel Eliot. *History of U.S. Naval Operations in World War II*. Vol. 1. *The Battle of the Atlantic, September 1939–May 1943*. Boston, MA: Little Brown, 1947 [1954].

Morris, Richard B. "Introduction," in *The American Navies of the Revolutionary War: Paintings*, ed. Nowland Van Powell. New York: G.P. Putnam's Sons, 1974.

Morriss, Roger, ed. *The Channel Fleet and the Blockade of Brest, 1793–1801.* Aldershot, Hants, UK: Ashgate for the Navy Records Society, 2001.

Morse, Hosea Ballou. *The International Relations of the Chinese Empire.* Vol. 3. Shanghai: Kelly and Walsh, 1918.

Mueller, G.O.W. and Adler, Freda. *Outlaws of the Ocean: The Complete Book of Contemporary Crime on the High Seas.* New York: Hearst Marine Books, 1985.

Muir, Ramsay. *Mare Liberum: The Freedom of the Seas.* London: Hodder & Stoughton, 1917.

Mukundan, P. "Scourge of Piracy in Southeast Asia—Any Improvements in 2004?" *Trends in Southeast Asia Series*: 3(2004). Singapore, Institute of Southeast Asian Studies, 2004.

Müller, Leos. *Consuls, Corsairs, and Commerce. The Swedish Consular Service and Long-distance Shipping,* 1720–1815. Uppsala: Uppsala universitet, 2004.

Mulligan, Timothy P. *Neither Sharks Nor Wolves: The Men of Nazi Germany's U-boat Arm, 1939–1945.* Annapolis, MD: Naval Institute Press, 1999.

Munemitsu, Mutsu. *Kenkenryoku: A Diplomatic Record of the Sino-Japanese War, 1894–95,* trans. Gordon Mark Berger. Princeton, NJ: Princeton University Press, 1982.

Murphy, Martin N. *Contemporary Piracy and Maritime Terrorism: The Threat of International Security.* IISS Adelphi Paper 388. London: Routledge, 2007.

Murphy, Martin. *Small Boats, Weak States, Dirty Money: Piracy and Maritime Terrorism in the Modern World.* New York: Columbia University Press, 2010.

Murphy, Martin. *Somalia: The New Barbary.* New York: Columbia University Press, 2011.

Murray, Dian H. *Pirates of the South China Coast, 1790–1810.* Stanford, CA: Stanford University Press, 1987.

Murray, Mary. *Cruel & Unusual Punishment: The U.S. Blockade against Cuba.* Melbourne, Australia: Ocean Press, 1993.

National Research Council. Committee on Potential Impacts of Ambient Noise in the Ocean on Marine Mammals. *Ocean Noise and Marine Mammals.* Washington, DC: National Academies Press, 2003.

National Research Council. *Low-Frequency Sound and Marine Mammals: Current Knowledge and Research Needs.* Washington, DC: National Academies Press, 1994.

National Research Council. *Marine Mammal Populations and Ocean Noise: Determining When Noise Causes Biologically Significant Effects.* Washington, DC: National Academies Press, 2005.

National Research Council. *Marine Mammals and Low-Frequency Sound: Progress Since 1994.* Washington, DC: National Academies Press, 2000.

Neilson, Keith, and Roy A. Prete, eds. *Coalition Warfare: An Uneasy Accord.* Waterloo, ON: Wilfrid Laurier University Press, 1983.

Nevins, Allan. *Henry White: Thirty Years of American Diplomacy.* New York: Harper and Brothers, 1930.

Newpower, Anthony. *Iron Men and Tin Fish: The Race to Build a Better Torpedo During World War II.* Westport, CT: Praeger Security International, 2006.

Nish, Ian. *The Origins of the Russo-Japanese War*. New York: Longman Inc., 1985.

Norman, L. *Sea Wolves and Bandits*. Hobart: J. Welch & Sons, 1946.

North, Douglass C. "The United States Balance of Payments, 1790–1860," in *Trends in American Economy in the Nineteenth Century*. Princeton, NJ: Princeton University Press, 1960.

O'Connor, Raymond G. *Origins of the American Navy: Sea Power in the Colonies and the New Nation*. Lanham: University Press of America, 1994.

O'Kane, Rear Admiral Richard H. *Wahoo! The Patrols of America's Most Famous World War II Submarine*. Novato: Presidio Press, 1987.

Offer, Avner. *The First World War: An Agrarian Interpretation*. Oxford: Clarendon Press, 1991.

Official Records of the Union and Confederate Navies in the War of the Rebellion, Series I, Vol. 5. Trial of the Officers and crew of the privateer *Savannah* on the charge of piracy, in the United States Circuit Court for the Southern District of New York, Hon. Judges Nelson and Shipman, presiding. Reported by A. F. Wharton, stenographer and corrected by the counsel. New York: Baker & Godwin, 1882.

Oh, Bonnie Bongwan. "The Background of Chinese Policy Formation in the Sino-Japanese War of 1894–1895," Ph.D. diss., University of Chicago, 1974.

Oi Atsushi. "Why Japan's Antisubmarine Warfare Failed," in *The Japanese Navy in World War II: In the Words of Former Japanese Naval Officers*, 2nd ed., trans. and ed. David C. Evans, with an introduction and commentary by Raymond O'Connor. Annapolis, MD: Naval Institute Press, 1986.

Olivier, David H. *German Naval Strategy 1856–1888: Forerunners of Tirpitz*. London: Frank Cass, 2004.

Ong-Webb, Graham Gerard, ed. *Piracy, Maritime Terrorism and Securing the Malacca Straits*. Leiden: International Institute for Asian Studies, 2006.

Ortzen, Len. *Stories of Famous Sea Raiders*. London: Arthur Barker Limited, 1973.

Owsley, Frank L., Jr. *The C.S.S. Florida: Her Building and Operations*. Tuscaloosa, AL: The University of Alabama Press, 1987.

Padelford, Norman J. *International Law and Diplomacy in the Spanish Civil Strife*. New York: Macmillan, 1939.

Padfield, Peter. *Dönitz. The Last Führer. Portrait of a Nazi War Leader*. New York: Harper & Row, 1984.

Paine, S.C.M. *The Sino-Japanese War of 1894–1895: Perceptions, Power, and Primacy*. Cambridge: Cambridge University Press, 2003.

Paine, S.C.M. *The Wars for Asia 1911–1949*. New York: Cambridge University Press, 2012.

Pares, Richard. *Colonial Blockade and Neutral Rights, 1739–1763*. Oxford: Oxford University Press, 1938.

Pares, Richard. *War and Trade in the West Indies, 1739–1763*. London: Frank Cass & Co. Ltd., 1963.

Parillo, Mark P. *The Japanese Merchant Marine in World War II*. Annapolis, MD: U.S. Naval Institute Press, 1993.

Parmelee, Maurice. *Blockade and Sea Power: The Blockade, 1914–1919, and Its Significance for a World State*. New York: Thomas Y. Crowell, 1924.

Patton, Robert H. *Patriot Pirates: The Privateer War for Freedom and Fortune in the American Revolution*. New York: Pantheon Books, 2008.

Payne, Roger. *Among Whales*. Scribner Press, 1995.

Pennell, C.R., ed. *Bandits at Sea: A Pirates Reader*. New York: New York University Press, 2001.

Pérotin-Dumon, Anne. "Economie corsaire et droit de neutralité. Les ports de la Guadeloupe pendant les guerres révolutionnaires," in *L'Espace Caraïbe, théâtre et enjeu des luttes impériales du XVIIe au XIXe siècle*. eds. Paul Butel and Bernard Lavallé. Bordeaux: Maison des Pays Ibériques, 1996.

Pérotin-Dumon, Anne. *La ville aux îles, la vile dans l'île, Basse-Terre et Pointe-à-Pitre, Guadeloupe, 1650–1815*. Paris: Karthala, 2000.

Peters, A. R. *Anthony Eden at the Foreign Office, 1931–1938*. New York: St. Martin's, 1986.

Pierce, James A. *Coalition War and Burden-Sharing: The President vs the Congress*. M.S. Thesis. Monterey: U.S. Naval Postgraduate School, December 1991.

Pinfold, John. "Introduction: Captain Hugh Crow and the Slave Trade," in *The Memoirs of Captain Hugh Crow: The Life and Times of a Slave Trade Captain*. Oxford: Bodleian Library, 2007.

Poe, Stacy A. *Rules of Engagement: Complexities of Coalition Interaction in Military Operations Other Than War*. Newport, RI: U.S. Naval War College, College of Naval Command and Staff, 13 February 1995.

Polson, Archer. "Law of Blockade," in *Principles of the Law of Nations, with Practical Notes and Supplementary Essays on the Law of Blockade and on Contraband of War to Which Is Added, Diplomacy*, eds. Archer Polson and Thomas H. Horne. London: John Joseph Griffin, 1848.

Poolman, Kenneth. *The Speedwell Voyage: A Tale of Piracy and Mutiny in the Eighteenth Century*. Annapolis, MD: Naval Institute Press, 1999.

Porter, David D. *Naval History of the Civil War*. Secaucus, NJ: Castle, 1984.

Powell, J. W. Damer. *Privateers and Ships of War*. Bristol: J. W. Arrowsmith Ltd, 1930.

Powell, Keith, II. *An Historical Examination of International Coalitions*. Strategy Research Project. Carlisle Barracks: U.S. Army War College, 6 April 1998.

Pritchard, James. *Louis XV's Navy: A Study of Organization and Administration*. Montreal, QC: McGill-Queen's University Press, 2009.

Pudas, Terry J. *Coalition Warfare: Preparing the U.S. Commander for the Future*. Newport, RI: U.S. Naval War College, 18 May 1992. Reprinted in *Essays on Strategy XI*, ed. John N. Petrie, pp. 109–32. Washington, DC: National Defense University Press, 1994.

Pyle, Kenneth B. *The Making of Modern Japan*, 2nd ed. Lexington, MA: D.C. Heath, 1996.

Rader, Karl A. *Blockades and Cyberblocks: In Search of Doctrinal Purity: Will Maritime Interdiction Work in Information Age Warfare?* Fort Leavenworth, KS: U.S. Army Command and General Staff College. School of Advanced Military Studies, 1995.

Raeder, E., and von Mantey, Eberhard. *Der Kreuzerkrieg in den ausländischen Gewässern*. 3 Vols. Berlin: E.S. Mittler, 1922–37.

Rahn, Werner. "The Development of New Types of U boats in Germany During World War II. Construction, Trials and First Operational Experience of the Type XXI, XXIII and Walter U boats," in *Les marines de guerre du dreadnought au nucléaire*. Paris: Service historique de la Marine, 1990.

Rahn, Werner. "German Naval Strategy and Armament, 1919–39," in *Technology and Naval Combat in the Twentieth Century and Beyond*, ed. Phillips Payson O'Brien. London: Frank Cass, 2001.

Rahn, Werner. "Long-range German U-boat Operations in 1942 and Their Logistical Support by U-Tankers," in *Die operative Idee und ihre Grundlagen. Ausgewählte Operationen des Zweiten Weltkrieges*. ed. Militärgeschichtliches Forschungsamt. Bonn: Herford, 1989.

Rahn, Werner, and Schreiber, Gerhard, eds. *Kriegstagebuch der Seekriegsleitung 1939–1945*, Teil A [part A]. 68 Vols. Bonn: Herford, 1988–97.

Ranft, Bryan. "Restraints on War at Sea Before 1945," in *Restraints on War: Studies in the Limitation of Armed Conflict*, ed. Michael Howard. Oxford: Oxford University Press, 1979.

Rapalino, Patrizio. *La Regia Marina in Spagna, 1936–1939*. Milan: Mursia, 2007.

Rawlinson, John L. *China's Struggle for Naval Development 1839–1895*. Cambridge: Harvard University Press, 1967.

Raymond, Catherine Zara. "Piracy in the waters of Southeast Asia," in *Maritime Security in Southeast Asia*, eds. Kwa Chong Guan and John K. Skogan. London: Routledge, 2007.

Recio, Jorge H. *Argentine Navy Units Participation in UN Haiti's Blockade: Permanent or Selective Engagement?* Newport, RI: Naval War College. Center for Naval Warfare Studies. Strategic Research Department, 1998.

Régent, Frédéric. *Esclavage, métissage, liberté. La revolution française en Guadeloupe, 1789–1802*. Paris: Grasset, 2004.

Rémy, Albert. *Théorie de la continuité du voyage en matière de blocus et de contre-bande de guerre: thèse pour le doctorat.* Paris: L. Larose & Forcel, 1902.

Reter, Ronald. "The Real versus Rhetorical Theodore Roosevelt in Foreign Policy Making." Ph.D. diss., University of Georgia, 1973.

Reynolds, J. E., and Rommel S. A., eds. *Biology of Marine Mammals*. Washington, DC: Smithsonian Institution Press, 1999.

Ribadieu, Henry. *Histoire maritime de Bordeaux. Aventures des corsaires et des grands navigateurs bordelais*. Bordeaux: Dupuy, 1854.

Rice, Anthony J. *Command and Control in Coalition Warfare: Does History Provide Us with Practicable Solutions for Today?* Strategy Research Project. Carlisle Barracks: U.S. Army War College, 11 March 1996.

Richardson, James D., ed. *Compilation of the Messages and Papers of the Presidents*. New York: Bureau of National Literature and the Arts, 1920.

Richardson, Michael. "Terrorism: The Maritime Dimension," *Trends in Southeast Asia Series*: 3(2004). Singapore, Institute of Southeast Asian Studies, 2004.

Ritter, Gerhard. *The Sword and the Scepter: The Problem of Militarism in Germany.* 4 Vols. English translation. Coral Gables: University of Miami Press, 1969–73.

Robidou, L. *Ler derniers corsaires malouins. La course sous la Révolution et l'Empire, 1793–1815.* Paris: Oberthür, 1919.

Robinson, Charles M., III. *Shark of the Confederacy: The Story of the C.S.S. Alabama.* Annapolis, MD: Naval Institute Press, 1995.

Robinson, Margaret. *Arbitration and the Hague Peace Conferences.* Philadelphia, PA: University of Pennsylvania, 1936.

Robinson, W. Courtland. *Terms of Refuge: The Indochinese Exodus & The International Response.* London: Zed Books Ltd., 1998.

Robinson, William Morrison, Jr. *The Confederate Privateers.* Columbia, SC: University of South Carolina Press, 1990.

Rodger, N. A. M. *The Wooden World: An Anatomy of the Georgian Navy.* New York: W. W. Norton & Company, 1996.

Rodger, N.A.M. *The Command of the Ocean: A Naval History of Britain, 1649–1815.* New York: W.W. Norton & Company, 2004.

Rodigneaux, Michel. *La guerre de course en Guadeloupe, XVIIIe-XIXe siècles, ou Alger sous les Tropiques.* Paris: L'Harmattan, 2006.

Rodman, Hugh. *Yarns of a Kentucky Admiral.* Indianapolis, IN: The Bobbs-Merrill Company, 1928.

Rodríguez-Salgedo, M.J., ed. *Armada, 1588–1988.* London: Penguin Books in association with the National Maritime Museum, 1988.

Rohwer, Jürgen. *Axis Submarine Successes 1939–1945.* Annapolis, MD: Naval Institute Press, 1999.

Rohwer, Jürgen. *The Critical Convoy Battles of March 1943.* Annapolis, MD: Naval Institute Press, 1977.

Røksund, Arne. *The Jeune École: The Strategy of the Weak.* Leiden: Brill, 2007.

Roosevelt, Theodore, and Morison, Elting Elmore. *The Letters of Theodore Roosevelt.* Cambridge: Harvard University Press, 1951.

Ropp, Theodore. *The Development of a Modern Navy: French Naval Policy 1871–1904,* ed. Stephen S. Roberts. Annapolis, MD: Naval Institute Press, 1987.

Roscoe, E. S., ed.. *Reports of Prize Cases Determined in the High Court of Admiralty . . . from 1745 to 1859,* 2 Vols. London: Stevens and Sons, Limited, 1905.

Roskill, S.W. *The War at Sea 1939–1945,* Vol. 1: *The Defensive.* London: H.M.S.O., 1954.

Roskill, S.W. *The War at Sea 1939–1945,* Vol. 2: *The Period of Balance.* London: H.M.S.O., 1957.

Ross, Steven T. *American War Plans 1890–1939.* London: Frank Cass, 2002.

Rössler, Eberhard. *The U-boat. The Evolution and Technical History of German Submarines.* London: Arms and Armour Press, and Annapolis, MD: Naval Institute Press, 1981.

Russell, John Robert. "The Development of a 'Modern' Army in Nineteenth Century Japan," Master's thesis, Columbia University, 1957.

Rybalkin, Iurii. *Operatsiya "X": Sovetskaya Voennaya Pomisch' Respublikanskoi Ispanii, 1936–1939.* Moscow: Aero-XX, 2000.

Sachs, William S. "The Business Outlook in the Northern Colonies, 1750–1775," Ph.D. dissertation, Columbia University, 1957.

Sakuye Takahashi. *International Law Applied to the Russo-Japanese War.* London: Stevens and Sons, Limited, 1908.

Salewski, Michael. *Die deutsche Seekriegsleitung 1935–1945.* 3 Vols. Frankfurt am Main: Bernard & Graefe, 1970–1975.

Scales, Robert H., Jr. "Trust, Not Technology, Sustains Coalitions." Chap. 11 in *Future Warfare: Anthology,* 187–99. Carlisle Barracks: U.S. Army War College, 1999. Reprinted in *Parameters* 28 (Winter 1998–99): 4–10.

Scalia, Joseph M. *Germany's Last Mission to Japan: The Failed Voyage of U-234.* Annapolis, MD: Naval Institute Press, 2000.

Schauff, Frank. *Der verspielte Sieg: Sowjetunion, Kommunistische Internationale und Spanischer Bürgerkrieg, 1936–1939.* Frankfurt am Main: Campus, 2005.

Scheck, Raffael. *Alfred von Tirpitz and German Right-Wing Politics, 1914–1930.* Boston, MA: Humanities Press, 1998.

Scheer, Admiral Reinhard. *Germany's High Sea Fleet in the World War.* London: Cassell, 1919.

Schimpf, Axel. "Der Einsatz von Kriegsmarineeinheiten im Rahmen der Verwichlungen des spanischen Bürgerkrieges 1936 bis 1939," in *Der Einsatz von Seestreitkräften im Dienst der auswärtigen Politik: Vorträge auf der Historisch-Taktischen Tagung der Flotte.* Deutsche Marine Institut. Herford: Mittler, 1983.

Schissler, Mark O. *Coalition Warfare: More Power or More Problems?* Newport, RI: U.S. Naval War College, 18 June 1993.

Schmalenbach, Paul. *German Raiders: A History of Auxiliary Cruisers of the German Navy 1895–1945.* Cambridge: Patrick Stephens, 1979.

Schmitt, Michael N. *Blockade Law: Research Design and Sources.* Buffalo, NY: William S. Hein, 1991.

Scott, Admiral Sir Percy. *Fifty Years in the Royal Navy.* New York: George H. Doran Company, 1919.

Scott, James B., ed. *The Declaration of London, February 26, 1909: A Collection of Official Papers and Documents Relating to the International Naval Conference Held in London December, 1908–February, 1909.* New York: Oxford University Press, 1919.

Semmes, Raphael. *Memoirs of Service Afloat, During the War Between the States.* Baltimore, MD: Kelly, Piet & Co., 1869; reprint Secaucus, NJ: The Blue & Grey Press, 1987.

Sengupta, Prasun K. "Japan Conducts First Bilateral Anti-Piracy Exercises in East Asia," *Asian Defence Journal,* no. 12 (December 2000): 10–11.

Sessions, Sterling D., and Carl R. Jones. *Coalition Command and Control: Defining by Casebook Studies.* Washington, DC: National Defense University, Institute for National Strategic Studies, Center for Advanced Concepts and Technology, November 1996.

Shalikashvili, John M. "Multinational Operations," in *Joint Vision 2010,* 9. Washington, DC: U.S. Joint Chiefs of Staff, 1996.

Shay, Shaul. *The Red Sea Terror Triangle*. New Brunswick & London: Transaction Publishers, 2005 [2007].

Sherry, Frank. *Pacific Passions: The European Struggle for Power in the Great Ocean in the Age of Exploration*. New York: William Morrow and Company, 1994.

Sherry, Frank. *Raiders and Rebels: The Golden Age of Piracy*. New York: Hearst Marine Books, 1986.

Silverstone, Paul H. *Civil War Navies, 1855–1883*. Annapolis, MD: Naval Institute Press, 2001.

Silverstone, Paul H. *The Sailing Navy, 1775–1854*. Annapolis, MD: Naval Institute Press, 2001.

Simpson, Benjamin Mitchell, III. *Admiral Harold R. Stark: Architect of Victory, 1939–1945*. Columbia: University of South Carolina Press, 1989.

Sims, William S. *The Victory at Sea*. London: 1920. [Garden City, NJ: Doubleday, Page, 1920]

Sinclair, Arthur. *Two Years on the Alabama*. Boston, MA: Lee and Shepard, 1895.

Siney, Marion C. *The Allied Blockade of Germany, 1914–1916*. Ann Arbor, MI: University of Michigan Press, 1957.

Sjaastad, Anders C. "Southeast Asian SLOCs and Security Options," in Kwa Chong Guan and John K. Skogan (eds.), *Maritime Security in Southeast Asia*. London: Routledge, 2007.

Snepp, Frank. *Decent Interval*. New York: Vintage Books, 1977.

Society of Friends, Philadelphia, Yearly Meeting, *An Exposition of the African Slave Trade, From the Year 1840, to 1850, Inclusive, Prepared from Official Documents, and Published by Direction of the Representatives of the Religions Society of Friends, in Pennsylvania, New Jersey, and Delaware*. Philadelphia, PA: J. Rakestraw, 1851; repub. Detroit, Michigan: Negro History Press, 1969.

Söderqvist, Nils. *Le blocus maritime: étude de droit international*. Stockholm: Centraltryckeriet, 1908.

Soley, James R. *The Blockade and the Cruisers*. New York: Charles Scribner's Sons, 1890.

Sondhaus, Lawrence. *Naval Warfare, 1815–1914*. London: Routledge, 2001.

Sondhaus, Lawrence. *Preparing for Weltpolitik: German Sea Power Before the Tirpitz Era*. Annapolis, MD: Naval Institute Press, 1997.

Spector, Ronald, *Admiral of the New Empire*. Baton Rouge, LA: Louisiana State University Press, 1974.

Spector, Stanley. *Li Hung-chang and the Huai Army: A Study in Nineteenth–Century Chinese Regionalism*. Seattle, WA: University of Washington Press, 1964.

Spindler, Arno. *Der Handelskrieg mit U-Booten*. 5 Vols. Berlin [Vol.V Frankfurt-am-Main]: E.S. Mittler, 1932–66.

Starkey, David J. *British Privateering Enterprise in the Eighteenth Century*. Exeter, Devon: University of Exeter Press, 1990.

Stegemann, Bernd. *Die Deutsche Marinepolitik, 1916–1918*. Berlin: Duncker & Humblot, 1970.

Stenzel, Alfred. *Kriegführung zur See. Lehre vom Seekriege*, ed. Hermann Kirchoff. Hannover and Leipzig: Hahnsche Buchhandlung, 1913.

Stern, Philip Van Doren. *The Confederate Navy: A Pictorial History*. Garden City, NY: Doubleday, 1962.

Still, William N., Jr., ed. *The Queenstown Patrol, 1917: The Diary of Commander Joseph Knefler Taussig, U.S. Navy*. Newport, RI: Naval War College Press, 1996.

Still, William N., Jr., Taylor, John M., and Delaney, Norman C. *Raiders & Blockaders: The American Civil War Afloat*. Washington, DC: Brassey's, 1998.

Stockton, Charles H. "Blockade," in *The Laws and Usages of War at Sea: A Naval War Code*, section VII, 22–25. Washington, DC: U.S. Gov't. Print. Off., 1900.

Stokesbury, James L. "The U.S. Army and Coalition Warfare, 1941–1945," in *Against All Enemies: Interpretations of American Military History from Colonial Times to the Present*, eds. Kenneth J. Hagan and William R. Roberts, 279–303. New York: Greenwood Press, 1986.

Stout, Neil R. *The Royal Navy in America, 1760–1775*. Annapolis, MD: Naval Institute Press, 1973.

Sumida, Jon Tetsuro. "Forging the Trident: British Naval Industrial Logistics, 1914–1918," in *Feeding Mars: Logistics in Western Warfare from the Middle Ages to the Present*, ed. John A. Lynn. Boulder: Westview Press, 1993.

Summers, Harry G., Jr. "Unity of Command and Coalition Warfare," in *On Strategy II: A Critical Analysis of the Gulf War*, 231–247. New York: Dell, 1992.

Swanson, Bruce. *Eighth Voyage of the Dragon: A History of China's Quest for Seapower*. Annapolis, MD: Naval Institute Press, 1982.

Swanson, Carl E. *Predators and Prizes: American Privateering and Imperial Warfare, 1739–1748*. Columbia, SC: University of South Carolina Press, 1991.

Symcox, Geoffrey. *The Crisis of French Sea Power, 1688–1697: From the Guerre d'Escadre to the Guerre de Course*. The Hague: Martinus Nijhoff, 1974.

Syrett, David. *Shipping and Military Power in the Seven Years War: The Sails of Victory*. London: University of Exeter Press, 2008.

Syrett, David. *The Defeat of the German U-Boats. The Battle of the Atlantic*. Columbia, SC: The University of South Carolina Press, 1994.

Syrett, David. *The Royal Navy in American Waters, 1775–1783*. Aldershot: Scolar Press, 1989.

Syrett, David. *Shipping and the American War, 1775–1783*. London: Athlone Press, 1970.

Tarling, Nicholas. *Piracy and Politics in the Malay World: A Study of British Imperialism in Nineteenth-Century South-East Asia*. Melbourne, Australia: F.W. Cheshire, 1963.

Tarrant, V.E. *The U-Boat Offensive, 1914–1945*. Annapolis, MD: Naval Institute Press, 1989.

Taylor, Richard K. *Blockade: A Guide to Non-Violent Intervention*. Maryknoll, NY: Orbis, 1977.

Taylor, Thomas E. and Wise, Stephen R. *Running the Blockade: A Personal Narrative of Adventures, Risks, and Escapes during the American Civil War*. Annapolis, MD: Naval Institute Press, 1995.

Terasawa, Katsuaki L., and Gates, William R. *Burden Sharing in the Persian Gulf: Lessons Learned and Implications for the Future*. Monterey, CA: U.S. Naval Postgraduate School, August 1992.

Terraine, John. *The U-boat Wars 1916 1945*. New York: Putnam, 1989.

Thayer, William R. *Life and Letters of John Hay*. Boston, MA: Houghton Mifflin, 1915.

The U-Boat War in the Atlantic, 1939–1945, ed. Ministry of Defense (Navy). Facs. Ed. with Introd. by Andrew J. Withers, 3 parts in 1 Volume. London: H.M.S.O., 1989.

Tilchin, William N. *Theodore Roosevelt and the British Empire: A Study in Presidential Statecraft*. New York: St. Martin's Press, 1997.

Toussaint, Auguste. *Les frères Surcouf*. Paris: Flammarion, 1979.

Traina, Richard P. *American Diplomacy and the Spanish Civil War*. Bloomington, IN: Indiana University Press, 1968.

Trocki, Carl A. *Prince of Pirates: The Temenggongs and the Development of Johor and Singapore, 1784–1885*. Singapore: Singapore University Press, 1979.

Truxes, Thomas M. *Defying Empire: Trading with the Enemy in Colonial New York*. New Haven, CT: Yale University Press, 2008.

Truxes, Thomas M., ed. *Letterbook of Greg & Cunningham, Merchants of New York and Belfast, 1756–57*. Oxford: Oxford University Press, 2001.

Tsamenyi, M., and Rahman, Chris, eds. *Protecting Australia's Maritime Borders: The MV* Tampa *and Beyond*, Wollongong Papers on Maritime Policy No. 13. Wollongong University, 2003.

Tucker, Spencer C. *Raphael Semmes and the Alabama*. Fort Worth, TX: Ryan Place Publishers, 1996.

Turbiville, Graham H., Jr. "Piracy Prompts Renewed Countermeasures," *Special Warfare* 14, no. 2 (Spring 2001): 44–45.

Turner, Maxine. *Navy Gray: Engineering the Confederate Navy on the Chattahoochee and Apalachicola Rivers*. Macon, GA: Mercer University Press, 1999.

U.S. Adjutant-General's Office. *Military Information Division. Notes on the War between China and Japan*. Washington, DC: Government Printing Office, 1896.

U.S. Department of Defense. *Conduct of the Persian Gulf War: Final Report to Congress*. Washington, DC: U.S. Department of Defense, April 1992.

U.S. Department of Defense. Office of General Counsel. *Critique of the Brief against the Egyptian Blockade of the Strait of Tiran*. Washington, DC: Department of Defense, 1967.

U.S. Department of Energy. *Piracy: The Threat to Tanker Traffic* (September 1992).

U.S. Department of State. *Foreign Relations of the United States Diplomatic Papers 1941: The Far East*, Vol. 4. Washington, DC: Government Printing Office, 1956.

U.S. Department of State. *Papers Relating to the Foreign Relations of the United States: Japan: 1931–1941,* Vol. 2. Washington, DC: Government Printing Office, 1943.

U.S. Department of the Army. *The Army in Multinational Operations*. Field Manual 100-8. Washington, DC: U.S. Department of the Army, 24 November 1997. 1 Vol. Mil. Pubs. FM 100-8.

U.S. Department of the Army. *Operations*. Field Manual 100-5. Washington, DC: U.S. Department of the Army, 14 June 1993. 1 Vol. (Mil. Pubs. FM 100-5). See especially the definition of coalition on page 5-1.

U.S. Naval Ordnance Laboratory. *Small Craft and Counterinsurgency Blockade*. White Oak, MD: Naval Ordnance Laboratory, 1972.

U.S. Naval War College. *International Law Topics: The Declaration of London of February 26, 1909*. Washington, DC: U.S. Gov't. Print. Off., 1909.

Underwood, Rodman L. *Waters of Discord: The Union Blockade of Texas During the Civil War*. Jefferson, NC: McFarland, 2003. (E 600 U53 W38 2003)

United States Strategic Bombing Survey, Summary Report (Pacific War). Washington, DC: Government Printing Office, 1946.

United States. Navy. Office of the Chief of Naval Operations. Operations Evaluation Group. *Efficiency of the UN Sea Blockade of the Korean Peninsula*. Washington, DC: Dept. of the Navy. Office of the Chief of Naval Operations. Operations Evaluation Group, 1951.

van Tuyll van Serooskerken, Hubert P. *The Netherlands and World War I*. Leiden: Brill, 2001.

Vandiver, Frank E., ed. *Confederate Blockade Running through Bermuda, 1861– 1865: Letters and Cargo Manifests*. Austin, TX: University of Texas Press, 1970.

Vigness, Paul G. "The British Blockade," in *The Neutrality of Norway in the World War*, chap. 4, 40–57. New York: AMS, 1971.

Villiers, Patrick. "La Guerre de Course," in *Napoléon et la Mer, un rêve d'Empire*, eds. J.M. Humbert and B. Ponsonnet. Paris: Seuil, 2004.

Villiers, Patrick. *Les corsaires: des origines au traité de Paris du 16 avril 1856*. Paris: J.P. Gisserot, 2007.

Villiers, Patrick. *Les corsaires du Littoral de P hilippe II à Louis XIV, Boulogne, Calais et Dunkerque 1560–1715*. Villeneuve d'Ascq: Presses universitaires du Septentrion, 1999.

Villiers, Patrick. *Marine royale, corsaires et trafic dans l'Atlantique de Louis XIV à Louis XVI*. Dunkirk, Société dunkerquoise d'histoire et d'archéologie, 1991.

Vincent, C. Paul. *The Politics of Hunger: The Allied Blockade of Germany, 1915– 1919*. Athens, OH: Ohio University Press, 1985.

Vladimir [Zenone Volpicelli]. *The China-Japan War Compiled from Japanese, Chinese, and Foreign Sources*. Kansas City, MO: Franklin Hudson Publishing, 1905.

Vo, Nghia M. *The Vietnamese Boat People, 1954 and 1975–1992*. London: McFarland & Company, Inc., 2006.

Wagenknecht, Edward. *The Seven Worlds of Theodore Roosevelt*. New York: Longman, Green, 1958.

Wagner, Gerhard, ed. *Lagevorträge des Oberbefehlshabers der Kriegsmarine vor Hitler 1939–1945*. Munich: J.F. Lehmann, 1972.

Wallach, Jehuda L. *Uneasy Coalition: The Entente Experience in World War I*. Westport, CT: Greenwood Press, 1993.

Walter, John. *The Kaiser's Pirates: German Surface Raiders in World War One*. London: Arms & Armour Press, 1994.

Wang, Yizhou. *Creative Involvement: The Evolution of China's Global Role*. Beijing: Peking University Press, August 2013.

Wannan, Bill. *Legendary Australians: A Colonial Cavalcade of Adventurers, Eccentrics, Rogues, Ruffians, Heroines, Heroes, Hoaxers, Showmen, Pirates and Pioneers*. Adelaide, Australia: Rigby Limited, 1974.

Warner, Denis, and Warner, Peggy. *The Tide at Sunrise: A History of the Russo-Japanese War, 1904–1905*. New York: Charterhouse, 1974.

Weber, Ludwig. "Blockade." In *Encyclopedia of Public International Law*, ed. Rudolf Bernhardt, Vol. 1, 408–12. Amsterdam: North-Holland, 1992.

Weber, Ludwig. "Blockade, Pacific," in *Encyclopedia of Public International Law*, ed. Rudolf Bernhardt, Vol. 1, 412–15. Amsterdam: North-Holland, 1992.

Weddle, Kevin J. *The Ottawa Treaty and Coalition Warfare: An Unholy Alliance?* Strategy Research Project. Carlisle Barracks: U.S. Army War College, 1 April 1999.

Weir, Gary E. *Building American Submarines, 1914–1940*, Contributions to Naval History, no. 3. Washington, DC: Naval Historical Center, 1991.

Weir, Gary E. *Building the Kaiser's Navy: The Imperial Navy Office and German Industry in the Tirpitz, 1890–1919*. Annapolis, MD: Naval Institute Press, 1992.

Wharton, Francis, ed. "Blockade," in *A Digest of the International Law of the United States, Taken from Documents Issued by Presidents and Secretaries of State, Decisions of Federal Courts, and Opinions of Attorneys-General*, 2nd ed., Vol. 3, chapter XVIII, parts 359–365, 352–410. Washington, DC: U.S. Gov't. Print. Off., 1887.

Whealey, Robert H. *Hitler and Spain: The Nazi Role in the Spanish Civil War, 1936–1939*. Lexington, KY: University of Kentucky Press, 1989.

Wheeler, Keith. *War Under the Pacific*. Alexandria, VA: Time-Life Books, 1980.

White, John. *The Diplomacy of the Russo-Japanese War*. Princeton, NJ: Princeton University Press, 1964.

White, Mark J. *The Cuban Missile Crisis*. Houndmills, Basingstoke, Hampshire, UK: Macmillan, 1996.

White, Philip L., ed. *The Beekman Mercantile Papers, 1746–1799*, 3 Vols. New York: The New-York Historical Society, 1956.

Whiteman, Marjorie M. "Blockade," in *Digest of International Law*, Vol. 10, chapter XXXI, parts 11–14, 861–79. Washington, DC: U.S. Gov't. Print. Off., 1968.

Williams, Glenn F. *U.S.S. Constellation: A Short History of the Last All-sail Warship Built by the U.S. Navy*. Virginia Beach, VA: Donning Company Publishers, 2000.

Williams, Gomer. *History of the Liverpool Privateers and Letters of Marque*. London: William Heinemann, 1897.

Williams, Greg H. *The French Assault on American Shipping, 1793–1813. A History and Comprehensive Record of Merchant Marine Loss*. Jefferson, NC: McFarland, 2009.

Williams, Samuel Wells, and Williams, Frederick Wells. *A History of China: Being the Historical Chapters from 'The Middle Kingdom'*. London: S. Low, Marston & Co., 1897.

Wilson, Charles. *Mercantilism*. London: The Historical Association, 1958.

Wilson, George G. *Provisional Instructions for the Navy: Defining the Rights of Belligerents and Neutrals, Laws of Blockade and Contraband of War*. Newport, RI: United States Naval War College, 1912.

Wise, Stephen R. *Lifeline of the Confederacy: Blockade Running during the Civil War*. Columbia, SC: University of South Carolina Press, 1989.

Wong, J. Y. *Yeh Ming-ch'en, Viceroy of Liang Kuang, 1852–8*. London: Cambridge University Press, 1976.

Woody, Lamont. *Coalition Logistics: A Case Study in Operation Restore Hope*. M.M.A.S. Thesis. Fort Leavenworth: U.S. Army Command and General Staff College, 1994.

Woolley, Mark S. *Coalition Warfare: Implications for the Naval Operational Commander in the Way Ahead*. Newport, RI: U.S. Naval War College, 19 June 1992.

Wylie, C. *Military Strategy: A General Theory of Power Control*, 3rd ed. Annapolis, MD: Naval Institute Press, 1989.

Young, Arthur N. *China and the Helping Hand 1937–1945*. Cambridge, MA: Harvard University Press, 1963.

Young, Arthur N. *China's Wartime Finance and Inflation, 1937–1945*. Cambridge, MA: Harvard University Press, 1965.

Young, Marilyn B. *The Vietnam Wars 1945–1990*. New York: HarperCollins, 1991.

Index

Note: Page locators in *italic* refer to case studies and **bold** refer to strategic terms.

9-11, 38, 68, **154**, **164**, **166**, **167**

Abhyankar, Jayant, 48
abolitionists, 97
aborigine, 39n5
active enemy, 62, 65, 86, 88, 102, 117, **143**
adaptability, 18, 25–26, 28, 29, 64, 84–86, **143**, **151**, **153**
Aegospotami, xvi
Afghanistan, xiii, 32, 34, 35, 38, 39n5, 60, 62, 67, 68, **164**
Africa, xv, 43, 47, 52, 93, 102, *140*
African American, 9–10
African slaves, 93
Age of sail, 84
aircraft carrier, 15, 26, 36, 38, 63–65, 112, 122, 123, **144**, **155**, **164**
Air Force, xiv, 26, 93, 122, **158**
airpower, 23, 25, 29, 31, 34, 35, 37, 58, 60, 68, 81, **143**, **164**
air superiority, 60, 64, **143**
Akhromeev, Sergei F., 123
Alaska, xi, 103, **148**
Aleutian Islands, 131
Alexander II, Tsar, xi–xii
alliance cohesion, 133

alliances, xiv, xvii, xviii, 32, 61, 63, 77, 82, 108, 109, 127, 130–33, *139*, **143**, **144**, **146**, **149–51**, **161**, **165**
allies, xv, xvi, xvii, 18, 20, 21, 25, 29, 36, 55, 57, 59–62, 64, 67, 78, 79, 82, 85, 86, 90, 94, 105, 108, 110, 111, 113, 118, 120, 129–35, *139*, **146**, **148–50**, **152**, **154**, **161**, **163**, **166**, **167**
Al Qaeda, 62, 68
alternate land route, 20, 21, 23, 26–28, 58, 86, **143**, **164**, **165**
Alvin, 101
American colonies, 42, 73, 82, 89, 129
American Revolution, 72, 74, 75, 77–80, 82, 83, 85–89, 119, 129
amphibious, 59, 64, 118, 119, 125, *141*, **144**, **162**
Amsterdam, xii
antipiracy operations, xvii, 41, 47, 50–53, 93, 95, 98–101, 104, *142*, **159**
Anti-submarine Warfare (ASW), 77, 79, 86, 112, **144**
Anvil, 61, **155**
Arctic Ocean, 130
Argentina, 1, 26, 63–65, 112, 122, **151**
armaments, 21, 134
Armenia, 66, 67, **154**

Army. *See* U.S. Army
Arrow War, *140. See also* Opium War,
    Second
Art of War, **169**
Arvid Pardo, 3n1
asymmetrical, 33, **144**
Athens, xvi
Atlantic, Battle of the, 86
Atlantic fleet, 121
Atlantic Ocean, xii, 73, 128, 129
atomic bombs, 77, 81. *See also* nuclear
    weapons
attrition, xvi, 34, 35, 39n5, 57, 61, 77,
    88, 108, 110, **144, 150**
audience, 94–98, 102, **144, 151, 166**
Aurora. See Chongqing
Australia, 2, 19, 22, 24, 28, 30, 33, 38,
    44, 50, 52, 59, 60, 66, 109, 114, 119,
    120, *137, 138*, **146**
Australia, HMAS, 11
Australian Maritime Information Fusion
    Center, 50
Austria, 102
Austro-Hungarian Empire, 7
Automatic Identification System (AIS),
    47, 51, 91
away game, 55, 133, **144, 156**
Axis Powers, 34, 37, 79, 109

Bacon, Sir Francis, xii
Bainbridge, 52
balance of power, 21, 36, 38, 55, 56, 89,
    108, 134, **144**
Balut Island, 44
Bangladesh, 44, 47, 101, *140*
bank robber, 125
Barbary, 42, *140*
barbed wire, 47
Base Action Network, 100
bastion, 123
Battle of the Atlantic, 86
Battle of the Coral Sea, 120
Battle of Trafalgar, 129
Battle of Tsushima, 112
Battle of Yorktown, 79

Bay of Bengal, 49
Beijing, 28, 35, 107, 122, 125, 135
Beiyang Fleet, *138*
Bekesy, Georg von, 101
Belgium, 94, 98, 102, 123, *142*
Belligerents, 18, 25, 37, 43, 62, 65, 72,
    75, 77, 79, 80, 90, 108, **145, 157,
    165**
Bering Sea, 130
Berlin, 75
Bismarck, Otto von, 64, *139*, **158**
Blackbeard the Pirate. *See* Thatch,
    Edward
Black Sea, 47, 66, 110, 130
Bligh, William, 5
Blitzkrieg, **145, 165**
Bloch, Felix, 101
blockade, xv, xvi, xvii, 3, 17–30, 34,
    35, 37, 56, 74, 77, 78, 82, 83, 88–90,
    94, 98, 102, 108, 110–12, 118–20,
    122, 123, 127, 128, 130–34, *137,
    138, 142*, **145, 146, 148, 150, 152,
    155–57, 160–64, 166, 167**
blogger, 95, **165**
blue water navy, xii, 100, **145**
Boat people, 44, *140*
boomerang effect, 62, 68, 95, 114, *142*,
    145
Border Protection Command, 50
Borneo, 42
Bosnia, 32, 35, 36, *139*
bottleneck, 23, 83, **145, 146, 154, 166**
bottleneck creation, 23, 83
Bounty, 5
Boxers, 35
Boxer uprising, 35, 129, *139*
BP (formerly British Petroleum), 94, 97
Brando, Marlon, 5
Brest, 119
Britain. *See* Great Britain
British Commonwealth, 56, 57, 65, 66
British Navigation Acts, (1651), 73
brown water, **145**
Brunei, 101, 125
buffer, 121, **145, 146, 161, 168**

Bugis, 42
Byzantine, xiii

C-130 transport plane, 120
Cambodia, 101, 125
Canada, xi, 8, 11, 13, 16, 19, 50, *137*
Cannon-shot rule, 76, **146**
carrier battle group, 28
Cattaro, 7, *137*
Celsus, xiii
Center for International Maritime
    Security, xi
Center of Gravity (COG), 19, 26, 34,
    63, 78, 112, **146**
Central Intelligence Agency, xiv
Central Powers, 63, 102, *139*
Chiang Kai-shek, 109, 123
Chile, 1, 16, *137*
China, xiii, xv, xvii, xviii, 2, 6, 9, 11, 13,
    17–30, 34–38, 41–45, 47, 52, 57–63,
    65, 67, 77, 78, 83–85, 94–96, 98–105,
    107, 109, 111–14, 117–25, 129–35,
    137–42, **153, 155, 159–61, 167**
Chinese civil war, 9, 34, 36, 103, 111,
    119, *137, 139*
Chinese Communist Party (CCP), xviii,
    36, *139*
Chittagong, 44
choke point blockade, 22, 29, 41, 90,
    118, 119, 124, 125, **146, 154**
Chongqing, 9, 11, 12, *137*
Christian, Mr., 5
Churchill, Winston, 66
Civil war, 9, 18–20, 24, 26, 27, 34, 36,
    71, 75–83, 85–89, 103, 111, 119,
    137, 139, 141, 142, **161**
Clancy, Tom, 14
clash of civilization, 56, **146**
Clausewitz, Carl von, 37, 121, **154**
climate change, 130, **154**. *See also*
    global warming
close blockade, 18, 20, 24, 30, 118, **145,
    146**
closed seas, xiii, 107, 110, 118, 128,
    146, 160

cluttered sea, 111, 112, **146**
coal, xiv, 27, 29, 72
coalitions, 3, 19, 20, 25, 27, 29, 31–39,
    56, 57, 60, 81, 83, 86, 104, 105, 109,
    110, 112, 113, 129, 130, 132–35,
    138, 139, **146, 147, 149, 151, 152,
    154–56, 160, 161, 163–68**
coastal states, xi, xv, 2, 29, 42, 46–50,
    52, 64, 65, 76, 97, 119, 121, 125,
    127, **145, 146, 159**
coast guard, 2, 94, 97, 100, *142*
coast watchers, 67, **146**
code breaking, 61
Cod wars, 2
Cold War, 14, 31, 33–36, 38, 43, 56, 59,
    64, 65, 93, 98, 105, 110, 117, 123,
    128–31, 133, 134, *139*, **159, 161**
colonies, xiv, 21, 25, 42, 73, 89, 129,
    148
combined, 20–23, 32, 34, 36, 52, 59–60,
    76, 80–82, 129, 130, *140*, **147, 152,
    154, 158**
Combined Task Force, 52
command and control (C2), 33, **147**
command of the sea, xvi, 31, 35, 83,
    107, 109, 112, **147, 150, 153, 165**
commerce raiding, xvi, xvii, 3, 71–91,
    93, 131, 133, 134, *141*, **144, 147,
    148, 157–58, 163, 166**
commercial tax, 46
Commission for the Relief of Belgium
    (CRB), 123, *142*
Committee on the Peaceful Uses of the
    Seabed, 2
commodity, 41, 90, 123
common heritage of mankind, 2, 3n1
common operating picture (COP), 50,
    147, 159
commons, xiii, xv, 37, 38, 80, 81,
    99–101, 104, 113, 117, 128, 132,
    134, **154**
communications, xii, xiii, xiv, xv, xvii,
    10, 11, 14, 17, 18, 23, 30–32, 35, 48,
    62, 82, 95, 99, 133, **143, 146, 148,
    149, 154, 155, 157–59, 161, 162, 165**

competitive advantage, 38, 44, 58, 62, 80, 108, 110–12, 119, 124, 125, 131, 135, **147**, **150**, **153**, **157**, **164**, **166**, **167**
computer, 50, **149**
concentration, 63, **147**, **151**, **159**
Confederacy, 19, 24, 76, 78, 82, 83, 85, 86, 89
Confederate Navy, 28, 88, *141*
confrontation, *141*
conquest, xi, xii, xiii, 22, 23, 61, **148**, **162**
Constellation, 15
constrainment, 38, **148**
container ships, 30, 45
containment, xvii, 121, **148**
contiguous zone, 43, **148**
continental blockade, 21, 24, 28, 82, 108, *138*, **148**
continental powers, xi–xviii, 17, 20, 33, 36, 38, 55, 72, 78, 86, 88, 89, 110, **148**, **157–59**. *See also* land power
continental shelf, 1, 2, **148**
control of population movements, 23
convoys, xv, 49, 64, 74, 77, 81, 84–86, 98, 118, **148**, **153**, **157**, **166**
cooperative adversary, 26, 85, 119, **148**
Cooperative Strategy for, 21ˢᵗ Century Seapower, A, 51, 105
coordination of land and sea, 56, 57, 60, 63, 64, 68
copper sheathing, 29, 72
Coral Sea, Battle of, 120
Corbett, Sir Julian, xii, 37, 55, 61, 67, 68, 75, 107, 110, **147**, **150**, **151**, **153**, **168**
corruption, 11, 16
cost escalation, 82, 83, **151**
Council of Economic Advisers, xiv
Covid-19, 16
Crimean war, 17, 18, 20–29, 56, 60, 61, 110, 111, 129, 130, *138*, *139*
critical vulnerability, 78, **148**
cryptography, 63, 67, 90
Cuba, 25, 26, 29, *138*

Cuban Missile Crisis, 17–19, 21, 22, 24–27, 29, 111, 112, 130, *138*
cultural choice, 44
cumulative effects, xiii, xvi, xviiin9, 10, 34, 39n4, 77, 78, 89, 134, **149**, **150**, **152**, **162**
cyber, xiii, 99, 132, **149**

Daily Mirror, 15
Dalian, 119
Dampier, William, 73
Dardanelles, 66
D-day invasion, 55, 58
death ground, 13, 103, **149**
decisive victory, xv, xvi, 25, 27, 38, 79, 88, 111, 118, 119, 134, *141*, **149**
Declaration of Paris, (1856), 74–75, 81
decolonization, xiv, 129
deconfliction, 31, **149**
decryption, 63, 67
deep-sea mapping, 99
Deepwater Horizon, 97, 99, 103, *142*
defection, 21, 34, 37, **149**
deliver victory, xvi, 19, 25, 108, 134, **149**
Denmark, 123
Department of Defense (DOD), xiv, 104, **143**, **146**
deployment, 21, 22, 35, 55, 57, 58, 60, 66, 67, 90, 96, 107, 108, 112, 118, 119, 121, 122, 134, **156**
Desert Storm, 34, 35
destruction of enemy forces, xvi, 23, 24, 82, 87, 94, 109, 110, *138*, **145–47**, **169**
detail, 119, **149**
deterrence, xv, 16, 19, 21, 23, 28, 35, 47, 52, 56, 77, 80, 95, 96, 98, 99, 103, 104, 120, *138*, *142*, **144**, **149**, **156**, **162**
diesel submarine, 125
Dili, 119
diplomacy, xvi, 2, 3, 26, 29, 32, 38, 56, 61, 64, 82, 88, 93, 96, 98, 100, 104, 114, 122, 128, *142*, **150**, **155**, **169**

direct effects, 94, 98–99, **144**, **150–52**

disaster relief, 93, 95, 103, 105, **150**, **151**, **155**, **156**, **159**

disposable force, 55, 67, **150**

disposal force, 55, 58, 67, 105, **150**

distant blockade, 18, 20, 24, 30, 118, 124, **145**, **150**

doctrine, 42, **150**

domino effect, 10, **150**, **164**

dream scenario, 25, 26, 29, 84, 85, **151**, **161**

drug trafficking, 42, 51, 105

dual-use equipment, 103–5, **150**, **151**

Duane, 100

Duke of Wellington. *See* Wellesley, Arthur

dumping, 99

duration, 18, 19, 22, 33, 56–58, 76, 77, **151**

Dutch, xiii, 41, 42, 73, 90, 99, 109, **154**

East Asia, 32, 43, 107, 109, 114, 118

East China Sea, 107, 112, 113

Eastern Europe, xvii, 130

Eastern front, 58

Eastern seaboard, 79

East Sea Fleet (PLAN), 132

East Timor, 119

East-West tensions, 56

economic interests, 32, 75, 129

economics, xiii, xiv, xvi, xvii, 2, 7, 12, 23, 25, 29, 32, 33, 42–44, 46, 55, 56, 61, 62, 68, 71–75, 82–84, 88, 91, 93, 97, 99, 101, 102, 104, 110, 111, 118, 124, 127, 129, 130, 132, 133, *138*, *140*, **147**, **150–53**, **155**, **157**, **164**

economic sanctions. *See* sanctions

economic sparkplug, 101, **151**

economic strangulation, 23, 83, **151**

Ecuador, 1

Edmonstone, William, 102

educational work, 15

Eisenhower, Dwight D., xiv

electric fencing, 47

electronic key-card, 48

embargo, 18, 26, 88, 94, 99, 103, 110, 117, 132–34, *142*, **151**, **154**, **167**

enemy adaptation, 18, 25–27, 29, 86, **143**, **151**

energy, 56

enforcement, xvii, 21–24, 28, 30, 45, 46, 51, 53, 83, 94, 103, 104, 110, 129, *138*, **162**, **164**

Enigma machine, 86

Entente, 18, 63, 66, 81, 87, 89, 109

EP-3 incident, 96

equipment, 33, 35, 53, 103–5, 134, **144**, **151**, **165**

escalation, 11–14, 16, 82, 90, 95, 99, 111, 123, **151**, **156**, **168**

Europe, xii, xiv, xvii, 17, 32, 36, 39n5, 42, 46, 47, 52, 63, 66, 74, 75, 80, 86, 96, 98, 103, 104, 108, 118, 129–31, 134, *138*, **148**, **169**

European Coal and Steel Community, xiv

European Economic Community, xiv, 46

European Union (EU), xiv

exclusion zone, xii, 30, 122, 127, 128, 132, **152**, **160**

exclusive economic zone (EEZ), 2, 43, 47, 132, **152**

expeditionary warfare, 3, 55–69, 93, 131, 133, *140*, **152**

extension packages, 105, **152**

external lines of communication, xiv, xvii

extortion, 42

face, gaining, retaining, and losing, 96, 114, 125, **152**, **163**, **169**

failed state, 90, **152**, **162**. *See also* pariah state

Faina, 51

Falklands, 18–20, 22, 24–29, 57, 59, 60, 63–65, 112, 122, *138*, *141*, **151**

Fascists, 76, 79, 82, 86

feint, 118, **150**, **153**

First Island Chain, 124, 131

First Sino-Japanese War, 18–20, 22–27, 76–81, 83, 85–88, 111, 118, 119, 132, *138*, *139*, *141*. See also Sino-Japanese War, (1894–1895)
flagship, 9, **153**
flags of convenience, 46, **153**
flexibility, 25, 38, 64, **153**
flipping China, 28, 61, **159**, **167**
Florida, xi, 100
food security, 56
foreign trade, 78
France, xvi, 7, 18, 22, 36, 38, 60, 61, 66, 67, 71, 74, 76–79, 82, 84–89, 94, 102, 108–10, 118, 119, 123, 128–30, 134, *137*, *139*, *141*, **146**
Freedom of Navigation (FON), 71, 99, 113, 122, 128, **154**
Freedom of Navigation Operations (FONOPS), 99, **154**
freedom of the seas, 1, 2, 42, 75, **154**
Freedom of the Seas, xiii, 41
free trade, 71, **154**
freight rates, 90, **154**
Frequent Wind, 95
friction, **149**, **152**, **154**

Gallipoli, 55–60, 63, 66, 67, *140*, **154**
gaps, 44, 45
gauntlet, 80
General Agreement on Tariffs and Trade, (1947), xiv, 130
Geneva Convention on the High Seas, (1958), 1, 46
genocide, xiv, xvii, 32, 67, **154**
geography, xii, xiv, 20, 25, 27, 29, 38, 43, 58, 66, 78–80, 86, 87, 89, 108, 110–12, 114, 117, 118, 124, 125, 127, 133, 134, **147**, **153**, **154**, **162**, **164**, **167**
Geography of the Peace, The, xii
Germany, 6, 7, 17, 18, 26, 29, 36, 56, 58, 60–62, 72, 75, 77–90, 94, 96, 98, 102, 109, 112, 114, 118, 120–23, 128, 131, *139*, *141*, **168**
ghost ship, **154**, **162**

Gibraltar, 129, 131. *See also* Strait of Gibraltar
Gibson, Mel, 5
global commons, 37, 38, 99, 101, **154**
globalization, 32, **155**
global order, xiii, xv, xvii, xviiin2, 71, 79, 113, 114, 128, 129, 133, 134, **154**
global prosperity, xviii, 99, 113, 114
global trade, 50, 74, 83, 88, 118
global warming, 97, 124, **154**. *See also* climate change
global war on terror (GWOT), 38, **154**
glue, 129, **155**. *See also* solvent
Gorbachev, Mikhail, xvii
Gotland, 14
grand strategy, xvi, 23, 56, 64, **155**, **157**, **158**, **166**
Great Britain, xi, xii, xvi, 2, 6, 8, 10, 14, 17, 18, 21, 22, 25–27, 37, 51, 56, 57, 61–67, 71–74, 79, 82, 83, 85, 88–90, 94, 96, 98, 99, 102, 108, 109, 112, 118, 121–23, 128, 129, 134, **148**, **154**, **157**, **165**
Great depression, xiv
Great game, *141*
great power, 28, 64, 80, 88, **148**, **155**
Great Wall, **155**
Greece, 41, 127
Green water, **145**
Grotius, Hugo, xiii, 1, 41, 42, 132, **154**
Guadalcanal, 57–63, 110, *140*, **145**, **146**
Guam, 95, **148**
Guerre de course, 71, 72, 75, 89, *141*, *142*, **147**, **155**
Guerrilla, 65, **155**
Gulf of Aden, 52, 100, 101
Gulf of Guinea, *140*
Gulf of Mexico, 94
Gulf of Thailand, 43
Gulf War, *139*
gunboat diplomacy, 38, **155**

Haiphong, 28, 120, 125
Hammer, 61, **155**
Han Chinese, 113

Hanoi, 59
hard extension package, 105, **152**
hard power, 103–5, **152, 155**
Harmonious Mission, 2013, 101
Harrier jets, 112, 122
Hawaii, **148**
hearts and minds, 32, **155**
Hermes, 112
heterogeneous coalitions, 31, 33, **155, 156, 160**
high seas, 1, 2, 41, 43, 51, 52, 80, 94, 110, 118, 122, 131, **154, 155, 157**
hijacking, 44, 49, 51, 52, 76
History of Imperial Defense, xii
home front, 38, **156**
home game, 55, 133, **156**
homeland security, 38, 58, **156**
homogeneous coalition, 33, **155, 156, 160**
Hoover, Herbert, 94, 102, *142*
horizontal escalation, 11, 13, **156, 168**
Horn of Africa, 52, *140*
humanitarian disaster, 93, 95, 103, 105, **150, 151, 155, 156, 159**
humanitarian relief, 3, 32, 93, 94, 98, 101–5, 123, *142*, **150, 151, 155, 156, 159, 166**
human trafficking, 51, 93, 99, 105, **156**
Hungary, 7
Hunt for Red October, The, 14
Hussein, Saddam, 25, 36, 57, 118

Iban, 42
Iberia, 58, 61, 66, 108, 129, **168**
Iceland, 1, 2
illegal immigration, 19, 30, 51, **156, 164**
Inchon landing, 55, 57, 60–62, 64, 65, 111, **160**
inclusive coalitions, 31, 33, **156, 160**
incremental, 56, **147, 153, 156**
Independence, 122
India, 10, 42, 47, 52, 101, 114, **164**
Indian Navy, 49, *137*
Indian Ocean, 38, 49
Indochina, 109. *See also* Vietnam

Indonesia, 32, 47, 101, 119, 125, **152**
Industrial revolution, xi, xiii, 50, 74, 113, 131, 132
Influence of Sea Power upon History: 1660–1783, The, xii, 88
information, xvii, 10, 41, 47, 50, 56, 61, 63, 67, 97, 100, 101, 117, **146, 147, 150, 152, 153, 157**
insurance, xv, 90, 124, **154, 157, 160**
intelligence, xiv, 50, 56, 61–64, 67, 68, 81, 85, 95, 96, **144, 157**
intermittent, 18, 19, 76–78, 121, **153, 157, 164**
internal lines of communication, xiii, xiv, 133
International Bank for Reconstruction and Development, xiv
International cooperation, 46
international law, xiii, xvi, 18, 42, 45, 52, 71, 80, 81, 101, 102, 107, 113, 128, 132, *137, 138*, **157, 162, 164**
International Maritime Organization (IMO), 45–48
International Monetary Fund, xiv, 130
International Ship and Port Facility Security (ISPS), 46, 47, 53
internet, 32, **149, 159, 165**
interoperability, 31, 33, 35, **157**
interruption of trade, 23
intervention, 20, 24, 27, 28, 35, 36, 45, 51, 59, 65, 77, 82, 84–88, 90, 98, 119, 120–22, *139*, **145, 157, 160, 167, 168**
invasion, xvi, 19, 22, 23, 26, 29, 57, 60–62, 81, 88, 108, 121–23, 125, 127, **148, 152, 167**
Invergordon, 8, 11, *137*
Iran, 85
Iran-Iraq Tanker War. *See* Tanker War
Iranun, 42
Iraq, 18–20, 22–29, 34–37, 57, 60, 62, 67, 68, 75, 80, 85, 110, 118, 121, *138, 139, 141*
Iraqi Freedom, 35, 36, *139*
Iroquois, 8

ISIS, 25
island-hopping, 120, **157**
Italy, 34, 90, 131, *139*

Japan, xii, xvi, 18–30, 35, 38, 47, 52,
    56–58, 60–65, 67, 68, 72, 75–90,
    95, 99, 103, 109–14, 118–20, 122,
    130–32, *138–42*, **145, 146, 156–58,
    162, 164–66, 169**
Jefferson, Thomas, 75–76
Jeune École, 71, 76–78, 87, 88
Joint Chiefs of Staff (JCS), xiv, **146,
    158**
jointness, 60, 62, 68
joint operations, 14, 20–23, 34, 59–64,
    68, 76, 80–81, 84, 119, 122, *140*,
    143, 147, 152, 158
joint sea-air operations, 23, 60, 84

Kamikaze, **158**
Kenya, 51, 52
Key Largo, 100
Kim Jung-un, xvii
Kitty Hawk, 15
Korea, xvi, xvii, 18–29, 47, 56, 57, 59–
    62, 65, 67, 111, 118, 122–24, 130,
    133, *138, 141*, **160**
Korean peninsula, 59, 65
Korean War, 22, 56, 60, 61, 65, 111,
    122, 123
Kosovo, 35, 36, *139*
Kowshing, 78, 84
Kuropatkin, Aleksei, 130
Kuwait, 118

Labuan Bajo, 101
land lines of communication (LLOC),
    17, 20, 26, 27, 29, 86, **143, 148, 149,
    154, 157, 158, 161, 162, 165**
land power, xii, xiii, xiv, xv, xvii, 3,
    17–21, 24, 25, 28, 29, 38, 55, 58, 59,
    67, 71, 78–80, 87, 107, 108, 110–13,
    118, 127–35, **144, 148, 153, 158,
    159, 165, 168**
Latvia, 14

Laughton, Charles, 5
Law of the Seas, 1, 2, **158**
Law of War and Peace, xiii
League of Nations, 132
letter of marque, 72, 85, **158, 163**
Liaodong peninsula, 35
Liberation Army Daily, 101
liminal space, 42, **158**
limited goals/objectives, 12, 23–25, 83,
    84, **158, 168**
limited wars, 24, 37, 83, 90, **151, 161,
    164, 168**
littoral, 47, 94, 108, 113, **158**
local population allegiance/alienation,
    59, 61, 66–68, 73, 109, **158**
logistics, xv, 25, 35, 55, 59, 61–63, 110,
    120, 122, *142*, **149, 159**
Lombok strait, 119
London, 64, 75, 83
Lord High Admiral, 72–73
Louisiana purchase, xi
Luhu-class, 104
Lüshun, 119

MacArthur, Douglas, 62, 65
Maersk Alabama, 52
Mahan, Alfred Thayer, xii, xv, 31, 75,
    88, 127, **157, 169**
main front, xvi, 58, 60, 61, 66, 133, 134,
    150, 152, 161, 162
Mainland China, 9, 36, 123. *See also*
    China; PRC
Malacca strait, 44, 47, 49, 81, 118, 124,
    140, **152**
Malay, 42, *141*
Malayan emergency, 121, *141*
Malayan peninsula, 59, 121
Malaysia, 47, 52, 125, **152**
Malaysia-Singapore-Indonesia
    (MALSINDO), 47, **152**
Maldives, 101
Manchuria, xvi, 35, 118, 119, *139*
Mandate of heaven, **159**
manifest destiny, **159**
Mao Zedong, 124, 132

Mare Liberum, 41, 42
marine mammals, 97
marine police, 44, 52, 75
maritime crime, 43–45, 76, *140*, **159**
Maritime Domain Awareness (MDA),
    50–52, **159**
maritime power, xi, xii, xiii, 34, 71, 78,
    87–90, 109, 132, **159**, **163**. *See also*
    sea power
maritime strategy, 105, 114
mass communications, xv, 10, 32, 95,
    159
Maury, Matthew Fontaine, 99
media, 14, 32, 38, 94, 95, **159**, **165**, **166**,
    169. *See also* social media
Mediterranean Sea, 42, 47, 66, 110, 128,
    129
megaship, xiv
Merchant marine, 63, 78, 85, 109, 111,
    124, 134
Mesopotamia, 60, 63, *140*
Mexico, xii, 94
Micronesia, 120
midair refueling, 60, **159**
Middle East, 36, 62, 84
military degradation, 23
Military Operations Other Than War
    (MOOTWA), 93, 105, **159**
missile blockade, 19, 21–24, 27–30, 34,
    122, **160**
mobility, 38, **143**, **160**, **161**
money sink, xiv, 25, **166**
Mongol, xiii
morale, 10, 23, 78
mother ship, 48, **160**
Muslim, 56
mutineers, 5–16, **165**
mutiny, 3, 5–16, *137*, **149**, **150**, **156**,
    158, **160**, **162**, **164**, **165**, **167–69**
Myanmar, 101

Napoleon, Bonaparte, xi, 17, 19, 21, 22,
    24, 25, 28, 35, 36, 60, 61, 72, 74, 76,
    82, 84, 108, 129, 134, *138*, **146**, **148**

Napoleonic Wars, xiii, xvi, 26, 66, 87,
    88, 108, 118, 128, 129, 131, 134,
    138, **168**
national goals, 23, 31, 56, 64, **147**, **149**,
    160
national interests, 90, 103, 108, 109,
    147, **155**, **160**
nationalism, xiv, 124
Nationalist navy, 111
Nationalists, 9, 22, 26, 119, 132, *138*
national prosperity, xiii, xviii, 114, 127,
    160
national security, xiii, 98, 127, **156**, **160**
National Security Council, xiv
national survival, 32, 65, 103, 129
naval coalition, 31, 32, 34–38, 60, 104,
    139, **160**, **164**, **165**, *166*
naval exercises, xviii, 105, **152**
naval strategy, 33, 35–36, 123, *141*
Nazi, xii, xiii, 21, 26, 35, 109, 130
negative incentive, 10, 12, 125
negative objective, 98, 99, 117, 118,
    163
negative space, 5, 19, 96, 121, 134, **160**,
    163
negative sum, xiii, xv, 132, 133
negotiated settlement, 18, 21, 23, 64, 80,
    83, 87, 90, **160**
Nelson, Horatio, 8, 75
Netherlands, The, xii, 109, 123
neutrality, *141*, **161**
neutrals, 30, 57, 64, 73–75, 77, 82, 84,
    85, 87, 90, 94, 98, 104, 107–9, 123,
    141, **161**, **166**, **169**
New England, 73
new front, **147**, **158**
New Guinea, 57, 59–63, 109, 110, 120,
    141
New Life, 95
new school, 71
newspaper, 32, 112, 114, 121
new theater, 60, 65, 67, 68, 133, **162**
New World, 45
New York City, 68

New Zealand, 66, 109
niche capabilities, 31, 33, **161**
Nicholas, II Tsar, xvi
nightmare scenario, 25, 26, 29, 84, 85, 128, **151**, **161**
Nimitz, 122
Nixon, Richard, **167**
Nobel Prize, 101
Non-Commissioned Officers, 10
non-contiguous, 55, **148**, **152**, **161**
non-military naval operations, 3, 56, 62, 93–106, 133. *See also* soft power
nonstate actor, xviiin2, 75, 96, 113
North Africa, xv
North America, xi, 42
North Atlantic, 47
North Atlantic Treaty Organization (NATO), xiv, 47, 51
Northern Fleet, Soviet, 123
North Korea, 19, 111
North Sea, 128, 129
North Sea Fleet (PLAN), 132
North Vietnam, 21, 103
nuclear powered submarines, xv
nuclear strike, xv, xvi
nuclear war, xv, xvi, xvii, 35, 62, 123
nuclear weapons, xv, 29, 58, 77, 81, 123

occupation of territory, xiii, 23, 58, 67, 109, 125, 129
ocean enclosure, 2, 41, 113, **161**
oceanic moat, 55, 58, 67, 68, 108, 127, **161**
oceanic trade, xiii, xv, 108, 127, 128, 134
Office of Naval Research, 101
Officer of the watch, 14
offshore islands, 131, **146**, **167**
oil exploitation, 97
oil exploration, 97
oil spill, 94, *142*
oil tankers, 45, 72, 76, **151**
Okhotsk, Sea of, 123, 130
Okinawa, 131
Old World, xii

open registries, 46, **161**
operational effectiveness, 27–28, 37; failure, 28, 37; goals, 18, 23, 57, 86, **161**; objective, 56, 114; risk, 64, 65, 87; success, 37, 55, 56, 61, 65; victory, 56
Operation Unified Assistance, 32, 101
opium trade, 42
Opium War, First, 43
Opium War, Second, 129, *139*
opportunistic crime, 43, 44, **162**
Organization of American States, xiv
Organized crime, 42–45
Ottoman Empire, 57, 62, 63, 66, 67
outcome, 19, 23, 25, 26, 28, 55, 61–65, 77–79, 82, 84, 87–89, 95, 100–103, 109, 119, **149**, **151**, **161**

pacific blockade, 18, **145**, **162**. *See also* blockade
Pacific Ocean, xii, 47, 57, 62, 63, 83, 95, 99, 109, 110, 120, 123, *140*, **156**, **168**, **169**
Pacific war, xv, 57, 62, 63, 67, 82–84, 89, 91, 95, 110, 120, *140*, **146**, **156**, **168**, **169**
Pakistan, 101
paper blockade, 18, **145**, **162**. *See also* blockade
Paracel Islands, 35, 57, 59, 120, 125, *141*
pariah state, 52, 81, 86, 90, **152**, **157**, **162**
Paris Declaration, (1856), 75, 81
Paris Memorandum of Understanding on Port State Control, 46
partial blockade, 18, 23, 24, 112, **145**, **162**, **163**
passive enemy, 62, 64, 68, **143**
Pax Americana, 128
Pax Britannica, 128
Peace Ark, 101
Pearl Harbor, 28, 60, 63–65, 68, 99, *140*, **153**, **166**, **167**
pearls, 76

Peirates, 41
Peninsular war, 57, 58, 60–62, 66, 108,
129, *140*
Pentagon, 68, **146**, **166**
People's Liberation Army (PLA), 101
People's Liberation Army Navy
(PLAN), 59, 95, 98–101, 112, 113,
117, 120, 124, 132
People's Republic of China (PRC), 9,
19–24, 26–29, 34, 35, 38, 111–14,
117, 118, 120–25, 129, 131, 132,
135, *138*, **161**, **167**. *See also* China;
Republic of China (ROC)
peripheral campaign, xv, xvi, 3, 34, 36,
44, 55–58, 60–64, 67, 68, 133, *140*,
141, **147**, **150**, **158**, **161**, **162**, **168**, **169**
Persian Gulf, 21, 81, 110
Peru, 1
Phantom ship, 41, **154**, **162**
Philippines, 44, 95, 99, 102, 103, 109,
125, 131
Phillips, Richard, 52
Piata, 41
piloting, 42
piracy, xv, xvii, 3, 41–53, 71, 72, 73,
74, 75, 76, 78, 81, 89, 93, 94, 95,
98, 99, 100, 101, 104, 105, *139*, *140*,
142, **144**, **154**, **156**, **159**, **160**, **162**
Piracy Reporting Center (PRC), 47
pirate, 41–53, 72–75, 81, 89, 95, 98,
101, 104, 105, *140*, **144**, **154**, **156**,
160, **162**
Politburo, 14
pollution, 46, 94, 99, 100, 113
porous, 18, 20, 27, 28, 76, 87, **145**, **163**
Port Arthur, 119
Port Chicago, 6, 9–11, *137*
Port Moresby, 120
ports, xvii, 26, 30, 43, 44, 46–48, 50,
77, 81, 82, 85, 100, 111, 118–20,
128, **145**
port states, 46, 52, 53, **163**
Portugal, 42, 45, 66
positive objectives, 98, 117, **163**; space, 5,
134, **160**, **163**; sum, xiii, 132–35, **169**

Potemkin, 7, 8, 11, 12, *137*
potted plant, 25, 36, **151**, **163**
PRC missile blockade, 19, 22, 23, 27–
29, 122. *See also* missile blockade
precision nuclear strike, xvi, 68
prestige, 25, 65, 84, **152**, **163**, **169**
prevent defeat, 108, 134, **149**, **163**, **169**
privateers, 41, 72–75, 81, 82, *141*, **147**,
163
Prize Act, 73
prize court, 81, **163**
prizes, 72–74
probes, 99
production, xv, xvi, xvii, 56, 85, 122
promotion of interest, 7–8, **164**
propaganda, 36, 133, **159**
protract, xv, xvi, 20, 22, 26, 38, 39n5,
55–59, 72, 81, 83, 90, 108, 127, 129,
131, 134, *141*, **150**, **151**, **159**, **162**,
164, **168**
provisioning, 42, 66
Prueher, Joseph Jr., 96, 114
punch above its weight class, 93, 103, 105
Pusan, 61

Qingdao, 104
Qing dynasty, (1644–1911), 111, 113,
118, 119
Quad coalition, 38, **164**

quarantine, 18, 26, 112, **164**

railway, 26, 29, 119
RAND, 93, 118–19
ransom, 44, 51, 52, **162**
rape, *140*
rebellions, 10, 14, *140*
Red Army, 130
Red Sea, 80, 90, 110
regime change, 57, 68, 83, 134, **164**,
168
Regional Cooperation Agreement
on Combating Piracy and Armed
Robbery against Ships in Asia
(ReCAAP), 47

regional fleets, 13–14
regional war, 57, 75, 79, 80, 90, 103, 123, 130
relative costs, 127, **164**
Republic of China (ROC), 19, 20, 22, 26, 28, **161**
reverse blockade, 19, 22, 30, **156**, **164**
Revolutionary France, 36, 38, 82
Rhodesia, 19, 20, 22–26, 28, *138*
Riau, 42
Riff, *140*
ringleaders, 10
rising seas, 113, 124
risk, 9, 11, 13, 14, 60, 64–68, 87–89, 124, **156**, **164**
risk averse, 64, **164**
Roberts, Bartholomew, 74
Roman Empire, 93
Roman Law, xiii
Roosevelt, Theodore, 96–98, 121
Root, Elihu, 96
Roughead, Gary, 104
Royal Air Force, 122
Royal Australian Navy, 119
Royal Canadian Navy, *137*
Royal Indian Navy, *137*
Royal Navy, 5, 8, 11, 71, 74, 77, 102, 112, 121, 122, 129, *140*, **151**
rules of engagement (ROE), 31, 33, 50, **164**
Russia, xi, xiii, xv, xvii, 6–8, 11, 14, 15, 20, 21, 24–26, 28, 29, 35, 36, 38, 51, 52, 57–62, 66, 67, 77, 80–82, 84–86, 89, 90, 108–12, 114, 118–23, 125, 128–34, *139*, *141*, **159**. *See also* Soviet Union; USSR
Russo-Japanese War, (1904–1905), 77, 80, 82, 84–86, 88–90, 112, 118, 119, 130, *141*

Sablin, Valery, 14
Safety of Life at Sea, International Convention for the (SOLAS), 46
sanction enforcement, 23, 83, **164**

sanctions, xvii, 18, 23, 29, 34, 83, 95, 108, 110, 133, 134, *138*, **154**, **164**, **167**
sanctuary, xvi, 55, 58, 59, 133, **164**
satellites, 68, 81, **154**
Satō Tetsutarō, xii
scientific research, 93
script writing, 26, 119, **164**
sea command, xvi, 31, 35, 83, 107, 109, 112, **147**, **150**, **165**. *See also* command of the sea
sea control, 3, 26, 107–15, 117, **147**, **165**
sea denial, 3, 35, 59, 60, 117–26, 133, 134, *139*, **165**
sea lab, 101
sea lift, 36, **165**
sea lines of communication (SLOC), 17, 18, 20, 25, 28, 43, 58, 59, 120, *138*, **146**, **149**, **157**, **161**, **162**, **165**
Sea of Japan, 130
Sea of Okhotsk, 123, 130
sea power, xii, 20, 21, 24, 30, 55, 58, 59, 67, 71, 72, 77, 79, 84, 88, 107, 108, 114, 118, 124, 128–31, 133–35, *138*, **150**, **165**, **168**, **169**
secession, 7, 8, **165**
Second Iraq War, 121. *See also* Iraq
Second Island Chain, 112
Second Opium War, 129, *139*
second order effects, 90, 124
Second Sino-Japanese War, 19–28, 30, 132, *138*. *See also* Sino-Japanese War, (1937–1945)
second theater, 68
second time, 27, 29, 85
secrecy, 96, 97, 117, 121, 125, **146**, **148**, **152**, **162**, **169**
secret diplomacy, **169**. *See also* whisper diplomacy
security architecture, xvii, xviii, 113, 114
seizure of power, 7, 8, **165**
sensors, 30, 47, **159**

sequential strategy, xvi, xviiin9, 39n4, 56, 87, **153**, **165**

Seventh Fleet, 114, 121. *See also* U.S. Navy

Seven Years' War, 77–79, 82, 85–90, *141*

Seychelles, 100

Shalikashvili, John, 93

Shandong peninsula, 29

Shelvocke, Captain, 74

shipowner, 47, 48, **147**, **163**

shipping industry, 42, 45–47, 49–51, 53, 72, 74, 75, 78, 82, 85, 90, 94, 97, 98, 101, 109, 124, *142*, **147**, **148**, **157**

shipping lanes, 43, 44

Short-Range Anti-ship Ballistic Missiles, 118–19, 144

Sierra Club, 100

Silk road, xiii

silver, 88

silver bullet, xv, 74, 88

simultaneous engagement, 56, 57, 66, 81, 82, **153**, **165**

Singapore, 47, 101

Sino-Japanese War, (1894–1895), 18, 20, 22–27, 76–81, 83, 85–88, 111, 118, 119, 132, 136, *138*, *139*, *141*

Sino-Japanese War, (1937–1945), 19–22, 25–28, 132, *138*

Sino-Soviet alliance, 61; conflict, 62, 121, 133; split, 56, 111

Sino-Vietnamese War, (1979), 35, 120, 125, *141*

Sirius Star, 51

slaves, 93, 94, 97, 102, *142*

smuggling, 22, 26, 27, 29, 30, 42, 118, **165**

social media, 95, **159**, **165**, **166**

soft extension package, 105, **152**

soft power, 103–5, *142*, **152**, **155**

solvent, **155**

Somalia, 51–53, 72, 75–83, 86, 88, 98, 100, 101, 104, *142*

sonar, 94, 97, *142*

sonic boom gun, 47, 52

South America, 96

South China Sea (SCS), 2, 43, 102, 107, 113, 120, 124, 125, *140*, *142*

Southeast Asia, 42–45, 47, 49, 101, *140*, *142*

South Sea Fleet, 132

South Vietnam, 37, 59, *142*, **167**

sovereign, xiii, 2, 22, 45, 72, 75, 128, **146**, **159**, **165**

Soviet Navy, 35, 130

Soviet Union, 25, 28, 38, 67, 111, 112, 120, 129, 131, 132, *139*. *See also* Russia; USSR

space-based weapons, 30, 91

Spain, xi, 18, 26, 37, 42, 45, 60, 66, 67, 73, 74, 79, 82, 84, *138*, *139*, *142*

Spanish-American War, (1898), 18, 20, 22–27, 29, 73, 74, 76–79, *138*

Spanish Civil War, 76, 78–83, 87–89, *142*

Spanish Fascists, 79

Spanish Republic, 77, 89

Spanish Succession, War of, 73

Sparta, xvi

Special Measures to Enhance Maritime Security, 46

special relationship, 98, **165**

sphere of influence, xii, 42, 75, 127, **165**

spice trade, 42

Spiegel Grove, 100, 102

spoiler, 29, **165**

sportsmen, 97

Spykman, Nicolas, xii, xviii

Sri Lanka, 32, 47

stability, 36, 51, 105

stability of coalitions, 34, 105, **146**, **165**

stakeholder, 45, 46, 94, 100, **165**

Stalin, Joseph, 111, 124

starvation blockade, 17, 94, 98, 102, 123, *142*, **166**

Storozhevoy, 14

Strait of Gibraltar, 44

straits, 28, 43, 44, 47, 49, 63, 81, 118, 121, 122, 124, 131, *140*, **146**, **152**, **158**, **160**, **161**, **166** strategic effectiveness, 27, 84, 86–88; failure, 34, 37, 55, 88; goals, 18, 19, 23–25, 57, 61, 62, 68, 82–84, 101, **155**, **161**, **166**; impact, 24; objective, 21, 23, 33, 35–36, 56, 83, **146**; risk, 64–66, 68, 87, 88; success, xv, 18, 20, 27, 57; victory, xv, 27, 31, 32, 37, 55, 56, 103, **166**; vision, **166**

submarine, xvi, 22, 23, 29, 60, 72, 75, 77, 79, 81, 82, 85, 86, 94, 109, 112, 117, 122–25, 131, *141*, *142*, **144**, **166**, **168**. *See also* U-boats

substitute market, 27, **166**

substitute product, xvii, 27, 87, **166**

Suez Canal, xiii

Sullivan, William, 103

Sulu, 42, 43

Sunda strait, 118

Sunzi, *169*

surveillance, 49, 50, 53, 91, 123, **159**

sustainability, 38, 55, 61, 110, 133, **165**

SWIFT code, xvii

symbolic target, 68, **164**, **166**

Syria, xiii, 37

Taipei, 122

Taiping, *140*

Taiwan, 17, 19, 21–24, 28–30, 34, 81, 121–24, 131, *138*, **161**, **167**, **168**

Taiwan Strait, 28, 81, 121, 122, **161**

Taliban, 38, 62

Tanker War, 75, 77, 78, 80–82, 84–88, 90, 121, *142*

targets, xv, 20, 24, 30, 35, 44, 76, 94–97, 117, 119, 123, **149**, **153**, **166**

tax, 46, 105, **153**, **158**

technology, 1, 10, 18, 29, 46, 72, 76, 79, 86, 89–91, **153**, **158**

territorial aggrandizement, 32, 129, 131, 133

territorial disputes, xv, 53, 129, 131, 135, **154**

territorial integrity, 113, **154**, **167**

territorial limit, 2, 41

territorial seas/waters, 1, 2, 43, 46, 51, 52, 76, 97, 117, **146**, **148**, **155**, **157**, **167**

terrorism, 38, 51, 104, 105, *141*, **149**, **154**, **167**

Texas, xii

Thailand, 32, 43, 109

Thatch, Edward, 74

theaters, xv, xvi, 18–20, 24–28, 33, 34, 36, 55–68, 76, 77, 79, 80, 82–87, 89, 104, 117, 119, 121, 124, 128, 131, 133, 134, **150**, **162**, **167**

Theodore Roosevelt, 16

Third Conference on the Law of the Seas, 2

third party intervention, xv, 24, 27, 34, 65, 85–88, 90, 122, **145**, **157**, **164**, **165**, **167**, **168**

third world war, xvii, 121

thirteen colonies, 42, 73, 89

threat, xvi, xviii, 5, 6, 9, 12, 13, 16, 19, 23, 26, 29, 35, 36, 49, 50, 65, 74, 75, 82, 90, 98, 105, 108, 109, 113, 124, 127, 129, 130, 132, 133, 135, **147**, **152**, **153**, **156**, **167**

threshold, 8, 9, 13, **158**, **167**

Thucydides, 127, **152**, **156**, **157**, **167**

Thucydides Trap, **167**

Titanic, 101

Tokyo, 57, 83, 95, 109

Torpedo, 76, 90, **167**

Torpedo Boat, **167**

total blockade, 18, 23, 24, 112, **162**, **163**, **167**

Toucey, Isaac, 97

Toulon, 119

tourists, 94, 96, 97, 102

trade restrictions, 18, 26, 110, **167**

Trafalgar, Battle of, xvi, 108, 129

transnational crime, 49

transnational terrorism, 121

transportation, xiii, 23, 29, 56, 82, 93, 99, 127, **154**, **157**

treasure ships, 45

trigger, 6, 7, 11, 90, **168**

Triple Intervention, 35, *139*
tripwire, 121, 133, **145**, **161**, **168**
troop concentration, 63
troop transports, 77, 81, 84, 85, 118
troublemaker, 9
Truk, 120
Truman, Harry S., xiv, 1
Tsarist Russia. *See* Russia
Tsushima, Battle of, xvi, 112
typhoon, 124

U-boats, 85, 86, 122, *141*, *142*, **168**. *See also* submarines
unconditional surrender, 25, 64, 65, **168**
unconditional victory, 23, **168**
unconventional warfare, 68, **168**
UN General Assembly, 2
Unified Assistance, Operation. See Operation Unified Assistance
Union (U.S. Civil War), 22, 24, 28, 78, 82, 85, 86, 88, *138*, **143**
United Kingdom (UK), xii, 2, 27
United Nations (UN), xiv, 1, 2, 19, 21, 22, 25, 30, 46, 51, 61, 122, 123, 129, 130, 132
United Nations Convention on the Law of the Seas (UNCLOS), 2, 41, 43, 46, 51, **148**, **152**, **158**
United States, xi, xii, xviii, 1, 6, 11, 15, 19–21, 24, 26–28, 32–38, 42, 46, 47, 49–52, 59–65, 67, 68, 72–90, 94–99, 102, 103, 109–13, 118–25, 128–30, 132–34, *141*, **146**, **148**, **154**, **158**, **159**, **164**, **165**, **167**
unlimited blockade, 23–25, **168**
unrestricted warfare, 75, 77, 81, 82, 84, 85, 109, *142*, **168**
UN Security Council, 25, 51–52, 129
Uragan, 15
U.S. Air Force, xiv, 93, **158**
U.S. Army, xii, 93, **158**
U.S. Civil War, 26, 71, 75, 76, 82, 85, 86, 88, 89, *141*
U.S. Coast Guard, 97, 100, *142*
U.S. government, 85, 95, 102, **167**

U.S. Marines, 121
U.S. military, 37, 105, **166**
U.S. Naval Observatory, 98
U.S. Naval War College, xx, **151**
U.S. Navy, xi, xviii, 2, 8, 10, 15, 29, 32, 34, 35, 49, 52, 59, 75, 81, 93, 94, 98, 99, 101–3, 105, 109, 110, 112–14, 121–23, 130, *141*, **168**
U.S. Senate, 2
USSR, 19, 26, 29, 34, 36, 37, 59, 61, 62, 119, 123, 132, 134. *See also* Russia; Soviet Union

value of the object, 36, 37, **168**
Vandenberg, 102
Venezuela, 96, 98
Venezuelan Crisis, (1902–1903), 96, 120, *142*
Versailles Peace Treaty, (1919), 46
Vertical escalation, 11–12, 16, **156**, **168**
very large crude carrier (VLCC), 51
Vietnam, 15, 19–22, 24, 26, 28, 29, 34–37, 42–44, 59, 61, 62, 67, 95, 102, 103, 120, 125, 130, 131, 133, *138*, *139*, *142*, **155**, **159**, **163**, **167**
virtual training environment, 99
visualization of battle spaces, 99
Vladivostok, 122
voters, 37, 63, 94, 96, 97, **166**
vulnerable landing period, 64, **168**

war by algebra, 23, 121, **153**, **168**
War of, 1812, xi, 19, 20, 22–24, 26, 74, 75, 77, 79, 80, 82, 83, 86, 87, 89, 102, *138*, *141*
war of the chase, 71, **155**. *See also guerre de course*
War of the Spanish Succession, (1702–1713), 73
war protraction, 22, 26, 39n5, 57–59, 90, 127, 129, **150**, **151**, **168**
war termination, *139*, **168**
Washington, 1, 28, 36, 37, 59, 75, 95, 98
Weak powers, xiii, 72, 82, 128

wealth accumulation, 38, **169**
Weapons of Mass Destruction (WMD), 24, 110, **169**
Weihaiwei, 19, 119, **153**
Wellesley, Arthur, 62, 66
West African Squadron, 102
Western allies, 62
Western capitalism, **164**
Western Europe, 42, 75
Western Front, 58
Western navies, 14, 15
Western order, 113
Western thinking, xiii
whisper diplomacy, 98, **169**
White Sea, 56, 57, 60, 61, 130, *140*
win without fighting, **169**
withdrawal, 36, 37, 58, 95, 99, 119, **152**, **155**, **169**
Wonsan, 65
wooden wall, 17
working conditions, 6–8, 11, 13, 15, 46, **169**
World Bank, 130
World Health Organization (WHO), 100
World Trade Center, 68, **166**

World Trade Organization (WTO), xiv
World War I, xiv, 17, 19, 21, 22, 26, 27, 29, 34, 35, 46, 60, 62, 63, 72, 77–89, 94, 98, 102, 109, 118, 122, 123, 130, 131, 134, *138*, **165**, **168**
World War II, xi, xiv, xv, xvii, 9, 14, 17, 19, 20, 22, 27, 29, 33–35, 37, 56, 58, 60–63, 65, 67, 72, 75–90, 98, 104, 109, 111, 120, 122, 128, 130, 131, 134, *139–42*, **146**, **156**, **157**, **162**, **165**, **166**, **168**
World War III, 121
worst-case scenario, 67, 109, **145**
Wounded Knee, xii

Xuzhou, 100

Yalu River, **160**
Yorktown, 77, 79, 89
Yorktown, Battle of, 79

zero sum, 132, 133, 135, **163**, **169**
Zhejiang Province, 101
Zhoushan Port, 101

Lightning Source UK Ltd.
Milton Keynes UK
UKHW010129140722
405812UK00002B/38

9 781538 161043